HANDY GUIDE TO
VIRGINIA
WINERIES

DONNA GOUGH

DEDICATION

To my family, with appreciation for their cheerful assistance in exploring Virginia wines and wineries, and their unfailing support while the 2013 edition of this guide was being updated.

CONTENTS

MAPS

WINE BASICS

ACKNOWLEDGMENTS

For this 2013 edition, my thanks and appreciation continue to go out to the winery owners and employees who graciously shared their time and information with me. Without your dedication and vision, this guide would not have been possible because there would be no Virginia wine industry to write about.

Toni Smith and Carl Sykes have been generous in sharing their time and expertise in helping me fine-tune my command of Adobe Illustrator.

And, of course, none of this would have been possible without the warm and continuous support of my family, who have all continued to join in exploring Virginia wineries with me, both revisiting familiar places and exploring new vineyards, as I updated my book. Thank you!

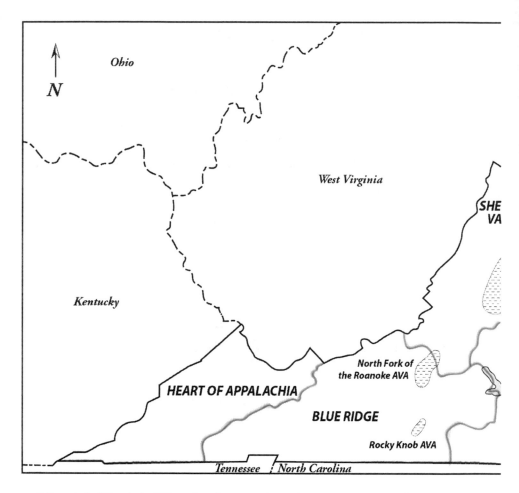

Map 1.1 Virginia Wine Regions & American Viticultural Areas
(AVAs)

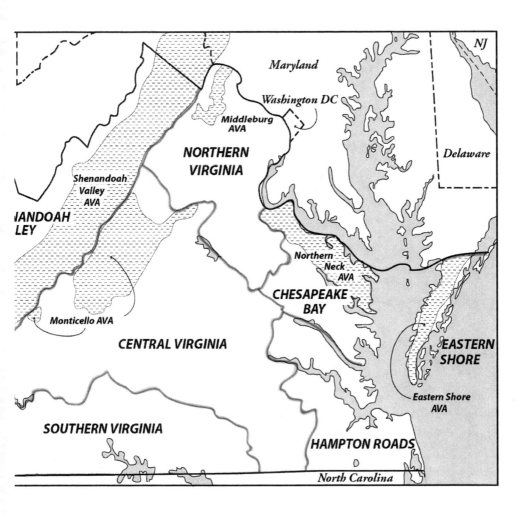

Map Legend

Roads and Road Symbols

▭	Interstate highway	🛡66	Interstate highway
—	U.S. Highway	🛡50	U.S. Highway
—	State or Local Route	(638)	State or Local Route
··············	Ferry Crossing	⌘	Interstate Exit

Administrative Divisions

— — — —	State Boundary	○ ○	City or Town
....	County Line	- - - - -	Military Base

Wineries & Points of Interest

☆	Winery	⬡	Points of Interest
	American Viticultural Area		Bodies of Water
	National or Local Park or Forest	△	Mountain Peak

1. INTRODUCTION TO VIRGINIA WINERIES

Virginia is the fifth-largest wine state in the country measured by the number of wineries. Yet it is still largely unknown to the American public, greatly overshadowed by the Big Three (California, Washington, Oregon), which dominate shelves in stores around the country.

While Virginia's winemaking roots reach back to the founding of the first permanent English colony on America's shores, its modern wine industry is comparatively young. Only within the past thirty years has winemaking truly blossomed in the state. There are over 185 wineries that now have regular tasting room hours, offering a variety of experiences and products that will suit every visitor's preference and taste.

There are large wineries and small. The biggest—such as Williamsburg, Chateau Morrisette, and Barboursville—boast large facilities, gift shops, and restaurants for the many visitors who come through their doors. But those opting for a more personalized experience can find that, too, at such tiny wineries as Twin Oaks Tavern or Vino Curioso.

Many of the state's wineries produce varietals familiar to any wine drinker, such as Chardonnay, Cabernet Sauvignon, and Merlot. Others are less common but are becoming more popular—Viognier and Cabernet Franc, for instance, Virginia's signature varietals.

Virginia's winemakers are also actively exploring grape varieties that are less widely known in the United States, often with excellent results. France's Tannat and Fer Servadou, Portugal's Tinta Cão and Touriga Nacional,

Georgia's Rkatsiteli and South Africa's Pinotage—all are being produced in Virginia's wine country.

No wine guide of the state would be complete without mentioning the Norton grape, the native American hybrid first propagated in Virginia and championed in particular by Horton and Chrysalis Vineyards. Today Norton can be found as a pure varietal, in blends, and in sweet wines, including several chocolate-flavored wines, such as those produced by Horton and Cooper Vineyards.

Virginia's widely varying topography, geologic diversity, and mesoclimates give rise to distinct differences in its wines. Vineyards are planted across the state, from the flat, sandy soils on the Eastern Shore to the high slopes of the Blue Ridge and limestone basin of the Shenandoah, producing wines that range from full-bodied to light.

Temperatures and precipitation vary not only from region to region but also from year to year, resulting in vintage differences that can be quite distinctive. The summer of 2010 was unusually hot and dry, for instance, and wineries across the state had one of the earliest harvests on record. The summer of 2011, by contrast, ended with a very cool and rainy period that prolonged the harvest. Such seasonal differences lead to very different expressions of a grape's character and personality.

❖ ❖ ❖

The goal of this guide is to serve as an introduction to the rich complexity of Virginia's wine country. It is not intended to be an encyclopedic collection of data and facts but rather a quick overview of the wineries now open to the public on a regular basis.

It starts with a brief review of the history of grape growing and winemaking in Virginia. An explanation of the elements included in each winery description then follows. Each of Virginia's nine wine regions has its own chapter. Each chapter begins with an introduction to that region with a snapshot of things to see and do, including the various wine trails available for that particular region. Detailed winery listings then follow, with information on the wineries themselves.

The guide also includes a bibliography, information on Virginia wine trails and wine blogs dealing with Virginia wineries and wines, a glossary of wine and wine-related terms (including the grape varieties currently used in Virginia wines), an alphabetical index of Virginia's wineries, and a general index at the very end.

For those readers who are already familiar with Virginia wines, this guide may introduce you to wineries and wines you might not otherwise have tried. For visitors who are new to the state, it provides a broad overview of the vibrancy and diversity of all that Virginia has to offer. For everyone, may this guide help you discover something new about Virginia and its wines.

2. THE HISTORY OF WINEMAKING IN VIRGINIA

Virginia is credited with a number of "firsts" in American history: the first permanent English settlement in North America; the site of the first representative assembly in the American colonies; the birthplace of the first President of the United States. What is less well known is that Virginia can also be called the birthplace of winemaking in the United States, although its rise as a wine-producing state was long in coming and, until recent years, marked more often by failure than success.

But why would English colonists in early Virginia even try to cultivate grapes, much less to make wine from them? After all, England was never one of the great wine-producing countries in Europe. It has no long history of grape cultivation and no deeply rooted wine culture. In the seventeenth century, as now, England's alcoholic production and consumption centered around beer, ale, and hard cider, not wines—and certainly not fine wines.

The answer lies both in the natural resources the colonists found in Virginia when they arrived and in the governing structures and aims of the Jamestown colony in its early years.

A COLONY IN SEARCH OF A PRODUCT

In the late sixteenth century, England lagged far behind other European countries—especially its archrival, Spain—in wealth, power, and prestige, and English leaders were determined to catch up. Trade offered the best prospect for doing just that, and English merchants and investors launched numerous ventures aimed at either breaking into trade relationships in

Africa and the East or exploring new opportunities in lands across the Atlantic. Nearly all these initiatives were set up in England as joint stock companies, a structure that allowed investors to pool their resources and finance projects in the expectation of sharing in the profits.

In 1606, the London Virginia Company was established to finance and direct an exploratory venture in the general Chesapeake Bay area. The company's goal was to establish a small colony that would uncover a marketable commodity—gold, spices, or dyes, for instance—to serve as a foundation for trade between the native peoples and England, much as the French had successfully done in establishing a lucrative fur trade with native tribes in Quebec some years earlier. One result of their efforts was the English colony at Jamestown, founded the year after the Virginia Company was launched.

As Jamestown passed its tenth anniversary, however, the colony was still searching for products that would help it become self-sufficient and profitable. Colonists shipped various goods back to England—sassafras, clapboard, and pitch, among others—but their marketability was limited because of distance and cost. Officers in the London Virginia Company offered ideas as well, sending to the colony silkworms and silk experts, ironworkers and refiners, and glassblowers from Italy, but none of these projects panned out. Tobacco was growing in popularity and importance as colonists became more skilled at its cultivation and processing, but it had not yet become the breakthrough crop that would fuel Virginia's future growth.

From the colony's earliest days, Jamestown settlers had also explored the production of one other commodity: wine. The region was rich in native grapevines, and the colonists soon turned to producing a quickly made and highly alcoholic wine. The fact that wine was being produced was noted by several of Jamestown's early leaders—as was the fact that this wine was not high in quality. Upon being appointed Governor of Virginia in 1610, for instance, Lord Delaware ordered that a cask of Virginia wine be sent to London, "sour as it is." About the same time, Colony Secretary William Strachey wrote about wine he had tasted in Jamestown made by a Doctor Bohoune, Virginia's first named winemaker, describing it as "strong and heady."

By 1619, Sir Edwin Sandys had taken over the leadership of the Virginia Company. It was Sandys who gave the colony greater control over its own political and economic affairs through the "Great Charter," which laid the foundation for the Virginia Assembly, the first representative body of government in America. During the Assembly's first session, delegates enacted several measures on land distribution, tobacco prices, mulberry cultivation for silkworms, and hemp production—all measures aimed at improving the colony's economic health.

Delegates also passed "Acte 12," a measure that required every householder to "yearly plante and maintaine ten vines, untill they have attained to the arte and experience of dressing a Vineyard, either by their owne industry, or by the Instruction of some Vigneron." The Virginia Company also arranged for eight French vignerons, or vineyardists, to go to Jamestown to help kick-start the effort. In 1621, King James I gave an extra push to the fledgling industry by ordering that translations of a French manual on cultivating vines be sent to the colonists.

All these efforts ultimately fizzled out, as the colonists increasingly turned to the much more lucrative tobacco as their cash crop of choice.

For roughly the next 50 years, Virginia's leaders continued to gently prod colonists toward vine cultivation, including dispatching more vineyard experts, importing European grape stock, even establishing a prize for anyone who could produce "two tunne of wine out of a vineyard made in this colony." Ultimately all their efforts proved unsuccessful. Some colonists dutifully planted vines and cultivated vineyards, but fungus and mildew—as well as the still unknown phylloxera louse—took their toll on the imported vines, while the appeal and profitability of the tobacco leaf lured others away.

Despite the frustrations and ultimate failures, however, the seeds of Virginia's future wine industry had been planted.

GENTLEMEN FARMERS AND THEIR VINES

In the decades that followed, records both public and private are largely silent about grape cultivation and wine production in Virginia. Judging from the occasional references to Virginia wine, some vineyards of native root-stock did exist and some wine was indeed produced. But ordinary farmers would not have been engaged in winemaking, since cultivating and tending to tobacco, the main cash crop of the colony, was a labor-intensive endeavor that demanded constant attention and time in the fields. They simply had no time to spare to indulge in an effort that had little to do with the hard business of eking out a living.

Instead, what winemaking occurred in Virginia during this period was through the efforts and interest of the well-to-do, particularly various members of Virginia's "First Families," a network of wealthy landowners often related by intermarriage. Only they would have had the time and financial resources to invest in planting a vineyard and attempting to make wine. As plantation owners whose fortunes rose and fell with the value of tobacco, these gentlemen farmers would also have had an economic interest in developing an alternative crop for export, such as wine.

One such individual was Robert Beverley, one of the colony's largest landowners and the author of the first history of Virginia. In 1709, Beverly planted a three-acre vineyard of native grapes on his estates in King and Queen County to the north of what is now Richmond. Six years later, the Irish diarist John Fontaine visited Beverley's home and reported that his vineyard had produced about four hundred gallons of wine, adding that they "were verry merry with the wine of his own making and drunk prosperity to his vineyard."

By 1722, Beverley was producing roughly 750 gallons a year of wine, which was described by a local pastor as being similar in taste to claret and as strong as port, suggesting it had been fortified with additional alcohol. Beverley died that same year, however, and his heirs proved less interested in viticulture than he had been.

About that same time, Beverley's brother-in-law, William Byrd, became intrigued with the idea of grape cultivation. In the 1720s, he planted a vineyard of about twenty native grape varieties at his Westover Plantation on the James River. Byrd was an astute businessman, and his initial successes helped persuade some of his neighbors to consider planting their own vines as well. Within ten years, however, his vineyards fell victim to harsh frosts and insect infestations, and his efforts at grape cultivation ended.

In the late 1750s, Charles Carter—another First Family member—also began cultivating grapes at his Cleve plantation in King George County. By 1762, Carter had planted around 1,800 vines and sent twelve bottles of wines made from a native American grape and from what he described as a "white Portugal summer grape" to the London Society for the Encouragement of the Arts to demonstrate the quality of his product.

Grape cultivation and wine production was not solely the purview of wealthy landowners, however. In 1769 Frenchman André Estave persuaded the Virginia House of Burgesses to provide him with land, money, and labor to establish a vineyard of both native and European grapes near Williamsburg. The endeavor ultimately collapsed when the European vines failed due to disease and pests, and Estave himself proved to be a failure at managing an estate.

Estave's chief rival was Colonel Robert Bolling from Buckingham County, who believed that Virginia's wine potential lay with European, not native American, varieties. Bolling wrote an unpublished treatise on grape cultivation in the middle colonies, one of the earliest studies on the subject written by an American. Unfortunately, his efforts to promote the cultivation of southern European grapes in Virginia were cut short by his sudden death in 1775.

THOMAS JEFFERSON

Perhaps the most well-known "gentleman farmer" involved in early Virginia viticulture was Thomas Jefferson, who has come to be emblematic of Virginia wine even though he met with little success during his lifetime. In 1773, Jefferson met Philip Mazzei, a Florentine exporter who had come to America by way of London in the hope of establishing commercial vineyards and olive farms in Virginia's back country. Captivated by the idea, Jefferson gave Mazzei two thousand acres near Monticello to build a house and establish a vineyard.

Mazzei spent several years bringing in workers and rootstock from Italy for his endeavor with Jefferson. The vineyard was planted with both European and native grape varieties. Mazzei wrote that the European vines had successfully fruited and produced flavorful grapes, but they soon withered on the vine. The vineyard fell into near-total neglect after Mazzei left for Europe in 1779 to raise funds for the American government during the Revolutionary War. He returned only once—briefly—and then spent the remainder of his days in Europe.

After leaving the White House in 1809, Jefferson revived his efforts to cultivate vines, corresponding frequently with John Adlum, often called the Father of American Viticulture. Adlum had succeeded in producing wine from both European and native grapes from his Georgetown vineyard in what is now the District of Columbia and provided Jefferson cuttings of various vines on several occasions. Jefferson's efforts invariably ended in frustration and failure, however, although he never lost interest and faith in the ultimate success of American viticulture.

POST-CIVIL WAR RISE AND DEMISE

In the nineteenth century, the American wine industry as a whole took root and expanded significantly, including in Virginia. The first commercially successful American winemaker was Nicholas Longworth, a wealthy Cincinnati businessman. Longworth's sparkling pink Catawba became wildly popular in the United States, and by the 1850s his winery was producing 100,000 bottles a year.

Although Longworth's vineyards had fallen victim to disease and withered by the time of his death in 1863, his success inspired potential American winemakers across the country, who began to try their hand at growing grapes and producing wine. In Virginia as well, farmers began considering their options for diversifying away from the labor-intensive tobacco. The most notable successes came from German immigrants who moved to Virginia after the Civil War.

The first of these vineyards was planted by William Hotopp, a Hanover native who had come to America around 1852. After establishing a successful business in New Jersey, Hotopp moved to Charlottesville in 1866 and purchased the Pen Park estate (the modern-day Pen Park and Meadow Creek Golf Course). Four years later, he began producing both red and white wines from his own vineyard in a winery he built to process his grapes.

In 1873, several other German grape growers led by Oscar Reierson founded the Monticello Wine Company, Virginia's first large-scale commercial winery. Their four-story winery located in the middle of what is now Perry Drive and McIntire Road in Charlottesville could process up to

200,000 gallons of wine, all from native American vines, including Virginia's own Norton grape, first cultivated in 1822.

Their success spurred others to follow suit in planting grapes, and by 1888, there were at least three thousand acres of vineyards in Albemarle County alone. By 1890, Virginia's wine industry ranked fifth in the United States, with a total production that year of 461,000 gallons.

Within two decades, however, wine production in the Commonwealth had all but disappeared. The Panic of 1893—second only to the Great Depression in its severity—struck Virginia hard, particularly its agricultural sector. Plant diseases also took their toll on the vineyards.

But it was the emerging temperance movement that ultimately played the greatest role in extinguishing Virginia's wine industry. The Anti-Saloon League was formed in Virginia in 1901 with the expressed purpose of banning the sale of alcoholic beverages. The League made rapid progress: by 1905, only thirty of the state's one hundred counties still allowed alcohol to be sold. And in September 1914, the Virginia legislature passed a state-wide prohibition law that made Virginia one of the earliest states to go "dry."

Five years later, the entire country followed suit with the ratification of the 19th Amendment, commonly termed Prohibition. Although Prohibition did not ban all commercial wine production—wine could still be produced commercially for sacramental and medicinal purposes—the net effect was the closure of most small wineries. States where small wineries predominated, such as Virginia, were particularly hard hit.

The ratification of the Twenty-First Amendment in December 1933 finally brought an end to Prohibition. Former wine-producing states throughout the country had to start almost from scratch to rebuild their wine industries. In Virginia, this rebuilding process was long in coming. From the end of Prohibition to the 1960s, Virginia regulators issued a grand total of twenty-two winery licenses, and all but four of these twenty-two wineries had closed their doors by 1970.

VIRGINIA VITICULTURE REBORN

In the early 1970s, Virginia's wine industry began to stir again. In 1973, Treville Lawrence helped found the Vinifera Wine Growers Association, which actively promoted the cultivation of European *Vitis vinifera* vines in Virginia and elsewhere on the East Coast. By 1980, half a dozen new wineries had opened, including several that are still in operation: Barboursville, Ingleside, Mountain Cove, Piedmont, Shenandoah, and Willowcroft.

The government of Virginia began to take an active interest in promoting the development of the state's wine industry. In 1980 the Virginia legislature passed a farm winery bill that required such wineries to have a producing vineyard in Virginia with facilities for bottling wine on the premises. The bill did not restrict the size of production and allowed sales at both the wholesale and retail levels, including on-site tasting rooms. Farm wineries were also permitted to buy grapes from other vineyards, as long as 75 percent of the grapes used in their wines were grown in Virginia.

This legislation allowed Virginia's wine industry to blossom. In 1980, Virginia had 286 acres under vine; by 2011, that figure had expanded nearly tenfold, reaching over 2,600 acres. From fewer than a dozen in 1980, Virginia now has over 200 licensed farm wineries, including over 170 that are routinely open to the public. It is once again fifth in the nation when measured by the number of wineries.

During this time, Virginia winemakers have become leaders in cultivating and exploring different grape varieties to use in their wines. Dennis Horton, founder of Horton Winery, was a pioneer in bringing Viognier to the United States and using it to produce a varietal that is now one of Virginia's signature wines. Horton and particularly Jennifer McCloud of

Chrysalis Vineyards also have actively cultivated and promoted the Norton grape, restoring it to greater prominence in its state of origin.

Virginia vineyardists now cultivate more than seventy different varieties of grapes for wine production, from the classic *Vitis vinifera* varieties grown in Europe to hybrids and crosses. These include grape varieties from Germany, Greece, Italy, Portugal, and Spain in addition to those traditionally cultivated in France. A number of Virginia winemakers also are cultivating native American varieties, both for blending with other grapes or for varietal production.

Virginia winemakers themselves come from across the country and even the world. Whether from Canada, France, Germany, Greece, Italy, Lebanon, Portugal, South Africa, or Turkey, all are drawn to a winemaking community that is characterized by the same energy, determination, and vision that marked the state's earliest winemaking efforts. This wide variety in background, training, and experience is contributing additional vitality to a wine industry that is vibrant and ever-growing.

From fine wines that can compete on an equal basis with Europe's classic varieties to more homegrown wines that have long been part of America's wine production, there is truly something for all wine tastes and preferences in Virginia.

3. HOW TO USE THIS BOOK

Virginia is divided into nine wine regions and includes seven American Viticultural Areas (AVAs) with the addition in 2012 of the Middleburg AVA. The wineries in this book are grouped mostly along those regional lines. For the larger wine regions, wineries are further sorted into geographic clusters for ease of reference. Each chapter includes information about the wine region itself and a brief snapshot of things to see and do. Only those wineries regularly open to the public are included in this guide.

For each winery, the address and contact information is provided, as well as usual business hours and seasonal closings. In addition, the Stay Tuned section indicates if a winery uses Facebook, Twitter, or a newsletter to share news with customers. A brief description of the facilities and features is offered, including a sampling of special events and festivals, whether the winery may be rented for special occasions, and whether children or pets may accompany visitors.

Wines: Each winery's wines are sorted by type, from sparkling to fortified; this information is current as of December 2012. While the wines actually available will vary as the year progresses, this list will provide a window into the styles and types of wines a given winery produces to help tailor your visit according to your interests and preferences. If a wine is a blend, the grape varieties used are included in parentheses if known; some wineries prefer to keep their blends a proprietary secret. Please be aware that even wines labeled as varietals may be a blend that includes up to 25 percent of another grape variety. While many Virginia wineries also produce reserve wines, these are not listed separately since their production and availability vary from year to year, depending on the quality of a given vintage. Similarly, library wines are not included, as their availability may vary considerably.

If you spot a specific varietal or blend that intrigues you, always call ahead to confirm if it is still available if that is one of the main goals of your visit. Many of Virginia's wineries are small producers and often run out of a given vintage. Advance research will help prevent disappointment.

Tastings: Most wineries charge a tasting fee that may vary depending on the number of wines or special vintages being sampled. In some cases, souvenir glasses convey with the tasting, particularly for groups. In addition, wineries occasionally offer a discount with the purchase of wine. If no tasting fee is specified, the tasting is complimentary. At small wineries, tastings are often handled informally, with guests paying for their tasting at the very end. However, many high-volume wineries require that a tasting ticket be purchased first. At many wineries, there is only one register to handle both incoming guests who want to pay their tasting fee and departing customers paying for their wine purchases. In such cases, it's best to be patient since the pourers will not start a tasting for anyone without a ticket.

Groups: Most wineries require advance reservations for groups, especially of eight or more. Please note that some wineries limit the size of groups they will accept, and several do not permit van, bus, or limo tours at all. Check the individual winery listings for more details. If you are planning to tour wineries with friends or family, call at least one day in advance to confirm that the tasting room can accommodate your group. This is especially helpful for smaller wineries with limited space in their tasting rooms. Weekends have become very popular times for group tours, particularly in the northern Virginia and Charlottesville areas. Early reservations can make all the difference.

Hours: Call ahead to confirm closing times and last pours if you are planning to arrive late in the day. A number of Virginia wineries rent out their spaces for private parties, dinners, or weddings, and may close earlier than the posted hours to accommodate a special event.

Food: Cheese, crackers, and often cold cuts are available for purchase at many wineries, especially those that also offer tables either inside the tasting area or outside on patios and decks. Some wineries also allow guests to bring their own food for a picnic on the grounds. Always call or e-mail first to determine a particular winery's restrictions if you are planning to bring food.

Alcoholic Beverages: Most wineries sell their wine by the glass or bottle. Please note, however, that Virginia state law prohibits the consumption of any alcoholic beverage on winery property that was not produced by that winery itself. If you are planning to snack or picnic at a winery, be prepared either to bring water or soft drinks, or to purchase wine on-site to have with your food.

Pets: A number of wineries are pet-friendly and allow leashed, well-behaved dogs on the winery grounds, though Virginia law prohibits dogs in the tasting rooms. A few, such as Breaux Vineyards, even host Dog Days that are very popular with two- and four-legged visitors alike. Even pet-friendly wineries may not allow pets during special events and festivals. Check the events calendar for any restrictions, or call ahead to confirm that your pet will be able to join you on the grounds. Pet-friendly wineries will be identified as such in the winery description.

Children: Rules on children vary from winery to winery. Many welcome children and families while others restrict access to adults twenty-one and older. Wineries can be boring places for children, and bored children often are eager to let adults know just how unhappy they are. If you are planning a family excursion to Virginia's wine country, it's easy to map out an itinerary that focuses on wineries offering adequate indoor and outdoor spaces for children to amuse themselves. Child-friendly wineries will be identified as such in the winery description.

Purchasing: All Virginia wineries offer their products for sale in the tasting room, but not all offer telephone or e-mail ordering, and their ability to ship to out-of-state customers can vary significantly. Differing state regulations and restrictions mean that each winery must apply for shipping permits on its own, and not all have decided to go this route. Since restrictions can quickly change with little warning, check with the winery to see if it is able to ship to your home state. If nothing is listed in the Purchasing section, the winery does not ship at this time; otherwise, current shipping guidelines are provided.

Directions: Basic driving directions to each winery are given from the closest major highway, either an interstate highway, U.S. highway, or major parkway. Please keep in mind that some winery addresses are not easily recognized by computer mapping sites or by GPS, particularly if the winery is located off the beaten track. Two good atlases to consider are the *Virginia State Road Atlas* (American Map) and the *Virginia Atlas and Gazetteer* (DeLorme). The *Virginia State Road Atlas* is easier to read and has more wineries marked; the *Gazetteer* is a topographic map that provides more details and a good sense of the terrain, but it is harder to decipher.

A Final Note: Wine tastings and tasting tours can be a fun and enjoyable way to spend a weekend afternoon. However, even small pours can add up to a considerable amount of alcohol when multiplied over numerous samplings. It is also worth noting that under Virginia law, all wineries have the right to refuse service to patrons who are noticeably intoxicated. Please be responsible and choose either a designated driver or use one of the many wine country tour groups now operating in Virginia.

Please also note that Virginia's Department of Alcoholic Beverage Control (ABC) has ruled that the only alcoholic beverages permitted on winery grounds are wines produced by that winery itself. Please leave any other alcoholic beverages, including wines from other wineries, in your car, limo, or tour bus.

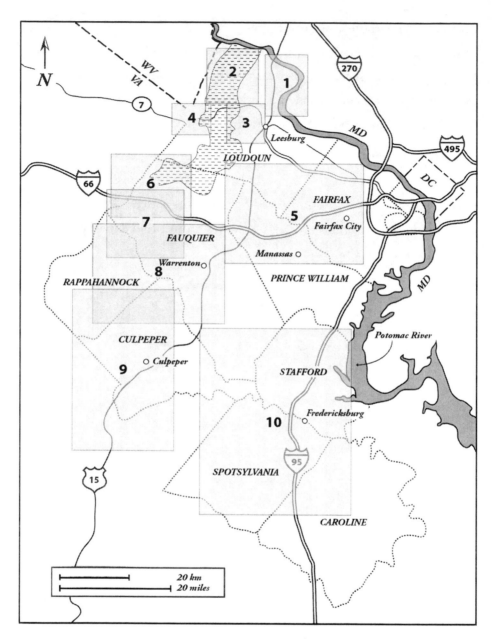

Map 4.1. Northern Virginia Region & Middleburg AVA:
(1) Leesburg North; (2) Northwest Loudoun; (3) Leesburg West;
(4) Bluemont; (5) Middleburg-Fairfax; (6) Delaplane;
(7) Northern Blue Ridge; (8) Warrenton; (9) Culpeper;
(10) Fredericksburg

4. NORTHERN VIRGINIA REGION & MIDDLEBURG AVA

The Northern Virginia wine region stretches from busy suburbs to small towns much calmer in pace and personality. Less than an hour's drive from our nation's capital are historic villages with deep colonial roots, working farms owned by the same families for generations, and winding country lanes that quickly go from paved to gravel.

Northern Virginia is home to just over 75 wineries, from small boutique operations that produce only a few hundred cases per year to larger wineries whose annual production is in the thousands. Given the region's proximity to Washington D.C. and its suburbs, wineries in this region can be crowded places on weekends, especially in summer months, with peak visiting hours from noon to 3:00 p.m.

The region's topography, soils, and climate are quite diverse. The crest of the northern Blue Ridge tops out at over 3,000 feet in elevation, sloping rapidly to the east in a sequence of rolling hills and broad basins. This pattern of mountains, hills, and valleys gives rise to numerous mesoclimates which help produce a rich variety of wines.

The Northern Virginia is also home to Virginia's newest American Viticultural Area, or AVA. The Middleburg AVA, approved in mid-2012, stretches from Loudoun County's border with Maryland down into Fauquier County at Little Cobbler Mountain.

<u>Things to See and Do</u>: There are numerous activities and sites available for visitors in the Northern Virginia region. Historic town centers, such as Old Town Alexandria and downtown Fredericksburg, are filled with Colonial- and Civil War-era homes along with numerous restaurants and cafes. George Washington's Mount Vernon, just south of Alexandria, gives visitors a thorough introduction to our nation's first president and his home.

Northern Virginia also is dotted with many small villages that allow visitors a glimpse of life in early rural Virginia. Among others, these include Waterford, founded in 1733 by Quakers; Hillsborough, the birthplace of Susan Koehner Wright, mother of aviation pioneers Orville and Wilbur Wright; and "little" Washington, whose town grid was surveyed by George Washington in 1749.

Northern Virginia also includes much of the "Journey Through Hallowed Ground" (www.hallowedground.org), a scenic 180-mile driving route from Charlottesville, Virginia to Gettysburg, Pennsylvania. The trail features over 10,000 sites, including presidential homes, African American and Native American historical sites, and battlefields from the French and Indian War, Revolutionary War, and War of 1812.

Those interested in the Civil War can tour a number of key battlefields, including Bull Run near Manassas, where two major battles were fought; Brandy Station, the war's largest cavalry encounter; and Chancellorsville, where Stonewall Jackson was accidentally felled by his own troops. Self-guided tour maps and guides can be downloaded from Virginia's Civil War Trails website (www.civilwartraveler.com/EAST/VA/).

Nature lovers can choose from among several state parks and nature preserves that offer hiking, horseback riding, camping, and boating. The Appalachian Trail crosses into Virginia at Clarke County and meanders south and west along the crest of the Blue Ridge Mountains. The

Shenandoah River is a popular rafting site, with several outfitters that will arrange a complete rafting trip for visitors.

<u>Wine Trails</u>: Over a dozen Virginia wine trails include at least one winery in the Northern Virginia region. Trails that focus predominately on Northern Virginia wineries include the Artisanal Wineries of Rappahannock, the Blue Ridge Whiskey Wine Loop, the Blue Ridge Wine Way, the Fauquier County Wine Trail, the Foothills Scenic Wine Way, Loudoun Wine Country, Tuskies Wine Trail, and Vintage Piedmont. See Appendix 1 for more details on these and other wine trails.

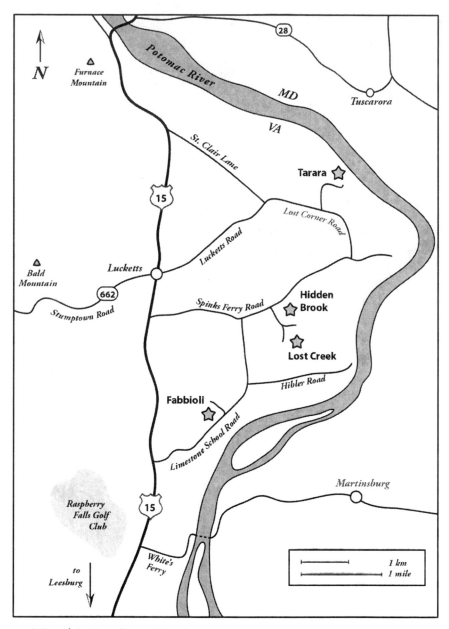

Map 4.2. Leesburg North

LEESBURG NORTH

Fabbioli Cellars
15669 Limestone School Road
Leesburg VA 20176

Hours: Daily 11:00–5:00

Closed New Year's, Thanksgiving, Christmas

Stay Tuned: Facebook, Twitter, newsletter

703-771-1197

www.fabbioliwines.com

E-mail: vinofab@aol.com,

Jen@fabbioliwines.com

Owner-winemaker Doug Fabbioli has been in the wine business in one way or another for nearly thirty years, beginning with his studies at the University of California, Davis, and work at Buena Vista Winery. After returning to the East Coast, Doug and wife Colleen Berg founded Fabbioli Cellars in 2000. The winery's tasting room is currently in the walk-out basement of their home and offers several tasting stations for visitors. Be sure to check in first at the cash register to purchase your tasting ticket. Bread and cheeses are available for purchase and enjoyment on the outdoor patio area, which overlooks part of the Fabbioli vineyards. Fabbioli also sponsors a range of events, including a home winemaking class, an annual customer harvesting day, and occasional charity benefits. Pets are welcome.

White Wines: Something White *(Traminette, Vidal Blanc)*.

Rosé Wines: Rosa Luna *(Sangiovese)*.

Red Wines: Cabernet Franc, Chambourcin, Fratelli *(Cabernet Sauvignon)*, Paco Rojo, Sangiovese, Tannat, Tre Sorelle *(Bordeaux-style blend)*.

Sweet/Dessert Wines: Raspberry Merlot.

Fortified Wines: Aperitif Pear Wine, Rosa Nera-Black Raspberry Wine.

Price Range: $16–$45

Tastings: $10 per person.

Groups: Reservations required for groups of 8 to 16; no groups over 16.

Speakeasy Wine Club members receive discounts on purchases, invitations to classes.

Purchasing: Online ordering available for residents of all states _except_ AL, AR, DE, ME, MD, MS, MT, NJ, OK, PA, RI, SD, TN, and UT.

Directions: From U.S. Route 15, turn onto Limestone School Road (Route 661) (portions unpaved) to the winery, 1.3 miles on the left.

Hidden Brook Winery
43301 Spinks Ferry Road
Leesburg VA 20176

Hours: Sa–Su 11:00–5:00; M, Th–F 12:00–5:00   703-737-3935
Closed New Year's, Thanksgiving, Christmas   www.hiddenbrookwinery.com
Stay Tuned: Newsletter   E-mail: hiddenbrookwine@aol.com

Eric and Deborah Hauck established Hidden Brook in 1999, literally next door to Eric's parents, Bob and Carol Hauck, who founded Lost Creek Winery. The rustic tasting room seats 48 and provides a calm atmosphere for visitors to relax, both indoors next to the fireplace or on the covered porch and deck under the trees. Hidden Brook sponsors a range of events, including live music on summer weekends, special brunches, and charity fundraisers, such as the Toast for Hope in support of the Susan G. Komen Race for the Cure. The winery's gift shop offers light fare for purchase, as well as gifts and works by local artists. Children and pets are welcome.

White Wines: Chardonnay, Reserve White *(Chardonnay, Vidal Blanc)*, Vidal Blanc.

Rosé Wines: Rosé *(Chambourcin, Vidal Blanc)*.

Red Wines: Cabernet Sauvignon, Chambourcin, Merlot, Reserve Red.

Sweet/Dessert Wines: Late Harvest *(Vidal Blanc)*, Sweet Amber *(Chambourcin)*.

Price Range: $12–$21

Tastings: $7 per person.

Groups: Reservations required for groups of 10 or more; $10 tasting fee per person, including cheese, crackers, and sausages.

Directions: From Leesburg, drive north on U.S. Route 15 for about 7 miles. Turn right onto Spinks Ferry Road (Route 657) (portions unpaved). Continue 2 miles to the winery entrance on right.

Lost Creek Winery & Vineyards
43277 Spinks Ferry Road
Leesburg VA 20176

Hours: Th–M, 11:00–5:00   703-443-9836
Closed New Year's, Thanksgiving, Christmas   www.lostcreekwinery.com
Stay Tuned: Facebook, Twitter, Newsletter   E-mail: winery@lostcreekwinery.com

   Bob and Carol Hauck founded Lost Creek in 1995, opening their tasting room seven years later. The winery is now owned by Todd and Aimee Henkle, who purchased Lost Creek in early 2013. The winery's mostly estate-grown production currently features a number of semi-sweet wines, and the Henkles plan to expand the offerings to include more dry wines in future vintages.. The tasting room includes a large fireplace and a number of tables in addition to the tasting bar. Visitors can purchase a glass or bottle of wine and snacks to enjoy either indoors or outside on the two patios. Lost Creek sponsors live music on select weekends. The winery can be rented for private events and weddings, and has a caterer's kitchen that can be used for special events. Children and pets are welcome.

White Wines: Chardonnay, Springtime *(Vidal Blanc, Viognier, Chardonnay, Muscat Canelli)*, Sweet Summer *(apple, Vidal Blanc, Chardonnay)*, Vidal Blanc.

Rosé Wines: Rosé *(Merlot, Chardonnay, Niagara)*.

Red Wines: Cabernet Sauvignon, Chambourcin, Chambourcin Gold, Merlot, Reserve *(Bordeaux-style blend)*.

Sweet/Dessert Wines: Late Harvest Alyce *(Vidal Blanc)*, Courtney's Christmas Blend.

Price Range: $14–$22

Tastings: $8 per person.

Groups: Reservations required for groups of 15 or more.

Directions: From Leesburg, drive north on U.S. Route 15 for about 7 miles. Turn right onto Spinks Ferry Road (Route 657) (portions unpaved). Continue 2 miles to the winery entrance on right, next to Hidden Brook Winery; continue another 1/2 mile to the Lost Creek parking lot.

Tarara Winery
13648 Tarara Lane
Leesburg VA 20176

Hours: Daily 11:00–5:00 (F–Su until 6:00, Apr–Nov)   703-771-7100
Closed New Year's, Easter, Thanksgiving, Christmas   www.tarara.com
Stay Tuned: Facebook, Twitter, newsletter   E-mail: specialevents@tarara.com

Carved into a bluff on the Potomac River, Tarara Winery was built in 1985 by Whitic and Margaret Hubert and produced its first wines four years later. Tarara's 475 acres currently include 60 acres of vineyards in addition to orchards and 6 miles of hiking trails. Winemaker Jordan Harris, who hails from Canada, has overseen Tarara's wine operations since 2007, focusing on small-lot production of classic French varietals. After sampling wines, visitors can enjoy a light picnic at the tables and benches on the two patios that overlook the river and the Maryland hills beyond. A self-guided tour of the wine cave is also available. Be sure to purchase your tasting tickets at the cash register at the entrance to the tasting room.

White Wines: Chardonnay, Charval *(Chardonnay, Sauvignon Blanc, Pinot Gris)*, Honah Lee White, Nevaeh White, Tarara White.

Rosé Wines: Rosé.

Red Wines: Cabernet Franc, Cabernet Sauvignon, Long Bomb *(Bordeaux-style blend)*, Merlot, Nevaeh Red, Pinot Noir, Tranquility.

Price Range: $15–$45

Tastings: $10 for 6 wines; $20 for 7 premier tasting (75 minutes, includes cheese plate).

Groups: Reservations required for groups of 10 or more on weekends; $35 per person fee.

Vine Club members receive quarterly shipments, discounts, invitations to special events; minimum one-year membership required.

Purchasing: Online or telephone purchases are available for AK, CA, CO, FL, LA, MN, MO, NV, NH, NC, ND, OR, VT, VA, WA, and DC.

Directions: From U.S. Route 15, turn onto Lucketts Road (Route 662) and continue 3 miles to the winery driveway on left; continue another 1/4 mile to the parking lot.

WINE ORIGINS

The *Oxford Companion to Wine* defines wine as the fermented juice of fruits or berries, a broad category that excludes ales, beers, and distilled liquors but includes fermented products flavored from flowers or herbs. Most frequently, wine refers specifically to the fermented beverage made from the juice of grapes.

The earliest archeological evidence of grape cultivation for the express purpose of winemaking was found in the southern Caucasus, the region between the Black Sea and the Caspian Sea in the areas of modern-day Georgia, Armenia, and Azerbaijan, according to Hugh Johnson in *Vintage: The Story of Wine.*

By 500 BC, vines were being cultivated and wine made throughout the eastern Mediterranean region. Tomb paintings from ancient Egypt include depictions of grape cultivation and winemaking, and ancient Greek historians such as Herodotus and Thucydides have left references to viticulture in their writings.

With the rise of the Roman Empire, winemaking began to expand to the areas of modern-day France, Spain, and Germany. Even in areas not as suitable for grape cultivation, such as modern-day Britain, wine was a much-prized commodity.

All of these wines would have been made from the *Vitis vinifera* species of grapevine (sometimes abbreviated as *V. vinifera* or simply *vinifera*). Widely adaptable to a broad range of climates and regions, *V. vinifera* includes over five thousand different varieties and accounts for the vast majority of wines made around the world today.

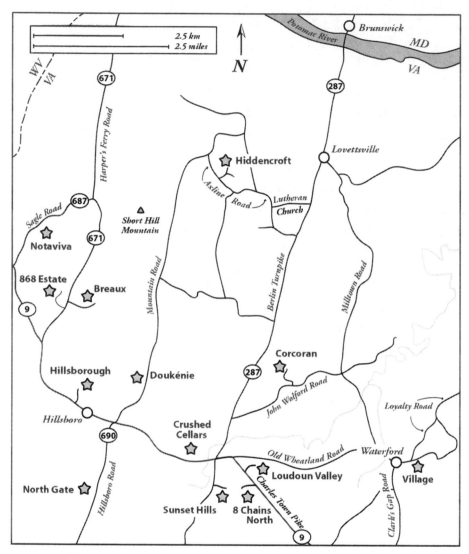

Map 4.3. Northwest Loudoun

NORTHWEST LOUDOUN

8 Chains North
38593 Daymont Lane
Waterford VA 20197

Hours: F 12:00–6:00 (8:00 in summer), Sa–Su 11:00–6:00   571-439-2255

Closed New Year's, Christmas   www.8chainsnorth.com

Stay Tuned: Facebook, Twitter   E-mail: info@8chainsnorth.com

Owner-winemaker Ben Renshaw opened his 8 Chains North Winery to the public in 2010 after producing and selling wine for several years, including through Fabbioli Cellars. The winery's tasting room is housed in a restored barn featuring a mobile tasting bar that can be reconfigured to suit various events. Visitors may purchase a glass or bottle to enjoy either inside at one of the tables or sofas, or outside on the patio overlooking one of the winery's vineyards. The winery features live music on Friday evenings in summer. Children and leashed pets are welcome.

White Wines: LoCo Vino *(Traminette, Vidal Blanc)*, Sauvignon Blanc.

Rosé Wines: Pink Link *(Merlot).*

Red Wines: Cabernet Sauvignon, Furnace Mountain Red *(Bordeaux-style blend)*, Merlot.

Price Range: $18–$22

Tastings: $5 per person.

Wheelchair accessible.

Directions: From Leesburg, take Route 7 West and drive 2 miles. Merge onto Route 9 West (Charles Town Pike). Drive 4 miles and turn left onto Daymont Lane (portions unpaved). The winery is on the left after ¼ mile.

868 Estate Vineyards
14001 Harpers Ferry Road
Purcellville VA 20132

Hours: W, Th, Su 11:00–6:00, Fr–Sa 11:00–7:00
Closed New Year's, Thanksgiving, Christmas
Stay Tuned: Facebook

540-668-7008
www.868estatevineyards.com
E-mail: info@868estatevineyards.com

Carl DiManno, Peter Deliso, and Wendy Charron opened 868 Estate Vineyards in May 2012 after working in the Maryland wine industry. The winery is located on the grounds of the Grandale Restaurant, just down the road from Breaux Vineyards, and its name comes from the elevation of the property's highest point. While 868's own vines mature, the winery is making wine from Chatham and Hague grapes that is produced at two Maryland wineries; several wines from Chatham Vineyards are also on offer. The winery features live music on select Friday evenings and is available for special events. The Grandale Restaurant is open for reservations Wednesday through Sunday. Children and leashed dogs are welcome.

White Wines: Chardonnay (Chatham), Gewurztraminer, Pinot Grigio.

Rosé Wines: Rosé of Merlot.

Red Wines: Cabernet Franc (Chatham), Merlot (Chatham), Meritage.

Price Range: $16–$28

Tastings: $8 per person with souvenir glass.

Wheelchair accessible.

Directions: From Route 7, merge onto Route 9 West (Charles Town Pike). Drive 9.8 miles and turn right onto Harper's Ferry Road (Route 671). Continue 0.8 mile to the winery entrance on left.

Breaux Estate Vineyards
36888 Breaux Vineyards Lane
Purcellville VA 20132

Hours: Daily 11:00–6:00 (May–Nov), 11:00–5:00 (Dec–Apr) 1-800-492-9961
Closed New Year's, Easter, Thanksgiving, Christmas www.breauxvineyards.com
Stay Tuned: Facebook, Twitter, newsletter E-mail: info@BreauxVineyards.com

Breaux [pronounced *bro*] Vineyards is located on a 404-acre estate with over one hundred fifteen acres of vineyards planted to eighteen different grape varieties. All their wines are from estate-grown grapes. The tasting room's patios offer visitors panoramic views of the vines, the valley, and nearby mountains. Tours are given daily when permitted by winery operations with a three-dollar per person fee. For tastings, last pours begin thirty minutes before closing. Gourmet snacks and breads are available for purchase. Breaux sponsors several festivals, including a Key West Festival, a Cajun Festival, and Dog Days. The winery can be rented for private events and weddings. Breaux will be opening a new ballroom and pub-style club room for special events in early 2013. Children and pets are welcome.

White Wines: Jennifer's Jambalaya, Jolie Blonde *(Seyval Blanc)*, Madeleine's Chardonnay, Sauvignon Blanc, Viognier.

Rosé Wines: Rosé.

Red Wines: Cabernet Franc, Equation *(Bordeaux-style blend)*, Marquis de Lafayette *(Cabernet Franc)*, Meritage, Merlot, Nebbiolo.

Sweet/Dessert Wines: Chère Marie *(Vidal Blanc)*, Nebbiolo Ice Late Harvest, Soleil *(late-harvest Muscat Blanc, Vidal Blanc)*.

Price Range: $13–$38

Tastings: $10 per person.

Groups: Reservations required for groups of 8 or more; limo tours are limited to 15 people, $13 per person fee.

Wheelchair accessible.

Cellar Club members receive regular wine shipments, free tastings, discounts on purchases, and members-only events.

Restrictions: Dogs are not permitted on the grounds during special events or festivals with the exception of Dog Day, when dogs are the stars.

Purchasing: Online or phone purchases for CA, LA, OH, OR, VA, WV, and DC.

Directions: From Route 7, merge onto Route 9 West (Charles Town Pike). Drive 9.8 miles and turn right onto Harper's Ferry Road (Route 671). Continue 1 mile to the winery entrance on right.

Corcoran Vineyards
14635 Corkys Farm Lane
Waterford VA 20197

Hours: Sa–Su 12:00–5:00   540-882-9073
Closed New Year's, Thanksgiving, Christmas   www.corcoranvineyards.com
Stay Tuned: Facebook, Twitter, newsletter   E-mail: info@corcoranvineyards.com

Jim and Lori Corcoran opened their winery just outside Waterford in 2002. Winemaker Lori focuses on producing high-quality wine using both her own estate-grown grapes and fruit from two neighboring vineyards. Corcoran's small tasting room is in a renovated 1750's-era house; it has room for about twelve guests around the tasting bar. Several picnic tables on the grounds offer a view of the nearby hills and pond. Corcoran offers free Wi-Fi, as well as occasional wine-tasting classes.

Corcoran wines are also available for tasting and purchasing at the Hunter's Run Wine Barn in Hamilton, Virginia (40325 Charles Town Pike). Tastings are held on the first Friday of each month (3:00-9:00) as well as Saturdays and Sundays (12:00-6:00). Corcoran now produces craft beers for sale at the Corcoran Brewing Company in a separate building on the property.

Fruit Wines: Apple.

White Wines: Riesling, Traminette, Viognier.

Rosé Wines: Rosé.

Red Wines: Cabernet Franc, Chambourcin, Petit Verdot, Pinot Noir, Tannat.

Sweet/Dessert Wines: Blackjack, Cello, RAZ.

Fortified Wines: USB *(port-style)*.

Price Range: $16–$20

Tastings: $7 per person.

Groups: Reservations required for groups of 6 or more; $10 per person fee.

Wheelchair accessible.

Directions: From Leesburg, drive west on Route 7 and merge onto Route 9 West (Charles Town Pike). Drive 5.7 miles and turn north onto Berlin Turnpike (Route 287). Drive 1 mile and turn right onto John Wolford Road (portions unpaved). Continue 1.5 miles and turn left onto Corkys Farm Lane (portions unpaved); the winery's gravel driveway will be 1/3 mile on the left.

Crushed Cellars
37938 Charles Town Pike
Purcellville VA 20132

Hours: Sa 11:30–5:00
Closed New Year's, Christmas
Stay Tuned: Newsletter

571-374-9463 (WINE)
www.crushedcellars.com
E-mail: info@crushedcellars.com

Bob Kalok opened Crushed Cellars in 2011 on the grounds of his family farm. Indeed, visitors may well spot a chicken or two strolling about the property, as well as one of the winery cats sunning itself on the porch. The family is currently using grapes from other Virginia vineyards while their own vines mature. The winery offers cheeses, spreads, and bread for purchase and enjoyment on the front porch or grounds. The two-story winery tasting room is available for small parties. Children are welcome.

White Wines: Seyval Blanc, Vidal Blanc.

Red Wines: Cabernet Sauvignon.

Price Range: $15–$20

Tastings: $3 per person.

Restrictions: No groups over 6.

Directions: From Route 7, merge onto Route 9 West (Charles Town Pike). Drive 5.8 miles to the winery's gravel driveway on the right.

Doukénie Winery
14727 Mountain Road
Purcellville VA 20132

Hours: Daily 10:00–6:00 (F to 9:00, Sa to 8:00, summer only)　　540-668-6464
Closed Thanksgiving, Christmas　　www.doukeniewinery.com
Stay Tuned: Facebook, Twitter, newsletter　　E-mail: info@DoukenieWinery.com

Doukénie Winery was founded by George and Nicki Bazaco and is named in honor of George's grandmother, Doukénie Bacos who arrived in the United States from Greece in 1920. Located on five hundred acres near the Blue Ridge Mountains, Doukénie offers scenic views of the surrounding hills, the vineyards, and winery pond from its tasting room and veranda. The winery hosts frequent events, including Taste of Greece and Taste of Italy festivals, barrel and harvest tastings, and cooking and art classes. Winemaker Sébastien Marquet occasionally leads trips to his native France, with a focus on winemaking regions. The winery may be rented for special events and parties. Children and pets are welcome.

Fruit Wines: Elderberry, Hope's Legacy Raspberry Wine.

White Wines: Chardonnay, Mandolin *(Traminette, Vidal Blanc)*, Pinot Grigio, Riesling, Sauvignon Blanc, Viognier.

Red Wines: Cabernet Franc, Cabernet Sauvignon, Cabernet/Syrah, Merlot, Petit Verdot, Sangiovese, Syrah, Vintner's Reserve *(Bordeaux-style blend)*, Zeus *(Merlot, Tannat, Petit Verdot)*.

Price Range: $21–$38

Tastings: $8 per person.

Groups: Reservations required for groups of 8 or more.

Restrictions: Limos and buses by appointment only.

Purchasing: Phone or e-mail orders for all states _except_ AL, AR, MA, ME, MD, MS, MT, NJ, NM, OK, PA, RI, SD, TN, UT, and WI.

Heritage Wine Club members receive regular wine shipments, free tastings, and discounts.

Directions: From Route 7, merge onto Route 9 West (Charles Town Pike). Drive 7.3 miles and turn right onto Mountain Road (Route 690 North). Continue 1 mile to the winery entrance on the left.

Hiddencroft Vineyards
12202 Axline Road
Lovettsville VA   20180

Hours: F–M 12:00–6:00 (Sa to 8:00, May–Oct)
Sa–Su, 12:00–5:00 (Oct–Apr)
Closed New Year's, Thanksgiving, Christmas
Stay Tuned: Facebook, Twitter

540-535-5367
www.hiddencroftvineyards.com
E-mail: hiddencroft@aol.com

The northernmost winery in Virginia, Hiddencroft is a family-run operation owned by Terry and Clyde Housel; Clyde also serves as wine-maker. The Housels have been cultivating grapes on six acres of their sixteen-acre property since 2001; they also produce several fruit wines from their own harvests. At this small winery, visitors probably will find themselves being served by the owners, who gladly share information about their wines and vintages. The tasting room is housed in an 1830s-era farmhouse with a deck with tables and umbrellas for seating. The farm-house's original laundry and smokehouse outbuildings provide a scenic backdrop for photos. The owners are planning to convert the smokehouse into a separate tasting room for private tastings. While no outside food is permitted, Hiddencroft offers snacks for purchase and enjoyment over a glass of wine on its patio. Children are welcome.

Fruit Wines: Grandma's Love Potion *(blueberry)*, Sweet Cherry, Vitis Rubus *(raspberry, Chambourcin)*.

White Wines: Chardonnay, Traminette, Vidal Blanc.

Red Wines: Cabernet Franc, Chambourcin, Dutchman's Creek *(Cabernet Franc, Cabernet Sauvignon, Petit Verdot, Tannat)*, Tannat.

Price Range: $18–$40

Tastings: $6 per person.

Groups: Reservations required for groups of 9 to 25; $10 per person with souvenir glass.

Restrictions: No groups over 25.

Directions: From Route 7, merge onto Route 9 West (Charles Town Pike). Drive 5.7 miles and turn right onto the Berlin Turnpike (Route 287) toward Lovettsville. Continue 5 miles and turn left at Lutheran Church Road (unpaved). At the end of the road, turn right onto Axline Road (Route 680) (portions unpaved). Drive 1.6 miles and turn right into the winery drive (unpaved). Bear left at the large red barn to the winery parking lot entrance on the right.

Hillsborough Vineyards
36716 Charles Town Pike
Purcellville VA 20132

Hours: F–M, 11:00–5:00

Closed Easter, Thanksgiving, Christmas

Stay Tuned: Facebook, Twitter

540-668-6216

www.hillsboroughwine.com

E-mail: info@hillsboroughwine.com

A family-owned farm winery, Hillsborough Vineyards was founded by Bora and Zeynep Baki who moved to the Washington, D.C., area from their native Turkey in 1979. The couple purchased the property in 2001 and began establishing the vineyard. Son Kerem serves as the winemaker as well as for Casanel, Dry Run, and Vintage Ridge Vineyards. Many of Hillsborough's mostly estate-grown wines bear the name of a gemstone, including two named after Bora and Zeynep's mothers. The tasting room is in a restored pre-Civil War barn, with two stone patios that offer a magnificent view of the Blue Ridge Mountains and adjoining valley. Hillsborough hosts several wine and live music events, including an annual Caribbean Nights festival, and is available for private parties and weddings.

White Wines: Carnelian *(Roussanne)*, Chardonnay, Opal *(Petit Manseng)*.

Rosé Wines: Serefina *(Viognier, Tannat)*.

Red Wines: Bloodstone *(Fer Servadou, Tannat)*, Garnet *(Bordeaux-style blend)*, Onyx *(Tannat)*, Ruby *(Tannat, Fer Servadou, Petit Verdot)*.

Sweet/Dessert Wines: Moonstone *(late-harvest Viognier)*.

Price Range: $22–$32

Tastings: $7 per person.

Groups: Reservations required for groups of 8 or more.

Wheelchair accessible.

Restrictions: No limos, buses, or vans on Saturdays. No food on patios unless purchased at the winery.

Frequent Winer club members receive discounts on wine, complimentary tastings, special events.

Directions: From Route 7, merge onto Route 9 West (Charles Town Pike) and drive 8 miles. The winery entrance will be on the right about 1/2 mile past the town of Hillsboro.

Loudoun Valley Vineyards
38516 Charles Town Pike
Waterford VA 20197

Hours: M, W–F 12:00–5:00, Sa–Su 11:00–6:00   540-882-3375
Closed Easter, Thanksgiving, Christmas   www.loudounvalleyvineyards.com
Stay Tuned: Facebook, Twitter, newsletter   E-mail: info@loudounvalleyvineyards.com

Loudoun Valley Vineyards is near the village of Waterford. Winemaker Bree Ann Moore and her husband Cameron purchased the winery after moving to the Washington, D.C., area from Bree's native Sonoma Valley. The tasting room has two tasting bars and a number of tables for extra seating, as well as an outdoor deck and picnic area that offer scenic views of the surrounding valley and nearby Blue Ridge Mountains. The winery is available for rental for private events, parties, and weddings. Children and pets are welcome.

Fruit Wines: Vin de Pommes *(apple)*.

White Wines: Chardonnay, Classic White *(Seyval Blanc, Traminette)*, Pinot Grigio, Seyval Blanc, Traminette, Viognier.

Red Wines: Cabernet Franc, Chambourcin, Dynasty *(Cabernet Franc, Merlot, Touriga Nacional)*, Merlot, Pinot Noir, Syrah, Vinifera Red.

Fortified Wines: Legacy *(Touriga Nacional)*.

Price Range: $17–$30

Tastings: $5 per person.

Vintner's Club members receive wine shipments, discounts, and special events.

Directions: From Route 7, merge onto Route 9 West (Charles Town Pike). Drive 5 miles to the winery's gravel drive on the right.

North Gate Vineyard
16031 Hillsboro Road
Purcellville VA 20132

Hours: Th–M 11:00–6:00 (F to 8:00 in summer) 540-668-6248
Closed Christmas, New Year's www.northgatevineyard.com
Stay Tuned: Facebook, Twitter, newsletter E-mail: vicki@north-gate.com;
fedor@north-gate.com

    Owner/vintners Mark and Vicki Fedor purchased their North Gate farm in 1997 and became interested in winemaking after discovering grape vines on the property. Their LEED-certified tasting room opened in 2011 and includes both indoor and outdoor seating. The winery sponsors live music on weekends. All the wines are from grapes grown either from North Gate's own vineyards or from other Loudoun County vineyards. The winery may be rented for private events. North Gate often participates in the annual Grapehound Wine Tour, a benefit for greyhound adoption.

Fruit Wines: Apple (proceeds go to Blue Ridge Greyhound Adoption, (http://brga.org)

White Wines: Chardonnay, Viognier.

Red Wines: Cabernet Franc, Meritage, Merlot, Petit Verdot.

Price Range: $13–$24

Tastings: $5 per person.

Groups: Reservations required for groups of 10 or more, $10 per person fee.

Restrictions: No smoking permitted.

Purchasing: Online sales for residents of AK, CA, CT, GA, LA, MI, NC, ND, NE, NH, NE, OH, SC, TX, VA, WY, and DC.

Trellis Club members receive regular shipments, discounts, members-only events.

Directions: From Route 7, merge west onto Route 9 (Charles Town Pike). Drive 7.6 miles and turn left onto Hillsboro Road (Route 690). The winery will be on the right in 1.7 miles.

Notaviva Vineyards
13274 Sagle Drive
Purcellville VA 20132

Hours: F–Sa 11:00–8:00, Su to 6:00; Th, M to 5:00 (Apr–Dec)   540-668-6756
Th–Su 11:00–5:00 (to 6:00 on Sa) (Jan–Mar)   www.notavivavineyards.com
Closed New Year's, Thanksgiving, Christmas   E-mail: info@NotavivaVineyards.com
Stay Tuned: Facebook, Twitter, newsletter

Stephen and Shannon Mackey established Notaviva Vineyards in 2004 in the secluded northwest corner of Loudoun County. The winery's two-story tasting room offers a scenic view of the winery pond and nearby hills; the grounds also include a number of benches and picnic tables for guests to use. Both Mackeys have backgrounds as musicians, and their winery frequently sponsors live musical performances on weekends. Notaviva is available for private parties and weddings, either in the tasting room or at their outdoor wedding site, The Glade. Children and leashed pets are welcome.

Notaviva also operates the Concertino tasting room at 1025 West Main Street in Berryville, Virginia (Th 12–8, F-Sa 12–10, Su 12–6).

White Wines: Calor Chardonnay, Ottantotto Viognier, Vincerò *(Viognier)*.

Red Wines: Cantabile Cabernet Franc, Celtico Chambourcin.

Dessert Wines: Gitano Chambourcin.

Price Range: $17–$28

Tastings: $8 per person.

Groups: Reservations required for groups of 8 or more; $12 per person fee for groups of 8-16; $32 per person for groups over 16, with bottle of wine.

Wheelchair accessible (some limitations).

Purchasing: Online ordering is available for VA and FL.

Directions: From Route 7, take Route 9 West (Charles Town Pike) for 11.6 miles. Turn right onto Sagle Road (Route 687) (portions unpaved). The winery will be on the right after 1 mile.

Sunset Hills Vineyard
38295 Fremont Overlook Lane
Purcellville VA 20132

Hours: M–Th 12:00–5:00, F–Su 12:00–6:00 (F to 8:00, Mar-Nov)   540-882-4560

Closed New Year's, Thanksgiving, Christmas   www.sunsethillsvineyard.com

Stay Tuned: Facebook, Twitter, newsletter   E-mail: information@sunsethillsvineyard.com

Located on a rise overlooking the Loudoun Valley and Blue Ridge Mountains, Sunset Hills Vineyard was established by Mike and Diane Canney, who now have over sixty acres under vine. The spacious two-story tasting room is in a 130-year-old Amish barn that includes a large four-sided tasting bar in the middle. The historic structure was carefully restored by Amish carpenters from Lancaster County, Pennsylvania, who have since returned to build an outdoor events gazebo next to the tasting room.

While no outside food is permitted, Sunset Hills offers a range of breads, cheeses, meats, and spreads for purchase. The winery sponsors live music on weekends, wine pairings, and special charity events, such as the Loudoun Therapeutic Riding fundraiser. An annual wine harvest tasting series is also offered in the fall. Sunset Hills may be rented for private functions or weddings. Children and pets are welcome.

White Wines: Chardonnay, Sunset White *(Chardonnay, Viognier)*, Viognier.

Rosé Wines: Sunset Rosé *(Cabernet Franc, Syrah, Mourvedre)*.

Red Wines: Cabernet Franc, Cabernet Sauvignon, Merlot, Sunset Red *(Cabernet Sauvignon)*.

Dessert Wines: Nettare di Tramonto.

Price Range: $22–$40

Tastings: $7 per person.

Groups: Reservations required for groups of 8 or more, $10 per person fee.

Restrictions: No group tastings on Saturdays or Sundays.

Estate Wine Club members receive regular wine shipments of wine, discounts on purchases and special events, and access to the reserved top floor of the tasting room.

Directions: From Route 7, merge onto Route 9 West (Charles Town Pike). Drive 5.7 miles to the Berlin Turnpike (Route 287). Turn left and drive 2.6 miles. Turn left into Fremont Overlook Lane (portions unpaved) to the winery parking lot on the right.

Village Winery
40405 Browns Lane
Waterford VA 20197

Hours: Sa 11:00–6:00, Su 12:00–5:00
Closed New Year's, Christmas

540-882-3780
www.villagewineryandvineyards.com
E-mail: info@villagewineryandvineyards.com

The Village Winery is a small family-owned farm winery located on a working farm in the historic village of Waterford. Kent and Karen Marrs opened the winery in 2005 and grow Cabernet Franc, Merlot, and Petit Verdot on their ten-acre vineyard. Winemaker Kent crafts his wines entirely by hand, using no mechanical pumps during the process. The tasting room is located in a small restored farm building on the property, with standing room at the tasting bar for about ten visitors; limited additional seating is available outside. Village Winery also offers several elderberry products for sale. Children are welcome.

Fruit Wines: Apple, Elderberry, Elderberry-Apple, Raspberry-Apple.

White Wines: Viognier.

Rosé Wines: Rosé *(Cabernet Franc)*.

Red Wines: Cabernet Franc, Merlot, Merlot-Cabernet Franc, Petit Verdot.

Price Range: $12–$20

Groups: Reservations requested for groups of 6 or more.

Directions: From Leesburg, take Route 7 and merge onto Route 9 West (Charles Town Pike). Drive 1/2 mile, then turn right onto Clarks Gap Road. Continue 3 miles through Waterford and bear right onto Loyalty Road. Take the second right onto Browns Lane and turn into the first drive on the right.

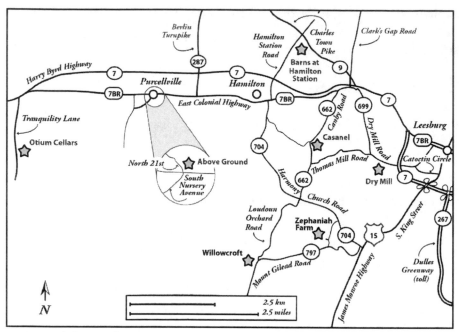

Map 4.4. Leesburg West

LEESBURG WEST

Above Ground Winery
105 East Main Street
Purcellville VA 20132

Hours: Th–M 10:00–6:00 (Fr–Sa til 9:00 in summer)   540-579-4467
Closed Thanksgiving, New Year's, Christmas   www.agwinery.com
Stay Tuned: Facebook, Twitter   E-mail: marybeth@agwinery.com

Above Ground Winery is owned and operated by Matt and Mary Beth Barbagallo, who housed their tasting room in a restored movie theater in the center of historic Purcellville. The Barbagallos supplement their own production with grapes from vineyards leased from nearby Tarara and Fabbioli. The winery sponsors various activities, including live music and potluck dinners, and offers a small retail shop in the tasting room. Above Ground is available for rental for parties and special occasions.

White Wines: Chardonnay.

Rosé Wines: White Chambourcin.

Red Wines: Chambourcin, Karma, Vintner's Reserve *(Bordeaux-style blend)*.

Sweet/Dessert Wines: Sweet Rebecca Lynn.

Price Range: $18–$32

Tastings: $10 per person ($1 for active-duty or retired military with ID).

Groups: Reservations required for groups of 8 or more, 3 days in advance; $15 per person fee.

Wheelchair accessible.

Directions: From Leesburg, take Route 7 West and drive about 9 miles. Turn left onto the Berlin Turnpike (Route 287) toward the town of Purcellville. Turn right onto East Main Street and drive 1.2 miles. The tasting room will be on the right; on-street parking as well as several town parking lots are available nearby.

Barns at Hamilton Station
6804 Hamilton Station Road
Hamilton, VA 20158

Hours: F 12:00–8:00, Th, Sa–M 12:00–6:00   540-338-5309
Closed New Year's Eve & Day, Easter,   www.thebarnsathamiltonstation.com
Thanksgiving, Christmas Eve & Day   E-mail: hamiltonstationvineyards@yahoo.com
Stay Tuned: Facebook, Twitter

The Barns at Hamilton Station opened in 2012 under the ownership of Craig and Kim Garten and Andrew and Marianne Fialdini, with Michael Shaps as winemaker. Located on an old dairy farm, the winery's tasting room is in a restored barn that can be rented for weddings and parties. The winery produces its wines from their own vineyards or a leased vineyard near Charlottesville. The winery features live music on select Friday evenings. Children and leashed dogs are welcome.

White Wines: Chardonnay, Viognier.

Red Wines: Cabernet Franc, Merlot, Meritage, Petit Verdot.

Price Range: $22–$26

Tastings: $5 per person with souvenir glass.

Groups: Reservations required for groups of 8 or more; $10 per person fee.

Wheelchair accessible.

Purchasing: Onling ordering available via VinoShipper to AK, FL, ID, LA, MN, MO, NE, NV, NH, N, ND, OH, OR, DC, WV, and WY.

Directions: From Leesburg, take Route 7 West and drive 7 miles. Turn right at the Hamilton exit and then left onto VA Route 704. Drive 0.7 miles to the winery entrance on the right.

Casanel Vineyards
17956 Canby Road
Leesburg VA 20175

Hours: Th 2:00–6:00, F–M 11:00–6:00 (Apr–Nov)   703-505-9674
F–M 12:00–6:00 (Dec–Mar)   www.casanelvineyards.com
Closed New Year's, Easter, July 4ᵗʰ,   E-mail: info@casanelvineyards.com
Thanksgiving, mid-Dec to mid-Jan
Stay Tuned: Facebook, Twitter

Casey and Nelson DeSouza opened Casanel Vineyards to the public in 2008, several years after Nelson retired as head of DeSouza Construction, which he had founded in the 1980s. Casanel is on forty scenic acres outside Leesburg on Catoctin Mountain and offers visitors a tranquil picnic area featuring several nineteenth-century buildings, including a barn that Nelson renovated to serve as a tasting room. Casanel's "Chegada" (Portuguese for "arrival") label was named in honor of Nelson's arrival in the United States in the 1960s from his native Brazil. Casanel also sponsors special events, including live music on summer weekends, and offers pizzas and light picnic snacks for purchase on the patio. Children and pets are welcome. Please note that last pours are twenty minutes before closing.

White Wines: Chardonnay, Don Lorenzo *(Pinot Gris, Chardonnay)*, Viognier.

Rosé Wines: Rosé *(Norton)*.

Red Wines: Cabernet Sauvignon, Merlot, Norton.

Sweet/Dessert Wines: Dulce *(late harvest Viognier)*.

Price Range: $21–$26

Tastings: $5 per person

Groups: Advance reservations required for groups of 8 to 20; $10 per person fee for groups of 10 or more.

Restrictions: No groups over 20; no limos or buses without advance reservations.

Wheelchair accessible.

Directions: From Leesburg, drive on Route 7 West and take the Route 9 exit (Charles Town Pike). Turn left at the bottom of the exit ramp onto Route 9 East. At the stop sign, turn right onto East Colonial Highway (Business Route 7). Drive 1/2 mile and turn left onto Canby Road (portions unpaved). The winery will be 1.4 miles on the left.

Dry Mill Vineyards & Winery
18195 Dry Mill Road
Leesburg VA 20175

Hours: Th 12:00–5:00; F 12:00–8:00;
Sa 11:00–6:00, Su 11:00–5:00
Closed Easter, Thanksgiving, Christmas
Stay Tuned: Newsletter

703-737-3930
www.drymillwine.com
E-mail: info@drymillwine.com

Dry Mill Vineyards & Winery, located just outside Leesburg, opened its doors in early 2009 in the renovated stable and barn of the former Loudoun Hunt Club. Owners Dean and Nancy Vanhuss source their wines from the Vanhuss's Short Hill Vineyards near Lovettsville, and winemakers Dean and Kerem Baki are gradually increasing the varietals under production. The tasting room offers visitors a pleasant setting in which to enjoy Dry Mill's wines, including a fireplace, balconies overlooking the grounds, and a patio that seats up to 30 for wine tastings. Light fare is available for purchase. The winery offers live music on weekends. Children are welcome.

White Wines: Chardonnay, Traminette, Viognier.

Rosé Wines: Rosé.

Red Wines: Cabernet Franc, Chambourcin, Merlot, Norton, Syrah.

Sweet/Dessert Wines: Dessert *(Chambourcin).*

Price Range: $15–$22

Tastings: $5 per person for groups up to 7; $10 per person for groups of 8 to 20.

Groups: Reservations required for groups over 20.

Wheelchair accessible.

Wine Club members receive discounts on wine purchases, invitations to special events.

Directions: From Leesburg, drive south on U.S. Route 15 (King Street) and turn west onto Catoctin Circle SE. Drive about ½ mile and turn left onto Dry Mill Road SW. The winery entrance will be two miles on the left.

Otium Cellars at Goose Creek Farms
18050 Tranquility Lane
Purcellville VA 20132

Hours: M, Th 11:00–5:00, F to 8:00; Sa, Su to 5:00   540-338-2027
Closed New Year's, Thanksgiving, Christmas   www.otiumcellars.com
E-mail: info@otiumcellars.com

Gerhard Bauer opened Otium Cellars in May 2012 on the grounds of his family's Goose Creek Farms, where the family breeds Hanoverian show horses. Gerhard serves as winemaker, working closely with Ben Renshaw of nearby 8 Chains North. The two-story tasting room is adjacent to the stables and offers seating both indoors and out. The tasting room includes a two-sided wood stove that adds a cozy touch on chilly winter days. Children and dogs are welcome.

White Wines: Chardonnay, Pinot Gris.

Red Wines: Blaufränkisch, Cabernet Sauvignon, Dornfelder, Malbec, Pinot Noir.

Price Range: $16–$36

Tastings: $5 per person.

Groups: Reservations recommended for groups of 6 or more.

Wheelchair accessible (some limitations).

Directions: From Route 7, take the Route 7 Business exit at Round Hill. Drive east on Route 7 Business (locally called East Loudoun Street) for 1.3 miles in the direction of Purcellville. Turn right onto Tranquility Road (portions unpaved) and drive 1.8 miles to the winery entrance on the left.

Willowcroft Farm Vineyards
38906 Mount Gilead Road
Leesburg VA 20175

Hours: F–Su 11:00–5:30   703-777-8161
Closed New Year's, Thanksgiving, Christmas   www.willowcroftwine.com
Stay Tuned: Facebook, newsletter   E-mail: info@willowcroftwine.com

Willowcroft is the oldest winery in Loudoun County and was founded in 1979 by owner-winemaker Lew Parker. The tasting room is in a weathered barn that predates the Civil War; light food is available for purchase. The winery grounds include several picnic tables and a one-mile walking trail that offers good views of Loudoun Valley. Willowcroft sponsors a range of events, including turkey chili weekends, an annual Oktoberfest, and an annual champagne special in December. Supplies and seminars for home winemakers are also available. Children and pets are welcome.

White Wines: Albariño, Chardonnay, Harmony, Riesling, Seyval Blanc, Traminette, Vidal Blanc.

Blush Wines: Cabernet Blanc *(Cabernet Sauvignon)*.

Red Wines: Cabernet Franc, Cabernet Sauvignon, Chambourcin, Fitzrada's Reward *(Bordeaux-style blend)*, Merlot, Petit Verdot.

Sweet/Dessert Wines: Claire *(Vidal Blanc)*.

Price Range: $17–$27

Tastings: $5 per person.

Groups: Reservations required for groups of 6 or more; $10 per person fee for groups of 10 to 15 ($12 with cheese or chocolate plate, $15 with hors d'oeuvres plate).

Restrictions: No groups over 15; reservations required for tour buses; no smoking on the grounds.

Purchasing: Online ordering to Virginia residents or via VinoShipper to AK, CA, FL, ID, LA, MO, NE, NV, NH, NM, ND, OH, OR, DC, WV, and WY.

Wine club members receive discounts, members-only events.

Directions: Take U.S. Route 15 South from Leesburg for about 3 miles. Turn right onto Harmony Church Road (Route 704) and make an immediate left onto Mount Gilead Road (portions unpaved). Continue 3 miles to the winery entrance on the right.

Zephaniah Farm Vineyard
19381 Dunlop Mill Road
Leesburg VA 20175

Hours: Sa, Su 12:00–5:30 (Apr to mid-Dec)　　　　703-431-2016
Closed mid-Dec to early Mar　　　　　http://zephwine.com/Z
Stay Tuned: Facebook, Twitter　　　　E-mail: bill@zephwine.com

Zephaniah Farm Vineyard is located on a 376-acre working farm that has been in the Hatch family for three generations. Owners Bill and Bonnie Hatch planted their first vines in 2002 and produced their first vintage six years later; Bill and son Tremaine are the winemakers. Zephaniah's tasting room is located in a first-floor room in the family's historic manor house that was constructed by the builder of President James Monroe's Oak Hill. The winery is named after Bill's great-grandfather, Zephaniah Jefferson Hatch, who founded the Monticello Steamboat Company in the San Francisco region in 1892. The winery's wine and farm products are also offered for sale at the Leesburg farmer's market.

White Wines: Chardonnay.

Red Wines: Cabernet Franc, Cabernet Sauvignon, Chambourcin, Merlot.

Price Range: $20–$27

Tastings: $3 per person.

Groups: Reservations required for groups of 6 or more.

Directions: Take U.S. Route 15 South from Leesburg for about 3 miles. Turn right onto Harmony Church Road (Route 704). Drive one mile and turn left onto Dunlop Mill Road (narrow, most portions unpaved). The winery will be 1/2 mile on the right.

౷

PHYLLOXERA

While Europe's grapes are from *Vitis vinifera*, native American grapevines are members of different *Vitis* species, including *Vitis labrusca*, *Vitis aestivalis*, or *Vitis riparia*. Many American grape varieties excel at producing table grapes or grape juice, but not all are well-suited for wine. Many have strong flavors, and some have a smell that professional wine tasters refer to as "foxiness," a colorful and self-explanatory term.

Native American rootstocks proved to be the salvation of *V. vinifera*—although it must be acknowledged that those same native rootstocks were at the origin of Europe's greatest vineyard crisis.

The mid-nineteenth century was a time of expanding interest in science, including botany, and wealthy Europeans brought back samples of American rootstocks for gardens and greenhouses. Unfortunately, those rootstocks also brought with them the almost microscopic phylloxera louse, which was (and still is) endemic to much of the United States. American grapevines had built up a resistance to phylloxera, but *V. vinifera* is highly vulnerable to phylloxera infestation. Europe's vineyards soon began dying off in an agricultural disaster second only to the Irish potato blight in terms of its impact.

In the 1870s, an American and a French scientist together found a solution. French scientist Jules Planchon was the first to identify the tiny phylloxera louse as the cause of the devastation spreading throughout European vineyards. Missouri state entomologist Charles Riley then uncovered a vital link by identifying the French louse as identical to the American one. Planchon came to Missouri in 1873 to study under Riley's guidance, and the two developed a new approach of grafting *vinifera* vines onto American rootstocks.

Today, roughly 85 percent of *vinifera* vines have been grafted onto native American rootstocks. Because phylloxera finds very dry and/or sandy soils inhospitable, however, ungrafted vines are still cultivated in such regions as South Australia, New Zealand, and Chile.

౷

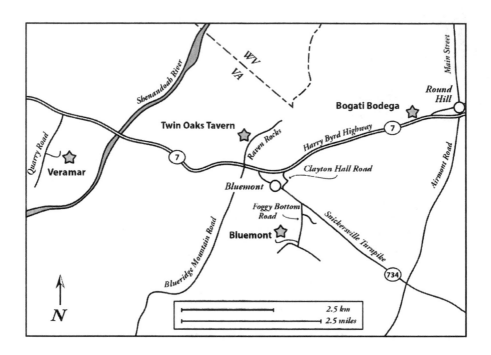

Map 4.5. Bluemont

BLUEMONT

Bluemont Vineyard
18755 Foggy Bottom Road
Bluemont VA 20135

Hours: Th–Su & holiday M 11:00–6:00 (Mar–Oct)   540-554-8439

Th–Su, 11:00–5:00 (Nov–Feb)   www.bluemontvineyard.com

Closed New Year's, Thanksgiving, Christmas   E-mail: 951@bluemontvineyard.com

Stay Tuned: Facebook, Twitter, e-newsletter

Bluemont Vineyard is Loudoun's highest winery, located on the eastern side of the Blue Ridge Mountains at 951 feet above sea level. The winery sources its wines both from its own vines and from other vineyards in the area. The main tasting area is upstairs in the two-story tasting room and features a window wall opening onto a wide deck with panoramic views of the valley toward Leesburg and Washington, D.C. Gourmet sandwiches and snacks are available for purchase and consumption in the tasting room or deck; outside food is not permitted. Children and pets are welcome.

Fruit Wines: Blackberry *(with red wine)*, Peach *(with Vidal Blanc)*, Strawberry *(with red wine)*.

White Wines: Vidal Blanc, Viognier.

Rosé Wines: Rosé.

Red Wines: Cabernet Franc, Cabernet Sauvignon, Merlot, Norton.

Sweet/Dessert Wines: Petit Manseng.

Price Range: $17–$25

Tastings: $7 per person.

Groups: Reservations required for groups of 6 or more for tastings and tours; $15 per person fee.

Directions: From Route 7, turn onto Clayton Hall Road (Route 760 South) toward the town of Bluemont. Take the first left onto Snickersville Turnpike and then turn at the first right onto Foggy Bottom Road to the winery driveway, 1/2 mile on the right. Continue up the hill to the winery parking lot.

Bogati Bodega & Vineyard
35246 Harry Byrd Highway
Round Hill VA 20142

Hours: Daily 12:00–5:00 (F to 9:00, Sa to 6:00) 540-338-1144
Closed New Year's, Thanksgiving, Christmas www.bogatibodega.com
Stay Tuned: Facebook, Twitter E-mail: info@bogatibodega.com

Bogati Bodega was opened to the public in 2010 by the Bogaty family, which also owns Veramar Vineyards. Justin Bogaty serves as winemaker for both; the wines offered at the Bodega are all from grapes grown at Veramar. The Bogatys opened the Bodega after a family trip to Argentina, and many of the winery's events and tastings reflect the inspiration of that wine-producing country. Tango Nights on summertime Friday evenings feature live music on the winery deck. The Bodega also offers daily Wine & Tapas tastings ($25), as well as periodic wine and food pairing menus ($45). The tasting room is available for rental for rehearsal dinners, parties, and corporate events.

White Wines: Seyval Blanc, Tango Blu *(Vidal Blanc, Viognier, Riesling)*, Viognier.

Red Wines: Cabernet Franc, Malbec, Syrah-Mourvedre.

Price Range: $17–$21

Tastings: $7 per person.

Groups: Reservations required for groups of 10 or more; $12 per person fee.

Purchasing: Online purchasing available to all states *except* AL, AR, DE, KY, MD, MA, MS, MT, NJ, OK, PA, SD, and UT.

Directions: From Leesburg, take Route 7 West for 15 miles. The winery will be on the right at the Hill High Orchard Building, about 3/4 mile past Airmont Road/Main Street in the village of Round Hill.

Twin Oaks Tavern Winery
18035 Raven Rocks Road
Bluemont VA 20135

Hours: Th, Su–M 12:00–6:00, F–Sa 12:00–7:00   202-255-5009, 540-554-4547
Closed Thanksgiving, New Year's, Christmas   www.twinoakstavernwinery.com
Stay Tuned: Tango's wine dog blog   E-mail: info@twinoakstavernwinery.com

Twin Oaks Tavern Winery is housed in a restored 100-year-old stone tavern of the same name at the northern edge of the Blue Ridge. Owners Donna and Bob Evers opened the winery to the public in 2008 and currently produce just under two hundred cases of wine annually. The tasting room is in a small restored outbuilding next to a comfortable deck where visitors can enjoy the scenic view of the valley below. Events include live music on Saturday afternoons. The property is available for rental for small private events and weddings. Children and pets are welcome.

Fruit Wines: Peach.

White Wines: Twin Oaks Tavern Chardonnay.

Red Wines: Cabernet Sauvignon, Norton, Raven Rocks Red (*Bordeaux-style blend*).

Price Range: $21–$23

Groups: Advance reservations required for groups over 6.

Directions: From Leesburg, drive west on Route 7 about 15 miles. Just past the village of Bluemont, turn right onto Raven Rocks Road to the winery, 1/3 mile on the left.

Veramar Vineyard
905 Quarry Road
Berryville VA 22611

Hours: Daily 12:00–5:00, Sa until 6:00   540-955-5510
Closed New Year's, Thanksgiving, Christmas   www.veramar.com
Stay Tuned: Facebook, Twitter, newsletter   E-mail: info@veramar.com

Jim and Della Bogaty opened Veramar Vineyard in 2001 on one hundred acres that border the Shenandoah River. Veramar produces about five thousand cases annually of estate-grown wines under the supervision of Justin Bogaty. The tasting room opens onto a covered deck overlooking a pond and the hills beyond. The winery is named after the Vera-Mar Steakhouse in North Carolina, where Jim and Della celebrated their honeymoon; their framed wedding photo and wedding dinner receipt are proudly displayed on the tasting room wall.

Veramar hosts a number of special events, including Friday evening "Wine Downs," Elvis weekends, Dog Day afternoons in August, movie nights, and an annual Taste of Tuscany. Jim Bogaty also offers a wine camp workshop on viticulture, tastings, and wine blending. Breads, cheeses, and other snacks are available for purchase. The facilities are available for weddings and private events. Children and pets are welcome.

White Wines: Chardonnay, Riesling-Vidal Blanc, Seyval Blanc, Très Blanc *(Viognier, Riesling, Vidal Blanc)*, Viognier.

Rosé Wines: Pink Chicken.

Red Wines: Cabernet Franc, Cabernet Sauvignon, Merlot, Mourvedre, Norton, Rooster Red *(Bordeaux-style blend)*.

Sweet/Dessert Wines: D'Oro *(Vidal Blanc)*.

Price Range: $19–$35

Tastings: $7 per person; $15 for reserve tasting (first and third Saturday of each month, reservations appreciated).

Groups: Reservations and prepayment required for groups of 10 or more; $10 per person fee.

Purchasing: Online purchasing available for CA, ID, IL, IA, MO, NM, OR, TX, VA, WA, DC, WI.

Estate Wine Club members receive quarterly shipments, discounts, members-only events, and wines not available to the general public.

Directions: From Leesburg, take Route 7 West for 22 miles. Once across the Shenandoah River, turn left onto Quarry Road (Route 612) and continue one mile to the winery entrance and driveway (portions unpaved) on the left.

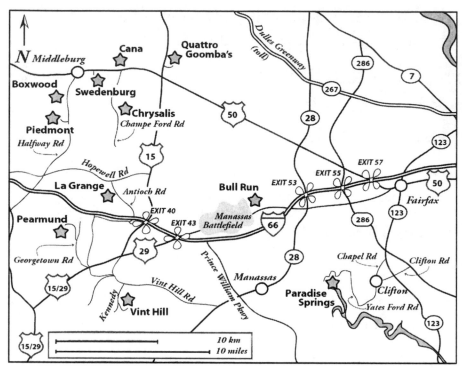

Map 4.6. Middleburg-Fairfax

MIDDLEBURG-FAIRFAX

Boxwood Winery
2042 Burrland Road
Middleburg VA 20118

Hours: F–Su 11:00–6:00

Closed New Year's, Thanksgiving, Christmas

Stay Tuned: Facebook, Twitter, newsletter

540-687-8778

www.boxwoodwinery.com

E-mail: contact@boxwoodwinery.com

Boxwood Winery was founded by John Kent Cooke at the historic Boxwood Estate, one of the earliest farms established in the Middleburg area. Adam McTaggart serves as the winemaker. Boxwood's wines are all Bordeaux-style reds, and its 16-acre vineyard is planted to the five classic Bordeaux grape varieties. Tastings are held either inside the small tasting room, which has several tables and chairs in addition to the circular tasting bar, or outdoors on the patio, weather permitting. Cheese plates and bottled water are available for purchase. Boxwood wines are also available at the winery's satellite tasting rooms in Reston Town Center (1816 Library Street, Reston, VA), Wisconsin Place (5330A Western Avenue, Chevy Chase, MD), and the National Harbor (137 Waterfront Street, Oxon Hill, MD).

Rosé Wines: Rosé *(Merlot, Cabernet Franc, Malbec).*

Red Wines: Boxwood *(Bordeaux-style blend)*, Topiary *(Bordeaux-style blend)*, Trellis *(Bordeaux-style blend).*

Price Range: $14–$25

Tastings: $10 per person.

Groups: Reservations requested for groups of 6 or more.

Restrictions: No tour buses permitted; no smoking on the grounds.

Purchasing: Online purchasing available for residents of AK, CA, CO, CT, FL, HI, MA, MD, MN, NC, NH, VA, and DC.

Directions: From I-66, take Exit 40 onto U.S. Route 15 North. Drive about 10 miles and turn onto U.S. Route 50 West. Continue 5 miles into the village of Middleburg and turn left onto Loudoun Road, which will become Halfway Road. Drive about 1 mile to the winery entrance on the right.

Cana Vineyards & Winery
38600 John Mosby Highway
Middleburg VA 20117

Hours: Th–M 11:00–6:00	703-348-2458
Closed New Year's, Thanksgiving, Christmas	www.canavineyards.com
Stay Tuned: Facebook, Twitter, Newsletter	E-mail: info@canavineyards.com

The Bell family opened Cana Vineyards to the public in mid-2012 on the grounds of an old farm property just outside of Middleburg. The tasting room is sited on a hill, offering a nice view and cooling breezes from the porch and decks; the winery's production facility is in the same building. Visitors may bring their own picnic lunches to enjoy on the grounds or purchase snacks in the tasting room. Cana's winemaker is Brenden McMahon, who works with consultant Alan Kinne. The winery sponsors live music on Saturday and Sunday afternoon year-round. The facilities are available for weddings and private parties. Children and leashed dogs are welcome.

Fruit Wines: Apple, Raspberry-Apple.

White Wines: Riesling, Viognier, Traminette.

Rosé Wines: Rosé.

Red Wines: Cabernet Franc, Le Mariage *(Bordeaux-style blend)*.

Sweet/Dessert Wines: Petit Manseng.

Price Range: $16–$34

Tastings: $10 per person.

Directions: From I-66 West, take Exit 57B onto U.S. Route 50 West toward Fair Oaks/Winchester. Continue on U.S. Route 50 for 20 miles and turn right into the winery driveway.

Chrysalis Vineyards
23876 Champe Ford Road
Middleburg VA 20117

Hours: M–Th 10:00–6:00, F–Su 10:00–6:30 (May–Oct);   540-687-8222
Daily 10:00–5:30 (Nov–Apr)   www.chrysaliswine.com
Closed New Year's, Thanksgiving, Christmas   E-mail: info@ChrysalisWine.com
Stay Tuned: Newsletter

Founded in 1998 by Jennifer McCloud, Chrysalis has over seventy acres of vineyards with plantings in over twenty varieties; most of its wines are estate-grown. McCloud has long had a special interest in the Norton grape and actively works to promote a greater appreciation of this native American variety; indeed, Chrysalis has the largest planting of Norton in the country. Chrysalis is a very popular destination for wine tourists, routinely welcoming over three hundred visitors on Saturdays and Sundays at its facilities. Tastings are held at various outdoor stations every forty-five minutes. The winery has several indoor and outdoor spaces that may be rented for weddings or private parties, including patios complete with barbecue grills. Visitors may purchase cheese and sausage platters, sandwiches, and salads to enjoy at the winery; menus are available online for ordering in advance. Please note that last tastings begin thirty minutes before closing.

White Wines: Albariño, Chardonnay, Sarah's Patio White, Traminette, Viognier.

Rosé Wines: Mariposa, Sarah's Patio Red *(Norton)*.

Red Wines: Norton, Papillon, Petit Verdot, Rubiana, Tannat.

Fortified Wines: Borboleta *(port-style Norton)*.

Sweet/Dessert Wines: Petit Manseng.

Price Range: $15–$35

Tastings: $5 per person; $10 per person for reserve tastings, with souvenir glass.

Groups: Reservations required for groups of 8 or more; group tastings are held before 12:00.

Restrictions: Children are permitted only in the children's outdoor play area and must be accompanied by an adult at all times. Reservations required for tour buses.

Wheelchair accessible.

VIP Wine Club members receive regular wine shipments, discounts on wine purchases, priority seating for special events.

Directions: From I-66 West, take Exit 57B onto U.S. Route 50 West toward Fair Oaks/Winchester. Continue on U.S. Route 50 for 19.7 miles and turn left onto Champe Ford Road (portions unpaved). The winery will be on the left after 1.4 miles.

Paradise Springs Winery & Vineyard
13219 Yates Ford Road
Clifton VA 20124

Hours: W–Su 11:00–7:00, F to 9:00 (Apr–Dec)   703-830-9463
F–Su 11:00–6:00 (Jan–Mar)   www.paradisespringswinery.com
Closed New Year's, Easter,   E-mail: wine@paradisespringswinery.com
Thanksgiving, Christmas
Stay Tuned: Facebook, Twitter, newsletter

Paradise Springs was founded in 2007 by Jane Kincheloe and her son Kirk Wiles on property that has been in their family for generations. Located on thirty-six acres next to Hemlock Regional Park, the winery opened to the public in 2009 in a restored early nineteenth-century log cabin before moving two years later to a new two-story tasting room next door. Paradise Springs sponsors Friday happy hours, live music on weekends, and a pumpkin carving festival in October. The tasting room offers light fare for enjoyment either inside or on the covered deck, which features an outdoor fireplace. The facilities are available for rental for private parties and dinners. Leashed dogs are welcome. Please note that last pours begin thirty minutes before closing.

Sparkling Wines: Après *(Viognier)*.

White Wines: Chardonnay, Petit Manseng, Sauvignon Blanc, Sommet Blanc, Viognier.

Rosé Wines: Nana's Rosé.

Red Wines: Cabernet Franc, Cabernet Sauvignon, Merlot, Meritage, Norton, Petit Verdot.

Price Range: $20–$43

Tastings: $10 per person.

Groups: Reservations required for groups of 8 or more; $15 per person charge.

Wheelchair accessible.

Purchasing: Online ordering is available via VinoShipper to AK, FL, ID, LA, MN, MO, NE, NV, NH, NM, ND, OH, OR, DC, WV, and WY.

Directions: From I-66, take Exit 55 onto southbound Fairfax County Parkway (Route 286 South). Drive about 5 miles and take the exit for Route 123 South. Turn right at the second traffic light onto Clifton Road (Route 645). Turn left onto Yates Ford Road before entering the village of Clifton and drive 1.7 miles to the winery on left.

Pearmund Cellars
6190 Georgetown Road
Broad Run VA 20137

Hours: Daily 10:00–6:00; F to 8:30 (Apr–Oct)   540-347-3475
Closed New Year's, Thanksgiving, Christmas   www.pearmundcellars.com
Stay Tuned: Facebook, Twitter, newsletter   E-mail: info@pearmundcellars.com

Chris Pearmund and Rick Tagg established Pearmund Cellars in 2003 after over a decade of selling grapes to wineries in the region from Pearmund's twenty-five-acre Meriwether Vineyard. The winery sponsors a number of special weekly events, including TGIF nights, Girls Night Out, winemaker dinners, and an SPCA fundraiser. The barrel room is available for rental for parties and dinners. Pearmund welcomes dogs and children, and has a special "Kid's Corner" inside the tasting room.

White Wines: Celebration (Washington state), Old Vine Chardonnay, Petit Manseng, Viognier.

Red Wines: Ameritage, Cabernet Franc, Cabernet Sauvignon, Merlot, Petit Verdot.

Sweet/Dessert Wines: Late Harvest Vidal Blanc.

Price Range: $20–$29

Tastings: $10 per person.

Groups: Reservations required for groups of 8 or more; tastings held between 10:00 a.m. and 3:00 p.m., with a $15 per person charge.

Wheelchair accessible.

Purchasing: Online purchases available for AK, AZ, CA, CO, CT, DC, FL, GA, HI, ID, IL, IN, IA, KS, LA, MI, MN, MO, NE, NV, NH, NM, NY, NC, ND, OH, OR, RI, SC, TX, VT, VA, WA, WV, WI, and WY.

Barrel Club members own a full barrel of wine and receive special tastings, mixed case shipments, discounts, and special members-only events.

Directions: From I-66, take Exit 43A (Gainesville/Warrenton) and merge onto U.S. Route 29 South. Drive 7.5 miles and take a right onto Old Alexandria Turnpike, staying straight to go onto Georgetown Road (Route 674) after 1/4 mile. The long winery driveway (portions unpaved) will be one mile on the left.

Piedmont Vineyards & Winery
2546-D Halfway Road
The Plains VA 20198

Hours: Sa 11:00–5:00, Su 12:00–5:00
Closed New Years Eve & Day,
Christmas Eve & Day

540-687-5528
www.piedmontwines.com
E-mail: piedmontwines@aol.com

Piedmont Vineyards was founded in 1976 by Elizabeth Furness, one of Virginia's pioneer viticulturists, on the pre-Revolutionary War estate of Waverly. Now operated by winemaker Gerhard von Finck, Piedmont supplements its estate-grown Chardonnay with grapes from nearby vineyards. The tasting room is in a renovated stable and offers snacks and gourmet sandwiches for purchase. Please note that groups over four are not currently permitted at the winery.

White Wines: Chardonnay, Little River White *(Seyval Blanc, Chardonnay)*.

Red Wines: Chambourcin, Hunt Country Red, Merlot.

Price Range: $18–$30

Tastings: $6 per person.

Directions: From I-66, take Exit 40 onto U.S. Route 15 North. Drive about 10 miles and turn onto U.S. Route 50 West. Continue 5 miles into the village of Middleburg and turn left onto Loudoun Road, which will become Halfway Road. Drive 2.8 miles to the winery entrance on the right.

Quattro Goomba's Winery
22860 James Monroe Highway
Aldie VA 20105

Hours: F–M 12:00–6:00   703-327-6052
Closed New Year's, Thanksgiving, Christmas   www.goombawine.com
Stay Tuned: Facebook, Twitter, newsletter   E-mail: qgw@goombawine.com

Quattro Goomba's is a micro commercial winery that sources its Mediterranean-style wines from grape-growing regions around the world.

After sampling wines, visitors can stay over a glass or bottle and enjoy freshly baked Sicilian-style pizza by the slice. Quattro Goomba's offers live music on Saturdays and Sundays, and can be rented for weddings and private parties. Children and pets are welcome.

White Wines: Sorelle (Virginia) *(Viognier, Chardonnay)*, Vino di Frascati (Italy) *(Malvasia Bianca, Trebbiano)*.

Red Wines: Vino di Nonni (California), Tradizione (Italy) (aged in bourbon barrels).

Sweet/Dessert Wines: Vino Dolce (California) *(Zinfandel)*.

Price Range: $18–$29

Tastings: $5 per person.

Groups: Reservations required for groups of 8 or more; $10 per person fee with souvenir glass and brief winery tour. Reservations required for private tastings, barrel sampling, and tours; $15 per person charge.

Wheelchair accessible.

Fourth Goomba Wine Club members receive quarterly wine releases, purchasing discounts, and invitations to special events.

Directions: From I-66, take Exit 57B onto U.S. Route 50 West. Follow U.S. Route 50 West for 17 miles through one roundabout. At the second roundabout, take the exit onto James Monroe Highway (U.S. Route 15 North) and drive 1.2 miles to the winery on right.

Swedenburg Estate Vineyard
23595 Winery Lane
Middleburg VA 20117

Hours: F, 11:00–5:00 (summers only), Sa-Su 11:00–5:00   540-687-5219
Closed New Year's, Christmas   www.swedenburgwines.com
Stay Tuned: Facebook   E-mail: info@swedenburgwines.com

The Swedenburg family first began making their estate-grown wine in 1987 on the historic Valley View Estate, which has been an working farm for over two hundred years. The late Juanita Swedenburg, the family matriarch, played a key role in reducing restrictions on interstate wine sales through a lawsuit that ultimately came before the U.S. Supreme Court; the Court's 2005 decision in her favor overturned laws that had restricted wineries from shipping direct to out-of-state customers.

The winery dog may be on hand to greet visitors to the small tasting room, which also offers light snacks for purchase. Visitors can relax outside at one of the picnic tables on the grounds to enjoy the view of the surrounding vineyards. Swedenburg sponsors live music on weekends, as well as pet adoption days, artisan jewelry fairs, and occasional book-signing parties for local authors. Children and pets are welcome.

White Wines: Chardonnay, Chantilly *(Seyval Blanc)*, Riesling.

Rosé Wines: C'Est La Vie.

Red Wines: Cabernet Sauvignon, Pinot Noir.

Price Range: $18–$28

Tastings: $5 per person.

Groups: Reservations required for groups of 6 or more.

Directions: From I-66, take Exit 57B onto U.S. Route 50 West and drive 21 miles to the winery on left.

Vint Hill Craft Winery
7150 Lineweaver Road
Warrenton VA 20187

Hours: F–Su 11:00–6:00
Closed New Year's, Thanksgiving, Christmas
Stay Tuned: Newsletter

703-991-0191
www.vinthillcraftwinery.com
E-mail: info@craftwinery.com

Vint Hill is a custom-crush winery that offers customers a unique opportunity to design and produce a half or full barrel of wine under the guidance of experienced winemakers. Founded in 2009 by Chris Pearmund (Pearmund Cellars) and Ray Summerell, the winery is housed in a restored 1900 dairy barn at Vint Hill Farms, once a secure listening post run by the U.S. military until the 1990s. The winery uses grapes from Virginia, California, and Washington in production; it has no vineyard of its own. Vint Hill's tasting bar overlooks the production floor, offering visitors the chance to see winemaking in action.

Price Range: $6,000 (and up) per barrel

Tastings: $6 per person for a flight of wines under production.

Purchasing: Services are available to residents of all 50 states, Washington DC, Puerto Rico, and the Virgin Islands.

Directions: From I-66, take Exit 43A (Gainesville/Warrenton) onto U.S. Route 29 South. Drive for 5.2 miles and turn left onto Vint Hill Road (Route 215). After 1.6 miles, turn right onto Kennedy Road (Route 652).

Take a left at the stop sign onto Aiken Road and drive 1/4 mile. Turn left onto Bludau Drive and then right onto Lineweaver Road to the winery entrance.

Winery at Bull Run
15950 Lee Highway
Centreville VA 20120

Hours: Daily 11:00–7:00; F to 8:00
Closed New Year's, Easter, Thanksgiving, Christmas
Stay Tuned: Facebook, Twitter, newsletter

703-815-2233
www.wineryatbullrun.com

The Winery at Bull Run was opened to the public in June 2012 by Jon and Kim Hickox on a historic property immediately adjacent to the Manassas National Battlefield Park; Civil War relics are on display in the main tasting room. Winemaker Chris Pearmund (Pearmund Cellars, Vint Hill) is using fruit from other Virginia vineyards while Bull Run's own vines mature. The tasting room features a number of tables and sofas inside, as well as tables and seating outdoors on the veranda and grounds. The winery sponsors live music on weekends and offers catered food for purchase for Friday night happy hours. The facilities are available to rent for private parties and events. Children are welcome but must be supervised at all times. Bull Run offers discounts for military personnel, police, and firefighters.

White Wines: Chardonnay, Delaney, Viognier.

Rosé Wines: Rosé.

Red Wines: Cabernet Franc, Meritage, Merlot, Norton.

Fortified Wines: Fort (Chambourcin).

Price Range: $24–$38

Tastings: $12 per person.

Groups: Reservations required for groups from 8 to 25; tastings held between 11:00 and 3:00 M–F and between 11:00 and 2:00 Sa–Su, $15 per person.

Wheelchair accessible.

General's Wine Club members receive wine shipments, discounts, and complimentary tastings (one-time $75 registration fee).

Purchasing: Online ordering available via VinoShipper to AK, FL, ID, LA, MN, MO, NE, NV, NH, NM, ND, OH, OR, DC, WV, and WY.

Directions: From I-66, take Exit 52 onto U.S. Route 29 South. Drive 2.8 miles to the winery entrance on the right.

Winery at La Grange
4970 Antioch Road
Haymarket VA 20169

Hours: Daily 11:00–6:00; Sa to 8:00 (summer only)   703-753-9360
Closed New Year's, Easter, Thanksgiving, Christmas   www.wineryatlagrange.com
Stay Tuned: Facebook, Twitter, newsletter   E-mail: info@wineryatlagrange.com

The Winery at La Grange was founded in 2006 by Chris Pearmund (Pearmund Cellars, Vint Hill) and is now owned by a group of Chinese investors, with Doug Fabbioli (Fabbioli Cellars) as consulting winemaker. The winery is located on the twenty-acre historic La Grange estate, whose manor house dates from the 1790s. The parlor and downstairs lounge rooms offer comfortable seating where guests can relax over a glass of wine or use the winery's Wi-Fi; outdoor seating is also available on the patios. La Grange sponsors a number of special activities and events, including movie nights, Sangria Saturdays, and winemaker dinners. The facilities are available to rent for private parties and weddings. Pets and children are welcome; children must be supervised at all times.

Sparkling Wines: Reserve Brut.

White Wines: Cuvée Blanc, Chardonnay, Pinot Gris, Viognier.

Rosé Wines: Rosé of Merlot.

Red Wines: Cabernet Franc, Cabernet Sauvignon, Meritage, Merlot, General's Battlefield Red, Tannat.

Fortified Wines: Snort *(Touriga Nacional, Tannat)*.

Price Range: $18–$49

Tastings: $10 per person for classic tasting, $10 per person for reserve tasting, with souvenir glass.

Groups: Reservations required for groups from 8 to 25; tastings held between 11:00 a.m. and 3:00 p.m. only, $15 per person.

Wheelchair accessible.

Manor House and Benoni's Reserve Wine Club members receive regular wine shipments and discounts.

Directions: From I-66, take Exit 40 (Haymarket) and turn onto U.S. Route 15 South. Turn right at the second light onto Route 55 and drive about one mile. Turn right onto Antioch Road and continue 3 miles to the winery on left.

꙰

READING A VIRGINIA WINE LABEL

All wine labels must be approved by the federal Bureau of Alcohol, Tobacco, Firearms, and Explosives (BATFE), which determines the specific guidelines governing each element on those wine labels, down to the font size of the print.

Let's decipher the label of an imaginary Virginia winery.

> *Sans Pareil*
> VINEYARDS
> Monticello
>
> 2010
> Viognier
>
> ESTATE GROWN
>
> PRODUCED AND BOTTLED BY
> SANS PAREIL VINEYARDS
>
> ALC. 13.0%
> BY VOL   CONTAINS SULFITES   750 ML

Below the winery name is the name of an American Viticultural Area (AVA). This means that at least 85 percent of the grapes in this particular wine were grown in that AVA. If a county name is included instead, at least 85 percent of the grapes must have come from that county. If the label reads simply "Virginia," then 75 percent or more of the grapes are from Virginia. Look (or ask) for "100% Virginia grown" if you are seeking a pure Virginia wine.

The vintage year and varietal name will also be displayed on the label. If the wine is a blend, the label will show the name of the wine, but the specific grape varieties and their proportions may or may not be listed, depending on the winery's preferences.

"Estate grown" means that all the grapes for this wine were grown on the winery's property.

This particular wine was produced and bottled at the winery itself. A number of small Virginia wineries work with a larger winery or use a "custom crush" facility, such as Virginia Wineworks, to produce their wines. In these instances, the winery will work closely with an expert winemaker to customize the wine and blend it to the winery's specifications.

꙰

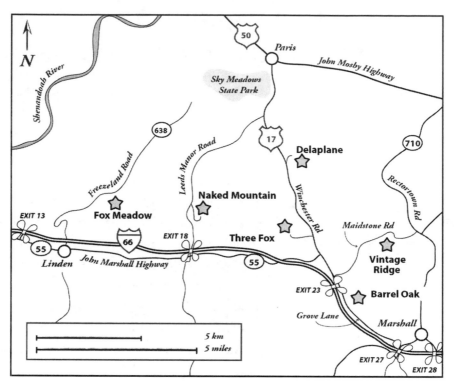

Map 4.7. Delaplane

DELAPLANE

Barrel Oak Winery
3623 Grove Lane
Delaplane VA 20144

Hours: W–M 11:00–6:00, F to 9:00 (Sa to 9:00, May–Nov) 540-364-6402
Closed New Year's, Thanksgiving, Christmas www.barreloak.com
Stay Tuned: Facebook, Twitter, Newsletter E-mail: info@barreloak.com

Barrel Oak was founded in 2008 by Brian and Sharon Roeder and has become a popular weekend wine destination. Tastings are held in the winery's modern two-story tasting room, with special curated tastings held next door at Oak Hill, the historic home of nineteenth-century Supreme Court Justice John Marshall (reservations required). In addition to live music and TGI Sunsets, Barrel Oak sponsors a range of special events, including breast cancer fundraisers and special pet adoption weekends. The winery may be rented for private parties. Children and leashed dogs are welcome.

White Wines: BowHaus White, Chardonnay, Petit Manseng, Seyval Blanc, Traminette, Viognier.

Rosé Wines: Barrel Oak Rosé.

Red Wines: BowHaus Red, Cabernet Franc, Cabernet Sauvignon, Merlot, Norton, Petit Verdot, Tour'ga Franc *(Touriga Nacional, Cabernet Franc)*.

Sweet/Dessert Wines: Late Harvest Vidal Blanc, Chocolate Lab Red.

Price Range: $21–$38

Tastings: $5 per person for white or red; $10 for full flight.

Handicapped accessible.

Purchasing: Phone orders accepted *except* from AL, AK, KS, MD, MA, MS, NJ, NY, PA, VT, and WI.

Wine Club members receive wine shipments, discounts, and members-only events.

Directions: From I-66, take Exit 27 (Marshall). Turn north in the direction of Marshall onto Free State Road (Route 55). Make an immediate left onto Grove Lane. The winery entrance will be about 2 miles on the right.

Delaplane Cellars
2187 Winchester Road
Delaplane VA 20144

Hours: Th–M 11:00–5:00 (Mar–Dec), F–Su 11:00–5:00 (Jan-Feb)   540-592-7210
Closed New Year's, Thanksgiving, Christmas Eve & Day   www.delaplanecellars.com
Stay Tuned: Facebook, Twitter, newsletter   E-mail: info@delaplanecellars.com

Delaplane Cellars was founded by Jim and Betsy Dolphin, whose love of wine sprang from years as home winemakers. The tasting room and the terrace offer a view of the Crooked Run valley to enjoy while trying Delaplane's 100 percent Virginia varietals. Light food is also available for purchase in the tasting room. In summer, Delaplane sponsors Sunset Saturdays and Easy Like Sunday Afternoons with live music. Vineyard tours ($15 per person) are available in summers (reservations required). Military, veterans, police officers, and firefighters receive a 10 percent discount on wine purchases. The winery is certified Virginia Green.

White Wines: Chardonnay, Mélange Blanc, Viognier.

Rosé Wines: Rosé.

Red Wines: Cabernet Franc, Cinq2, Left Bank Reserve, Mélange Rouge, Springlot Reserve, Syrah, Williams Gap Reserve.

Sweet/Dessert Wines: Late Harvest Petit Manseng.

Price Range: $20–$30

Tastings: $5 per person.

Winemaker's Dozen Club members receive regular wine shipments, discounts on purchases, and invitations to special events.

Wheelchair accessible.

Restrictions: No buses or limos permitted; no groups over six; no outside food in tasting room.

Purchasing: Online purchasing available for VA residents; please contact the winery for shipping restrictions to all other states.

Directions: From I-66, take Exit 23 onto Winchester Road (U.S. Route 17 North) toward Delaplane and Paris. Continue on U.S. Route 17 North for 4 miles and turn right onto the winery's single-lane gravel driveway.

Fox Meadow Winery
3310 Freezeland Road
Linden VA 22642

Hours: Su–F 11:00–5:00, Sa 11:00–6:00   540-636-6777
Closed New Year's, Easter, Thanksgiving, Christmas   www.foxmeadowwinery.com
Stay Tuned: Facebook, Twitter   E-mail: info@foxmeadowwinery.com

Perched on a hillside over 1,700 feet above sea level, Fox Meadow Winery offers guests a spectacular vista of vineyards and the Blue Ridge from its tasting room and outdoor deck. Originally part of the Freezeland Orchards, Fox Meadow was founded by Dan and Cheryl Mortland and opened to the public in 2006. The tasting room offers visitors two tasting bars from which to sample Fox Meadow's wines, many of which are paired with food samples for extra effect. A side tasting room may be rented for small events. Fox Meadow is available for weddings or private parties.

White Wines: Chardonnay, Freezeland White *(Chardonnay, Vidal, Rkatsiteli)*, Le Renard Gris *(Chardonnay, Vidal Blanc, Pinot Gris)*, Pinot Gris, Riesling, Viognier.

Red Wines: Cabernet Franc, Freezeland Red *(Cabernet Franc, Mourvedre)*, Le Renard Rouge *(Bordeaux-style blend)*, Merlot, Syrah.

Price Range: $19–$29

Tastings: $6 per person.

Groups: Reservations required for groups of 8 or more, $10 per person fee; cellar tastings (reservations required), $12 per person.

Wheelchair accessible.

Friends of Foxes Wine Club members receive discounts on wine purchase, special events.

Purchasing: Phone orders available for residents of FL, MD, and VA.

Directions: From I-66 West, take Exit 18 (Markham) and turn south onto Leeds Manor Road. Turn west onto John Marshall Highway (Route 55) and drive 4 miles toward Linden. Turn right onto Freezeland Road (Route 638) and continue 3 miles to the winery up the hill and on the right.

Naked Mountain Vineyard
2747 Leeds Manor Road
Markham VA 22643

Hours: Daily 11:00–5:00   540-364-1609
Closed New Year's Eve & Day, Thanksgiving, Christmas   www.nakedmtnwinery.com
Stay Tuned: Facebook, Twitter, newsletter   E-mail: drinknaked@nakedmtnwinery.com

Founded in 1982, Naked Mountain is owned by Randy and Megan Morgan. Located on forty-two acres, Naked Mountain is best known for its Chardonnays. The winery now produces over six thousand cases of wine each year. Naked Mountain's tasting room opens onto a deck offering a splendid view of mountains, valleys, and vines. The winery hosts various special events each year, including winemaker dinners and open houses. Guided tours are offered on weekends at 1:00 p.m.

White Wines: Chardonnay, Chardonnay-Riesling, Riesling.

Rosé Wines: Make Me Blush *(Cabernet Franc, Merlot).*

Red Wines: Cabernet Franc, Cabernet Sauvignon, Catamount Run Red, Merlot, Raptor Red, Scarlet Oak Red *(Syrah, Mourvedre, Tannat).*

Sweet/Dessert Wines: Old Vine Riesling, Soar.

Price Range: $18–$22

Tastings: $5 per person.

Groups: Reservations required for groups of 8 to 15 (maximum size), with a $10 per person fee (includes souvenir glass); long vehicles and stretch limos may have difficulty managing the driveway's blind curve.

Wheelchair accessible.

Purchasing: E-mail purchases available for residents of TX and VA only, and through VinoShipper to residents of AK, CA, FL, ID, LA, MO, NE, NH, NV, NM, ND, OH, OR, WV, WY, and DC.

Directions: From I-66, take exit 18 (Markham) and drive north on Leeds Manor Road (Route 688) for 1.6 miles. The long winery driveway will be on the right (watch out for the blind curve!).

❖ ❖ ❖

Three Fox Vineyards
10100 Three Fox Lane
Delaplane VA 20144

Hours: Th–Sa, M 11:00–5:00, Su 12:00–5:00

Closed New Year's Eve & Day,

Thanksgiving, Christmas Eve & Day

Stay Tuned: Facebook, Twitter, newsletter

540-364-6073

www.threefoxvineyards.com

E-mail: info@threefoxvineyards.com

Three Fox Vineyards acquired its name when Holli and Jon Todhunter saw three foxes on a hill while first visiting the property. The winery sits on fifty acres of gently rolling hills and includes over ten acres of vines. Three Fox sponsors a range of events, including Vin-Olympics, wine dinners, SPCA fundraisers, and an annual Blessing of the Harvest. At 1:00 p.m. on summertime Sundays, winemaker Jon leads Winemaker Walkabouts through the vineyard and winery (reservations required). Three Fox may be rented for weddings or private events. Children and dogs are welcome.

White Wines: Appassionata Vidal Blanc, Calabrese Pinot Grigio, Gatto Bianco, La Bohème Viognier, La Giocosa Chardonnay, Leggero Chardonnay.

Rosé Wines: Cano Passo Rosé.

Red Wines: Alouette Cabernet Franc, La Trovatella Merlot, Maestro *(Sangiovese, Cabernet Franc, Chambourcin)*, Piemontese Nebbiolo, Signor Sangiovese Reserve, Sirius, Volpe Sangiovese.

Fortified Wines: Rosso Dolce Chambourcin.

Price Range: $21–$29

Tastings: $3 per person for whites, $3 for reds.

Groups: Reservations required for groups of 8 to 50; $10 per person charge.

Restrictions: No buses after 2:00 p.m.

Purchasing: Online purchases for residents of AK, FL, ID, LA, MO, NE, NV, NH, NM, ND, OH, OR, VA, DC, WV, WY through VinoShipper.

Vintner's Club sponsorship includes discounts on purchases, priority reservations for special events, special members' only events. See the website for more details.

Directions: From I-66, take Exit 23 (Delaplane/Paris). Turn onto U.S. Route 17 North and continue about one mile. After crossing the railroad tracks, turn left onto Three Fox Lane and the winery entrance on the left.

Vintage Ridge Vineyard
8517 Maidstone Road
Delaplane VA 20140

Hours: F–Su 11:00–5:00 (Apr–early Dec)

Closed mid-Dec-Mar

Stay Tuned: Facebook, Twitter

540-364-3371

www.vintageridgewine.com

E-mail: info@vintageridgewine.com

Vintage Ridge is a small family farm winery owned and operated by Bill and Vicki Edmands; the winemaker is Kerem Baki. Visitors may choose a wine-only tasting or, on the first weekend of each month, a wine-food tasting. On Saturdays and Sundays at 10:00 a.m., Vintage Ridge offers tours (reservations required) of the vineyard, winery, and a concluding tasting; there is a limit of sixteen participants at a cost of twenty-five dollars per person..

White Wines: Maiden Voyage *(Vidal Blanc, Mourvedre)*, Summer Night *(Vidal Blanc)*.

Red Wines: Cabernet Franc, Merlot, Petit Verdot, Syrah.

Price Range: $18–$28

Tastings: $10 per person.

Groups: Reservations required for groups of 5 or more.

Restrictions: No tours buses or limos; no outside food.

Wine Club members receive discounts and special members-only events.

Purchasing: Phone orders for Virginia residents.

Directions: From I-66, take Exit 23 (Delaplane/Paris) onto U.S. Route 17 North. Turn right onto Maidstone Road (Route 713) and drive 3 miles to winery entrance on right.

WHITE, RED, AND PINK WINES

Peel back the skin of a *V. vinifera* grape, and you will find, with few exceptions, that the fruit underneath is light, regardless of the color of the grape skins. It is easy to see that white wines get their color from the grape itself. The color for red and pink wines comes from a different step in the winemaking process.

The juice for red wines becomes red by keeping the grape skins in contact with the juice. This skin contact may range from less than a day to a week or more, depending on the wine being made. In addition to color, the skins also convey flavor and tannins, helping give the finished wine body and structure.

This also means that white wines may be made even from dark-skinned grapes, as long as the juice does not come in contact with the skins. The most well-known such wine is Champagne, which is made from Pinot Noir and Pinot Meunier (both dark-skinned grapes) as well as from Chardonnay (a light-skinned grape).

Rosé, or pink, wines are generally made through one of several methods. As with red wines, the juice may be left in contact with the grape skins but only for a matter of hours, not days. Another common practice is to blend white and red wines together after fermentation.

Yet another method is to break the grape skins by barely crushing them and then allowing the grapes to rest for 12 to 48 hours before drawing the juice off. The resulting wine may be a pale blush or a light pink, depending on how long the grapes were allowed to rest.

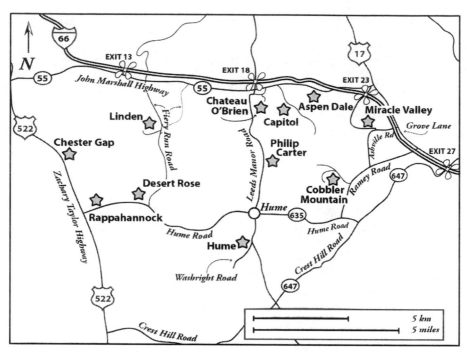

Map 4.8. Northern Blue Ridge

NORTHERN BLUE RIDGE

Aspen Dale Winery at the Barn
3180 Aspen Dale Lane
(GPS address: 11083 John Marshall Highway)
Delaplane VA 20144

Hours: M, Th–F 11:00–5:00, Sa 11:00–6:00, Su 12:00–5:00   540-364-6178, 202-297-9517
Closed New Year's, Thanksgiving, Christmas   www.aspendalewinery.com
Stay Tuned: Twitter   E-mail: reservations@aspendalewinery.com

Aspen Dale Winery is located on a two-hundred-year-old country estate that once belonged to the family of nineteenth-century Supreme Court Chief Justice John Marshall. Owners Larry and Kelly Carr are currently producing five wines using grapes from their own vineyard as well as from nearby Breaux Vineyard. Aspen Dale's tasting room is in a restored barn, with scattered tables, sofas, and wing chairs adjoining the tasting bar; live music is featured on many weekends. Tastings are paired with small samplings of food; cheese, sausage, and other foods are also available for purchase. The facilities may be rented for weddings and private events. Children and dogs are welcome.

White Wines: Hildersham *(Sauvignon Blanc)*, Sarah's Chapeau *(Vidal, Sauvignon Blanc)*, Seyval Blanc.

Rosé Wines: Mary Madeleine's Rosé *(Vidal Blanc, Cabernet Sauvignon).*

Red Wines: Parris Country Blend *(Merlot, Cabernet Franc)*, Rockawalkin' *(Bordeaux-style blend).*

Price Range: $22–$42

Tastings: $8 per person.

Groups: Reservations required for groups of 8 or more.

Purchasing: Online ordering for VA residents.

Stable Club members receive wines, special seating, and member events.

Directions: From I-66, take Exit 23 (Paris/Delaplane) onto U.S. Route 17 North for 1/2 mile. Turn west onto John Marshall Highway (Route 55). Drive 2.4 miles to the winery entrance on the left.

Capitol Vineyards
3600 Sage Road
Delaplane VA 20144

Hours: Sa–Su 9:00–5:00 (Mar–Oct) 845-598-2662
Closed Nov–Feb www.capitolvineyards.com
Stay Tuned: Facebook, Twitter E-mail: Cellar@capitolvineyards.com

Lauren Shrem and Matthew Noland founded Capitol Vineyards in 2009 on a thirty-acre property, opening to the public two years later. The tasting room is housed in a building once occupied by the first African-American postmaster in Virginia. While Capitol's own vineyards are maturing, the winery is using grapes purchased from other Virginia vineyards to produce its wines. The winery may be rented for small, private parties and events.

White Wines: Traminette, Viognier.

Red Wines: Cabernet Franc, Cabernet Sauvignon, Meritage, Merlot.

Price Range: $21–$29

Tastings: $10 per person.

Wine club members receive wine shipments, free tastings, and members-only events.

Directions: From I-66, take Exit 18 (Markham) and drive south on Leeds Manor Road. Turn left onto John Marshall Highway (Route 55). Take the third right onto Sage Road and continue 1.3 miles to the winery on right.

Chateau O'Brien at Northpoint
3238 Rail Stop Road
Markham VA 22643

Hours: Th–M 11:00–5:00
Closed New Year's, Easter,
Thanksgiving, Christmas Eve & Day
Stay Tuned: Facebook, Twitter, newsletter

540-364-6441
www.chateauobrien.com
E-mail: howard@chateauobrien.com

Howard and Debbie O'Brien opened their winery and vineyard to the public in 2006, four years after purchasing the property. Chateau O'Brien's French-style farmhouse home is on a hilltop and can be seen long before they pull into the parking lot. The farmhouse includes three separate tasting rooms and a covered deck with sweeping views of the countryside and vines. Chateau O'Brien regularly hosts a variety of events, including murder mystery dinners, an annual crab boil, an Ancient Order of Hibernians festival, and an Irish Stew weekend. The winery is also available for private parties or dinners. Active duty military receive a 15 percent discount.

Fruit Wines: Virginia Apple Wine.

White Wines: Northpoint White *(Pinot Grigio, Chardonnay)*, Petit Manseng, Virginia Chardonnay.

Rosé Wines: Northpoint Rosé.

Red Wines: Buddy's Bistro Red, Cabernet Franc, Northpoint Red *(Bordeaux-style blend)*, Paddock Red *(Bordeaux-style blend)*, Petit Verdot, Syrah.

Sweet/Dessert Wines: Late Harvest Tannat.

Price Range: $20–$79

Tastings: $7 per person; cellar collection tastings at $12 per person, Saturdays and Sundays only.

Groups: Reservations required for groups of 8 or more, $20 per person fee. Buses and limos are by appointment only.

Wheelchair accessible.

Restrictions: No one under 21 permitted in the tasting room or on the winery grounds; buses, vans, and limos by appointment only.

Cork Club members receive special gifts, depending on how many winery corks they have accumulated.

Directions: From I-66, take Exit 18 (Markham). Turn south onto Leeds Manor Road and cross John Marshall Highway (Route 55). Turn left onto Old Markham Road and then make a hairpin right onto Rail Stop Road. Drive up the hill to the winery entrance.

Chester Gap Cellars
4615 Remount Road
Front Royal VA 22630

Hours: F 12:00–5:00 (6:00 in summer), Sa 11:00–6:00   540-636-8086

Su, Memorial Day & Labor Day 11:00–5:00   www.chestergapcellars.com

Closed New Year's, Christmas   E-mail: Bernd@ChesterGapCellars.com

Chester Gap is located near the Shenandoah National Park at over one thousand feet in elevation, offering a lovely view from the tasting room and deck of the gap for which it is named. Owners Bernd and Kristi Jung got their start in the wine business in Florida before moving to Virginia and establishing Chester Gap. The couple planted their first vines on their eight-acre vineyard in 2000 and produced their first wines four years later. A native of Munich, Germany, Bernd also serves as the winemaker and vineyard manager.

White Wines: Roussanne, Viognier.

Red Wines: Cabernet Franc, Merlot, Petit Verdot.

Sweet/Dessert Wines: Cuvée Manseng *(Petit Manseng)*.

Price Range: $16–$24

Tastings: $7 per person.

Groups: Reservations required for groups over 6.

Restrictions: No buses or limos permitted.

Purchasing: Online shipping for VA residents only.

Directions: From I-66, take Exit 13 (Linden). Turn south onto Apple Mountain Road (Route 79) and then right onto John Marshall Highway (Route 55). Drive 4.7 miles and turn left onto U.S. Route 522 (Remount Road/Zachary Taylor Highway). The winery will be 4.7 miles on the left.

Cobbler Mountain Cellars
5909 Long Fall Lane
(GPS address: 10363 Moreland Road)
Delaplane VA 20144

Hours: Th–M 11:00–5:00

Closed New Year's, Christmas

Stay Tuned: Facebook

540-364-2802

www.cobblercellars.com

E-mail: shop@cobblercellars.com

Jeff and Laura McCarthy Louden established Cobbler Mountain Cellars on a ninety-acre farm that Laura's father had originally purchased in 1959. They opened to the public in 2011, one year after bringing in their first vintage. Located high on a hill overlooking Little Cobbler Mountain, the winery offers seating on the patio at the side of the house, as well as on the lawn where visitors may enjoy a glass of wine. Signs along the long winery driveway point guests to a creekside picnic area and a hiking trail. Bread and artisanal cheeses are available for purchase. Cobbler Mountain also offers live music on some weekends. The facilities may be rented for weddings. Children are welcome.

Ciders: Hard Apple Cider.

White Wines: Chardonnay, Cobblestone White.

Red Wines: Cabernet Franc, Cabernet Sauvignon, Malbec, Meritage, Merlot, Petit Verdot.

Price Range: $18–$26

Tastings: $9 per person.

Purchasing: Online ordering via VinoShipper to AK, FL, ID, LA, MN, MO, NE, NV, NH, NM, ND, OH, OR, DC, WV, and WY.

Directions: From I-66, take Exit 27 (Marshall) and turn north in the direction of Marshall onto Free State Road (Route 55). Make an immediate left onto Grove Lane. Take the first left onto Ramey Road. Drive 3.2 miles and turn right onto Moreland Road (portions unpaved). Cobbler Mountain's driveway (also unpaved) will be about 1/3 mile on the left; continue up the hill to the tasting room entrance on the left side of the house.

Desert Rose Ranch & Winery
13726 Hume Road
Hume VA 22639

Hours: F–Su 1:00–6:00   540-635-3200
Closed New Year's, Christmas   www.desertrosewinery.com
Stay Tuned: Facebook   E-mail: info@desertrosewinery.com

Bob and Linda Claymier established their Desert Rose Winery on an eighty-acre farm the couple had purchased with the aim of starting a horse ranch. They eventually decided to establish a vineyard as well and opened their winery to the public in 2011. The tasting room's Western theme reflects Bob's own background growing up on a ranch in eastern Oregon. The name of the winery is from the desert rose crystalline formations often found in arid regions. Desert Rose offers live music on weekends. Children have a special place of their own in the tasting room's Kiddie Korner. Pets are welcome.

Fruit Wines: GiGi Peachi *(peach)*.

White Wines: Hitch Hollow *(Chardonnay)*, Ole Moo-Moo.

Rosé Wines: Sparky *(Cabernet Franc, Cabernet Sauvignon, Merlot)*.

Red Wines: Cabernet Franc, Merlot, R.E.D. *(Chambourcin)*.

Sweet/Dessert Wines: Desert Delight *(Vidal Blanc)*, Starboard *(Norton)*.

Price Range: $18–$30

Tastings: $5 per person.

Groups: Reservations required for groups of 6 or more, $10 per person fee.

Wheelchair accessible.

Restrictions: No buses.

Directions: From I-66, take Exit 18 (Markham) and turn south onto Leeds Manor Road. Cross John Marshall Highway (Route 55) and continue following Leeds Manor Road for 5 miles. Turn right onto Hume Road and continue another 5 miles to the winery entrance on the right, just past Fiery Run Road.

Hume Vineyards
5396 Washwright Road
Hume VA 22639

Hours: F–Su, M holidays 11:30–5:00

Closed New Year's, Christmas

Stay Tuned: Facebook, Twitter

540-364-2587

www.humevineyards.com

E-mail: info@humevineyards.com

Hume Vineyards is a small boutique winery located just south of the village of Hume. Owners Stéphane and Andrea Baldi purchased the 1880s homestead in 2007 and began planting their five-acre vineyard in Viognier, Chambourcin, Merlot, and Petit Verdot, with plans for another six acres to follow. Their goal is to produce wine that is half from their own vineyard and half from other Virginia vineyards to give them greater flexibility in their production. Stéphane's interest in wine came from his experience working at wineries in his native France before moving to the United States. Outdoor seating and picnic grounds are available for visitors.

White Wines: Seyval Blanc, Viognier.

Red Wines: Cabernet Franc, Cabernet Sauvignon, Chambourcin, Merlot.

Price Range: $17–$26

Tastings: $5 per person.

Wine Club members receive discounts, wine shipments, and complimentary tastings.

Directions: From I-66, take Exit 18 (Markham) and turn south onto Leeds Manor Road. Drive 6.6 miles and make a right onto Washwright Road (portions unpaved). The winery driveway will be 1/2 mile on the right.

Linden Vineyards
3708 Harrels Corner Road
Linden VA 22642

Hours: W–Su 11:00–5:00 (Apr–Nov)
Sa–Su 11:00–5:00 (Dec–Mar)
Closed New Year's, Easter,
Thanksgiving, 19 Dec–5 Jan

540-364-1997
www.lindenvineyards.com
E-mail: wine@lindenvineyards.com

Owner-winemaker Jim Law founded Linden Vineyards in 1983 and opened his winery to the public five years later. A highly respected vintner, Law is considered a mentor by many fellow Virginia winemakers. He offers a two-year wine apprenticeship program for those who want an intensive, hands-on exposure to winemaking. Visitors to Linden may also choose a special reserve cellar tasting on weekends (sign up upon arriving). Vineyard and cellar tours are offered at 11:30 a.m. on Saturday and Sunday in the summer (maximum of six). Bread and cheeses are available for purchase. While there are no chairs in the tasting room, weekday visitors may sit on the deck overlooking the vineyard.

White Wines: Chardonnay, Sauvignon Blanc, Seyval, Vidal-Riesling.

Rosé Wines: Rosé.

Red Wines: Avenius Red, Boisseau Red, Claret, Hardscrabble Red, Petit Verdot.

Sweet/Dessert Wines: Late Harvest Vidal.

Price Range: $19–$42

Tastings: $5 per person for basic tasting; $20 per person for cellar tasting (maximum of 4 per group, register upon arrival).

Restrictions: No limos, buses, or groups over 6. Case Club members only on the deck and grounds on weekends, maximum 3 guests per member.

Purchasing: Online ordering for VA residents only.

Case Club members receive invitations to barrel and pre-release tastings, vintner's dinners.

Directions: From I-66, take Exit 18 (Markham). Turn south onto John Marshall Highway (Route 55) and drive 4.2 miles to the village of Linden. Turn left onto State Route 638 which will become Harrels Corner Road. The winery's gravel driveway will be 2.2 miles on the right.

Miracle Valley Vineyard
3661 Double J Lane
(GPS: 3841 Cobbler Mountain Road)
Delaplane VA 20144

Hours: Th–M 11:00–5:00
Closed mid-Dec-Feb
Stay Tuned: Facebook, Twitter, newsletter

540-364-0228
www.miraclevalleyvineyard.com
E-mail: vineyardbusiness@aol.com

Established by Mary Ann and Joe Cunningham, Miracle Valley Vineyard opened in 2007. The winery's tasting room is in a restored 1880's farmhouse featuring a handcrafted wooden tasting bar and an adjoining parlor with a fireplace, tables, and chairs for visitors. The winery's stone patios offer a good view of the vineyards and Cobbler Mountain beyond. Miracle Valley sponsors various events, including Taste of Italy, Sangria Sundays, and live music. The owners also actively support several wounded warrior support groups and events. The winery may be rented for private parties and events. Children are welcome.

White Wines: Chardonnay, Viognier.

Red Wines: Cabernet Franc, Cabernet Sauvignon, Meritage, Merlot.

Sweet/Dessert Wines: Sweet Michelle *(Rkatsiteli)*.

Price Range: $16–$30

Tastings: $7 per person.

Groups: Reservations required for groups of 8 or more, $10 per person fee.

Wheelchair accessible.

Restrictions: Groups of 12 or more only at 11:00 am, 12:00 pm, or 1:00 pm. No pets.

Purchasing: Online purchases for VA residents or via VinoShipper for residents of AK, FL, ID, LA, MO, NE, NV, NH, NM, ND, OH, OR, DC, WV, and WY.

Directions: From I-66, take Exit 27 (Marshall). Turn onto Free State Road (Route 55 East) and make an immediate left onto Grove Lane. Drive 2.5 miles and turn left onto Ashville Road, crossing under I-66. Drive about 1/2 mile and turn right onto Cobbler Mountain Road (Route 731). Continue 0.7 mile to Double J Lane and the winery on the right.

Philip Carter Winery
4366 Stillhouse Road
Hume VA 22639

Hours: Daily 11:00–6:00 (Sa until 7:00) 540-364-1203
Closed New Year's, Easter, Thanksgiving, Christmas Eve & Day www.pcwinery.com
Stay Tuned: Facebook, Twitter, newsletter E-mail: info@pcwinery.com

Philip Carter Strother purchased the former Stillhouse Winery in 2008, renaming it in honor of the Carter family's long role in Virginia's history. The winery sponsors a range of events, including SPCA fundraisers,

Sangria weekends, Movies in the Vineyards, book signings for local authors, and an annual Blessing of the Vines. Winery facilities are available to rent for private dinners and weddings. Pets and children are welcome.

White Wines: Chardonnay, Governor Fauquier, Sabine *(Viognier)*.

Rosé Wines: Danielle's Rosé *(Tinta Cão)*.

Red Wines: Cabernet Franc, Chambourcin, Cleve *(Bordeaux-style blend)*, Meritage

Dessert Wines: Late Harvest Vidal.

Price Range: $16–$29

Tastings: $5 per person

VIP club members receive wine shipments, discounts, and members-only events.

Directions: From I-66, take Exit 18 (Markham) and turn south onto Leeds Manor Road. Continue to follow Leeds Manor Road for 4 miles and turn left onto Stillhouse Road (portions unpaved) to the winery on right.

Rappahannock Cellars
14437 Hume Road
Huntly VA 22640

Hours: Daily 11:30–5:00, Sa to 6:00	540-635-9398
Closed New Year's, Easter, Thanksgiving, Christmas	www.rappahannockcellars.com
Stay Tuned: Facebook, Twitter, newsletter	E-mail: info@rcellars.com

John and Marialisa Delmare founded Rappahannock Cellars in 1998 after selling their Saratoga Vineyards in California's Santa Cruz Mountains. The Delmares have since expanded their vineyard to over twenty acres of vines. Light food is available for purchase and enjoyment on the grounds.

The winery is available for rental for private parties and weddings. Rappahannock's tasting room includes a children's corner with books and games, as well as outdoor spaces where children can play. Dogs are welcome.

White Wines: Chardonnay, Noblesse Blanc, Seyval Blanc, Vidal Blanc, Viognier.

Rosé Wines: Rosé.

Red Wines: Cabernet Franc, Meritage, Merlot, Noblesse Rouge, Norton, Super Meritage.

Sweet/Dessert Wines: Late Harvest Vidal, Solera *(Vidal Blanc, sherry style)*.

Fortified Wines: Port *(Norton)*.

Price Range: $19–$32

Tastings: $8 per person.

Groups: Reservations and prepayment required for groups of 8 or more; $12.50 charge per person.

Wheelchair accessible.

Purchasing: Online purchasing available for residents of CA, CO, FL, GA, IL, LA, ME, MD, MN, NH, NY, NC, TX, VA, WA, and DC only, or via VinoShipper to AK, ID, MO, NE, NV, NM, ND, OH, OR, WV, and WY.

Wine of the Month Club members receive wine shipments, discounts, and members-only events.

Directions: From I-66, take Exit 13 (Linden/Front Royal) onto John Marshall Highway (Route 55) toward Front Royal. Drive 4.7 miles and turn left onto U.S. Route 522 South (Remount Road). Drive 6.9 miles and turn left onto Hume Road (Route 635). The winery will be on the left.

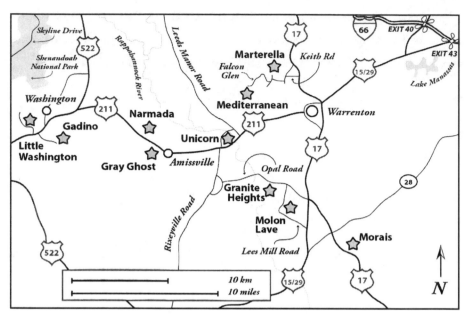

Map 4.9. Warrenton

WARRENTON

Gadino Cellars
92 School House Road
Washington VA 22747

Hours: F–M 11:30–5:00, Sa to 6:00 (Feb–Dec)   540-987-9292
Closed New Year's, Easter, Thanksgiving, Christmas   www.gadinocellars.com
Stay Tuned: Facebook, Twitter, newsletter   E-mail: steph@gadinocellars.com

Longtime wine enthusiasts Bill and Aleta Saccuta Gadino first planted their fifteen-acre vineyard in 1989. Sixteen years later, the couple opened Gadino Cellars to the public outside the historic town of Little Washington, with Bill and daughter Stephanie serving as winemakers. The tasting room also offers cheese and sausage for purchase to enjoy either inside or on the trellised deck that overlooks the vines and gardens. Guests can also test their skills on the two regulation-size bocce ball courts. Gadino sponsors a number of special events, including fundraisers, live music, and harvest picnics. Gadino is a certified Virginia Green winery. Pets and children are welcome.

White Wines: Chardonnay, Pinot Grigio, Luminoso *(Petit Manseng, Vidal Blanc)*, Sunset *(Traminette, Chardonnay)*, Viognier.

Rosé Wines: Moonrise.

Red Wines: Antiche Viti Riserva Cabernet Franc, Cabernet Sauvignon, Delfino Rosso *(Bordeaux-style blend)*, Imagine *(Chambourcin, Cabernet Franc, Cabernet Sauvignon)*, Petit Verdot.

Sweet/Dessert Wines: Dolce Sofia *(Petit Manseng, Vidal Blanc)*.

Price Range: $16–$33

Tastings: $5 per person.

Wheelchair accessible.

Purchasing: Online ordering via VinoShipper to AK, FL, ID, LA, MD, MN, MO, NE, NV, NH, NM, ND, OH, OR, VA, DC, WV, WY.

PMI Wine Club members receive regular wine shipments and discounts on purchases.

Directions: From Warrenton, take U.S. Route 29 South. Turn onto U.S. Route 211 West toward the Shenandoah National Park. Drive 23.3 miles and turn left onto School House Road (Route 636). The winery driveway (portions unpaved) will be about 1/2 mile on the left.

Granite Heights Vineyards
8141 Opal Road
Warrenton VA 20186

Hours: Sa–Su 11:00–5:00 (Apr–Nov)   540-349-5185
Closed Dec–Mar   www.graniteheightsorchard.com
Stay Tuned: Facebook   E-mail: tasting-room@graniteheightsorchard.com

Granite Heights was established by Luke and Toni Kilyk on a working farm and orchard that has now expanded to 53 acres. Granite Heights produced its first vintage in 2010 and opened to the public two years later. Luke serves as the winemaker for the winery's all-Virginia grown wines; the wines are made either from estate-grown fruit or grapes from Loudoun and Albemarle vineyards. The tasting room is in a restored farmhouse and includes several tasting areas for visitors. Sandwiches and other light fare are available for purchase, as are several jams from Granite Heights Orchard fruit and honey from beehives on the property. Well-behaved children are welcome.

White Wines: Petit Manseng.

Rosé Wines: Rosé *(Petit Verdot, Merlot)*.

Red Wines: Evening Serenade *(Bordeaux-style blend)*, Merlot, Lomax Reserve *(Bordeaux-style blend)*, End of the Road *(Bordeaux-style blend)*.

Sweet/Dessert Wines: Ashby *(Touriga Nacional, Merlot)*.

Price Range: $18–$36

Tastings: $5 per person.

Groups: Reservations required for groups of 8 or more, with one week advance notice; $8 per person for groups of 8 to 11, $10 per person fee for groups of 12 or more.

Restrictions: Reservations required for buses, limos, and vans.

Directions: From Warrenton, drive south onto U.S. Route 15/17/29 about 7 miles to the village of Opal. Turn right onto Opal Road and continue 2.7 miles to the winery driveway on the left.

Gray Ghost Vineyards & Winery
14706 Lee Highway
Amissville VA 20106

Hours: F–Su, M holidays 11:00–5:00 (Mar–Dec), 540-937-4869
also Tu–Th 11:00–5:00 (Jun–Aug) www.grayghostvineyards.com
Sa-Su, M holidays 11:00-5:00 (Jan-Feb)
Closed New Year's, Easter, Thanksgiving, Christmas
Stay Tuned: Facebook, newsletter

Gray Ghost was founded by Al and Cheryl Kellert, who named their winery after Confederate Colonel John S. Mosby, known during the Civil War as the Gray Ghost. (Al's family is related to the Mosbys.) The winery first opened to the public in 1994 and now produces about a dozen estate-grown wines. Seating is available upstairs on the second floor of the tasting room or outdoors on the deck or gazebos. Visitors may enjoy cheese and crackers purchased at the winery or may bring their own picnic fare. Gray Ghost offers a range of activities at the winery, including a Valentine's Day tasting, a volunteer harvest program, an annual food drive, and a Civil War authors day. In December, the winery also puts on a Holiday Open House that features statues and scenes made from over sixty thousand wine corks. Children are welcome.

White Wines: Chardonnay, Gewurztraminer, Riesling, Seyval Blanc, Victorian White, Vidal Blanc.

Red Wines: Cabernet Franc, Cabernet Sauvignon, Merlot, Ranger Reserve *(Bordeaux-style blend)*, Victorian Red *(Cabernet Franc, Chardonnay)*.

Sweet/Dessert Wines: Adieu (late harvest Vidal Blanc).

Price Range: $15–$40

Groups: Reservations required for groups of 8 or more.

Directions: From Warrenton, take U.S. Route 29 South and turn onto U.S. Route 211 West toward the Shenandoah National Park. Drive 11.5 miles to Woods Edge Lane at the Amissville Volunteer Fire & Rescue. Make a U-turn on the highway to the winery entrance on the right.

Little Washington Winery & Vineyards
72 Christmas Tree Lane
Washington VA 22747

Hours: F–Su 11:00–5:00
Closed New Year's, Christmas
Stay Tuned: Facebook, Twitter, newsletter

540-987-8265
www.littlewashingtonwinery.com
E-mail: info@littlewashingtonwinery.com

Little Washington Winery is located just outside the historic town of "little" Washington. Opened in 2011 by Carl and Donna Henrickson, the winery is on a twenty-five-acre farm with scenic views from its decks. As its own vines mature, the winery is using fruit from other Virginia wineries. Tastings include Little Washington's own wines as well as wines from other small-lot producers in the United States and elsewhere, amd may include such exotic offerings as pineapple wine from Hawaii. Visitors are welcome to bring their own picnic lunches to enjoy on the grounds. Art and jewelry by local artists are often available in the tasting room. Light fare is available for purchase. Children and pets are welcome.

White Wines: Chardonnay, Mesmerized, Solstice *(Chardonnay, Sauvignon Blanc, Vidal Blanc, Viognier).*

Red Wines: George *(Cabernet Sauvignon, Merlot).*

Price Range: $16–$27

Tastings: $7 per person.

Groups: Please call ahead for groups for 8 or more.

Wheelchair accessible.

Dirt Road Wine Club members receive shipments of wines from around the United States.

Purchasing: Online orders are available via VinoShipper to AK, FL, ID, LA, MN, MO, NE, NV, NH, NM, MD, OH, OR, DC, WV, and WY.

Directions: From Warrenton, take U.S. Route 29 South. Turn onto U.S. Route 211 West toward the Shenandoah National Park. Drive 24 miles and turn right onto Christmas Tree Lane. The winery driveway will be about 1/2 mile on the right.

❖ ❖ ❖

Martarella Vineyards
8278 Falcon Glen Road
Warrenton VA 20186

Hours: Th–Su 11:00–6:00   540-347-1119
Closed New Year's, Easter, Thanksgiving, Christmas   marterellawines.com
Stay Tuned: Facebook, newsletter   E-mail: kate@marterellawines.com

Owned and founded by Jerry and Kate Marterella, Marterella Winery is located in the Fauquier County countryside just down the road from Mediterranean Cellars. Marterella produces all Virginia-grown wines, both from their own eight-acre vineyard and from other Virginia fruit. The winery includes an indoor tasting area with tables and chairs for guests, as well as additional seating outdoors on the patio overlooking the winery's vineyard. Light food is available for purchase to accompany wines by the glass or bottle. Children and leashed pets are welcome.

White Wines: Chardonnay, Pinot Grigio, Vidal Blanc, Viognier.

Rosé Wines: Heritage Dry Rosé, Rosalie's Rosé *(Merlot)*.

Red Wines: Cabernet Franc, Meritage, Merlot.

Sweet/Dessert Wines: Grace *(Vidal Blanc, Riesling)*, Sweet Nothings *(Chambourcin)*.

Price Range: $18–$36

Tastings: $5 per person for white or red flight; $10 for full flight.

Groups: Reservations required for groups of 6 or more. Upon request, group tastings can also include a full glass of wine and souvenir glass for $19 per person. Private barrel room tastings for 10 or more, $30 per person fee.

Wheelchair accessible.

Restrictions: Reservations required for buses, limos, and vans.

Purchasing: Online sales to Virginia residents only.

Directions: From Warrenton, take U.S. Route 17 North for 3 miles. Turn left onto Keith Road (Route 628) and drive 1.1 miles. At the end of the road, turn left onto Cannonball Gate Road and drive about 1 mile. Turn right onto Falcon Glen Road (portions unpaved) to the winery on the right.

Mediterranean Cellars
8295 Falcon Glen Road
Warrenton VA 20186

Hours: Th–M 11:00–6:00; F-Sa to 8:00, Su to 7:00 (Jun–Aug only)   540-428-1984
Closed New Year's, Thanksgiving, Christmas   www.mediterraneancellars.com
E-mail: info@mediterraneancellars.com

Mediterranean Cellars was opened in 2003 by Louis Papadopoulos, who first began making wine in his native Greece before moving to Virginia in 1984. The winery is located on a hillside that offers visitors a charming view of the valley and vineyards below from its stone patio. Inside the tasting room are a small tasting bar and larger tasting room with several tables and chairs for seating. In addition to its wide selection of mostly estate-grown varietals, Mediterranean offers a retsina-style white wine in a tribute to the Papadopoulos family's ancestral origins. Light fare is available for purchase. Children and pets are welcome.

White Wines: Belleview Blanc *(Vidal Blanc)*, Chardonnay, Rechina *(retsina-style)*, Vidal Blanc, Viognier.

Rosé Wines: Matina's Rosé.

Red Wines: Cabernet Franc, Cabernet Sauvignon, Chambourcin, Merlot, Romance.

Sweet/Dessert Wines: Sweet Lucia *(late harvest Vidal Blanc)*, Sweet Romance Reserve.

Price Range: $16–$45

Tastings: $5 per person.

Groups: Please call ahead for groups for 8 or more.

Wheelchair accessible.

Winemaker's Selections members receive discounts, quarterly shipments, free wine tastings.

Directions: From Warrenton, take U.S. Route 17 North for about 3 miles. Turn left onto Keith Road (Route 628) and drive 1.1 miles. At the end of the road, turn left onto Cannonball Gate Road and drive about 1 mile. Turn right onto Falcon Glen Road (portions unpaved) to the winery driveway 1/2 mile on the left.

Molon Lave Vineyards
10075 Lees Mill Road
Warrenton VA 20186

Hours: Daily 11:00–6:00   540-439-5460
Closed New Year's, Easter, Thanksgiving, Christmas   www.molonlavevineyards.com
Stay Tuned: Facebook   E-mail: info@molonlavevineyards.com

Molon Lave was founded by Louis Papadopoulos, son of the owner of nearby Mediterranean Cellars. The winery's name is rooted in ancient Greek history in honor of the family's heritage: At the battle of Thermopylae, Persian King Xerxes called on Spartan King Leonidas to surrender his greatly outnumbered force. Leonidas replied, "Come and take them [molon lave]." The winery's tasting room includes two spacious areas with several tasting bars as well as a wraparound patio and outdoor pavilion. As at Mediterranean Cellars, Molon Lave offers a retsina-style wine in honor of the family's Greek heritage. Tastings also include small food pairings. Snacks are available for purchase at the winery, which may be rented for weddings and private events.

White Wines: Chardonnay, Vidal Blanc, Vidal Blanc Semi-Sweet.

Rosé Wines: Kokineli *(retsina-style)*.

Red Wines: Autumn Nectar, Cabernet Franc, Cabernet Sauvignon, Chambourcin, Kate's Charm, Merlot.

Price Range: $18–$36

Tastings: $5 per person.

Groups: Reservations required for groups of 6 or more. Upon request, group tastings can also include a full glass of wine and souvenir glass for $19 per person. Private barrel room tastings for 10 or more, $30 per person fee.

Wheelchair accessible.

Restrictions: Reservations required for buses, limos, and vans.

Purchasing: Online sales to Virginia residents only.

Directions: From Warrenton, drive south onto U.S. Route 15/17/29 about 7 miles to the village of Opal. Turn right onto Opal Road and continue one mile. Turn left onto Lees Mill Road. Winery entrance will be on the left in 0.7 miles.

Morais Vineyards
11409 Marsh Road
Bealeton VA 22712

Hours: Sa–Su 12:00–6:00   703-369-2241
Closed New Year's, Easter, Thanksgiving, Christmas   www.moraisvineyards.com
Stay Tuned: Facebook, Twitter   E-mail: moraisvineyards@aol.com

José and Josephine Morais [*more-ice*] established Morais Vineyards in 2004, when they planted the first vines on the property. The winery opened to the public eight years later, offering all estate-grown wines from grapes grown on the 100-acre property. Several of the wines honor the family's Portuguese heritage, including Battlefield White, made in the *vinho verde* style, and Jeropiga, a Portuguese-style dessert wine. The winemaker also crushes the grapes by foot in the traditional Portuguese manner. Visitors can relax in the tasting area around a fireplace or outside on the patios, which feature a view of the vines. The facilities include a ballroom for weddings and other events.

White Wines: Select White *(Rkatsiteli)*, Battlefield White *(Vidal Blanc, Albariño)*.

Rosé Wines: Rosé *(Cabernet Franc)*.

Red Wines: Red Select *(Merlot, Cabernet Franc)*, Merlot, Cabernet Franc, Touriga Nacional.

Sweet/Dessert Wines: Jeropiga *(Merlot)*, Moscatel *(Muscat)*.

Price Range: $9–$20

Tastings: $8 per person.

Groups: Reservations appreciated for groups of 6 or more.

Wheelchair accessible.

116

Restrictions: Reservations required for buses, limos, and vans.

Directions: From Warrenton, drive south onto U.S. Route 15/17/29 about 7 miles to the village of Opal. Turn left to continue following U.S. Route 17. Drive 4.9 miles and make a U-turn at the Sunoco station; the winery driveway will be 0.1 mile on the right.

Narmada Winery
43 Narmada Lane
Amissville VA 20106

Hours: Th–M 12:00–6:00, Sa until 7:00 Sa (May–Nov); 540-937-8215
F–Mo 11:00–5:00, Sa until 6:00 (winter) www.narmadawinery.com
Closed New Year's, Thanksgiving, Christmas E-mail: info@narmadawinery.com
Stay Tuned: Facebook, Twitter, newsletter

Narmada brings a taste of India to Virginia's wine country. The winery was established by Sudha and Pandit Patil, who planted their first vines in 2005. Sudha, a full-time endodontist in neighboring Culpeper, serves as the winemaker, and Pandit handles the business end. The Patils named their winery in honor of Pandit's mother, Narmada. In addition to cheeses, cold cuts, and breads, Narmada occasionally also offers Indian food for visitors to enjoy either in the tasting room or on the patios (please note that the kitchen is closed on Thursdays and Mondays). The winery is available for rental for private parties of up to one hundred people. Children and pets are welcome.

White Wines: Chardonnay, Dream *(Traminette)*, MOM *(Chardonel, Vidal Blanc)*, Viognier.

Red Wines: Cabernet Franc, Gulabi *(Chambourcin, Chardonel)*, Mélange *(Bordeaux-style blend)*, Midnight *(Chambourcin)*, Reflection *(Chambourcin)*, Tannat, Yash-Vir *(Bordeaux-style blend)*.

Sweet/Dessert Wines: Lotus *(Vidal Blanc)*, Primita *(Chambourcin, raspberry)*.

Fortified Wines: Allure *(Chambourcin, Tannat, Cabernet Sauvignon)*.

Price Range: $20–$38

Tastings: $7 to $9.

Wheelchair accessible.

Purchasing: Online shipping is available for Virginia residents and through VinoShipper to AK, FL, ID LA, MO, NE, NV, NH, NM, ND, OH, OR, DC, WV, and WY.

Maharaja Wine Club members receive regular shipments, discounts, members-only events.

Directions: From Warrenton, take U.S. Route 211 West for 13 miles to the winery entrance on the right.

Unicorn Winery
489 Old Bridge Road
Amissville VA 20106

Hours: M–F 12:00–5:00, Sa–Su 11:00–6:00 (Apr–Oct) 540-349-5885
F 12:00–5:00, Sa–Su 11:00–5:00 (Nov–Mar) www.unicornwinery.com
Closed Thanksgiving, Christmas E-mail: info@unicornwinery.com
Stay Tuned: Facebook, Twitter, newsletter

Owned by Richard and Sandy LePage, Unicorn Winery is located on twenty acres on the banks of the Rappahannock River. The cozy tasting room includes several tasting bars, as well as a shaded deck outdoors with a view of the winery's pond. Light fare is available for purchase and consumption on the grounds, or visitors may bring their own food for family picnics. The winery also offers a horseshoe pit and picnic area near the river. The facilities are available for rental for private events. Children and pets are welcome.

White Wines: Chardonnay, Pinot Gris, Table Rock White *(Chardonel, Seyval Blanc, Vidal Blanc)*, Traminette.

Blush Wines: Slightly Embarrassed *(Seyval Blanc, Chardonel, Vidal Blanc)*.

Red Wines: Cabernet Franc, Cabernet Sauvignon, Chambourcin, Crimson Sunset *(Chambourcin)*, Meritage, Merlot.

Sweet/Dessert Wines: Obsidian.

Price Range: $14–$25

Tastings: $5 per person.

Wheelchair accessible.

Purchasing: Online ordering via VinoShipper to AK, FL, ID, LA, MO, NE, NV, NH, NM, ND, OH, OR, DC, WV, and WY.

Directions: From Warrenton, take U.S. Route 211 West for about 5 miles. Turn right onto Leeds Manor Road (Route 688) and drive 3/4 mile. Turn left onto Jeffersonton Road, which becomes Old Bridge Road. Winery entrance will be on the left after 1/2 mile.

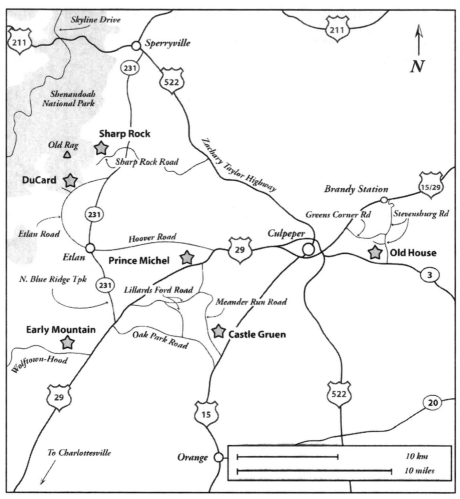

Map 4.10. Culpeper

CULPEPER

Castle Gruen Vineyards & Winery
1272 Meander Run Road
Locust Dale VA 22948

Hours: Temporarily closed; see the website for details

540-229-2498
www.castlegruenwinery.com
E-mail: CastleGruen@aol.com

Owner/winemaker Dean Gruenburg opened his boutique winery and tasting room in August 2008 in what is one of the most unique structures in the Virginia wine community. Built to resemble a small castle, complete with crenellated top and purple doors, Castle Gruen houses (at the moment) both the winemaking facilities and tasting bar. Dean, who works at Prince Michel Vineyard during the week, currently produces about five hundred cases of estate-grown wine annually and works the vineyards and winery himself. Children and pets are welcome.

White Wines: Chardonnay, Queen's White.

Red Wines: King's Red *(Bordeaux-style blend)*, Merlot, Norton.

Price Range: $15–$20

Purchasing: Online purchases for VA residents only.

Directions: From Culpeper, drive south on U.S. Route 15 for about 10 miles. Turn right onto Meander Run Road (Route 631) and drive 1.25 miles to the winery entrance on right at the purple mailbox.

DuCard Vineyard
40 Gibson Hollow Lane
Etlan VA 22719

Hours: F–Su, M holidays 11:00–6:00

Closed 20 December–6 January

Stay Tuned: Facebook, Twitter

540-923-4206

www.ducardvineyards.com

E-mail: scott@ducardvineyards.com

Scott and Karen Elliff started their vineyard on the site of an old apple orchard in Madison County, opening their winery to the public in 2010 after ten years of producing wines for private sale. The Elliffs named their winery by flipping the name of one of Scott's favorite single malt scotches, Cardhu. The winery offers visitors a scenic view of the nearby Blue Ridge Mountains from the tasting room and the outdoor patios. Winery and vineyard tours are also available for groups up to ten. Light food is available for purchase in the tasting room. DuCard sponsors occasional live music festivals; check the website for details. Pets and children are welcome.

White Wines: Gibson Hollow White, Signature Viognier.

Rosé Wines: Rosé.

Red Wines: Cabernet Franc, Norton, Petit Verdot, Popham Run *(Bordeaux-style blend)*.

Sweet/Dessert Wines: Sweet Virginia Vidal Blanc.

Fortified Wines: C'Est Trop *(Norton)*.

Price Range: $18–$30

Tastings: $6 per person.

Groups: Reservations required for groups of 10 or more.

Wheelchair accessible.

Purchasing: Online purchasing available for CA, VA and DC residents.

Case Club members receive discounts and members-only events.

Directions: From U.S. Route 29, turn north onto North Blue Ridge Turnpike (Route 231) and continue for about 6 miles to the village of Etlan. Turn left onto Etlan Road (Route 643). Drive 2.7 miles and turn right onto Gibson Hollow Lane. The winery entrance will be immediately on the right.

Early Mountain Winery
6109 Wolftown Hood Road
Madison VA 22727

Hours: Daily 11:00–5:00 (F until 8:00)
Closed New Year's Eve & Day, Easter,
Thanksgiving, Christmas Eve & Day
Stay Tuned: Newsletter

540-948-9005
http://earlymountain.com
E-mail: cheers@earlymountain.com

Early Mountain is owned by Steve and Jean Case who purchased the winery in late 2011. The winery was originally named Sweeley Estate, and the Cases renamed it in honor of Revolutionary War patriot Joseph Early, who was the original owner of the land on which the winery now stands. The facilities include a tasting room with numerous sofas and chairs, a small gift shop, and an events room for weddings and private parties. Wine tastings include both Early Mountain's own production and select wines from other Virginia wineries. Early Mountain sponsors various activities, including live music on Friday evenings. Food is available for purchase at the winery; menus are listed on the website. Children and leashed pets are welcome.

White Wines: Chardonnay, Petit Manseng, Pinot Gris, Viognier.

Red Wines: Handshake Red *(Bordeaux-style blend)*, Merlot.

Sweet/Dessert Wines: Muscat Dolce *(port-style)*.

Price Range: $16–$32

Tastings: $12 per person for a red, white, or mixed flight.

Groups: Reservations required for groups of 10 or more.

Wheelchair accessible

Directions: From Culpeper, take U.S. 29 South for about 17 miles. Turn right onto Wolftown Hood Road (Route 230). The winery will be 1.2 miles on the right.

Old House Vineyards
18351 Corkys Lane
Culpeper VA 22701

Hours: M–F 12:00–6:00, Sa 11:00–6:00,
Su 12:00–5:00 (Memorial Day–Labor Day)
M, W–F, Su 12:00–5:00,
Sa 11:00–6:00 (Labor Day–Memorial Day)
Closed New Year's, Thanksgiving, Christmas

540-423-1032
www.oldhousevineyards.com
E-mail: info@oldhousevineyards.com

Old House was founded in 1998 by Patrick and Allyson Kearney on a farm within the boundaries of the Brandy Station Civil War battlefield. They opened their tasting room in the restored 1800s-era farmhouse, which offers a distant view of the house where George Armstrong Custer honeymooned with his bride in 1864. Old House offers several tables on the grounds, which are open for family picnics. The winery sponsors a range of special events, including live music, an annual chili cook-off, and Harvest

Days festivals. Old House is also available for rental for private parties, weddings, and corporate events. Children are welcome.

Sparkling Wines: Pétillante.

White Wines: Chardonnay, Clover Hill, Vidal Blanc.

Rosé Wines: Rosie's Rosé *(Cabernet Franc)*.

Red Wines: Bacchanalia *(Cabernet Franc, Chambourcin, Tannat)*, Cabernet Franc, Wicked Bottom *(Chambourcin)*.

Sweet/Dessert Wines: Arctica *(Vidal Blanc)*.

Fortified Wines: Chambourcin Dessert.

Price Range: $15–$35

Tastings: $5 per person.

Groups: Reservations required for groups of 8 or more and include winery tour, private tasting, souvenir glass; $10 per person fee.

Wheelchair accessible.

Restrictions: No pets.

Wine Club members receive wine shipments, discounts, members-only events.

Directions: From U.S. Route 15/29 at Brandy Station, turn south onto Alanthus Road. Make an immediate left onto Brandy Road and take the first right onto Mount Dumpling Road, which will bend to the left and become Stevensburg Road. Drive 3.2 miles and turn right onto Corkys Road (narrow, gravel drive), which is the driveway to the winery. Continue about 1/2 mile to the winery parking lot.

❖ ❖ ❖

Prince Michel Vineyard & Winery
154 Winery Lane
Leon VA 22725

Hours: Daily 10:00–6:00 (Apr–Dec);
M–Th 10:00–5:00, F–Su 10:00–6:00 (Jan–Mar)
Closed New Year's, Thanksgiving, Christmas
Stay Tuned: Facebook, Newsletter

1-800-800-WINE (9463)
www.princemichel.com
E-mail: info@princemichel.com

Established in 1982, Prince Michel is one of the largest commercial wineries in Virginia, producing well over forty thousand cases annually under the Prince Michel and Rapidan River labels. Now owned by Kristin Holzman, Prince Michel offers private labels for resorts, companies, and special events, such as weddings. Winemaker Brad Hansen has overseen Prince Michel's production since 1999. The tasting room includes a tasting bar in the middle of an extensive gift shop and free Wi-Fi. The winery offers a free self-guided tour, as well as private group tours by reservation only. Prince Michel has several suites for overnight stays. The facilities may be rented for private meetings, parties, and weddings.

Prince Michel wines are also available for tasting at the Carter Mountain Wine Shop at 1435 Carter's Mountain Trail in Charlottesville. The shop is open from June through November (M-Sa 11:00-6:00, Su to 5:00).

Fruit Wines: Rapidan River Blackberry, Rapidan River Peach, Rapidan River Raspberry.

Sparkling Wines: Prince Michel Sparkling.

White Wines: Chardonnay, Mount Juliet Chardonnay, Mount Juliet Petit Manseng, Pinot Grigio, Rapidan River Chardonnay, Rapidan River Dry Riesling, Rapidan River Semi-Dry Riesling.

Rosé Wines: Dry Rosé, Rapidan River Rosé.

Red Wines: Cabernet Franc, Cabernet Sauvignon, Crown Orchard Cabernet Sauvignon, Merlot, Mountain View Cabernet Franc, Mount Juliet Petit Verdot, Quaker Run Farm Syrah, Symbius *(Bordeaux-style blend)*, Rapidan River Merlot.

Sweet/Dessert Wines: Très Bien *(Petit Manseng)*, Prince Michel Dessert, Rapidan River Sweet White Reserve, Rapidan River Sweet Red Reserve, Rapidan River Chocolate.

Price Range: $13–$50

Tastings: $5 per person.

Groups: Reservations required for groups of 8 or more; $20 per person for groups of up to 10, $10 per person for groups of 10 to 50.

Wheelchair accessible.

Purchasing: Online purchasing is available for residents of AK, AZ, CA, CO, FL, GA, IA, IL, LA, MI, MN, MO, NC, ND, NE, NH, NM, NV, NY, OH, RI, SC, TX, VA, WA, DC WV, and WY.

Wine Club members receive regular shipments of wine, special members-only offers.

Directions: From Culpeper, take U.S. Route 29 South for 8 miles to the winery on right.

Sharp Rock Vineyards
5 Sharp Rock Road
Sperryville VA 22740

Hours: F–Su, M holidays 11:00–5:00 (mid-Feb–Dec)   540-987-8020
Th–M 11:00–5:00 (Oct)   www.sharprockvineyards.com
Closed Jan–mid-Feb, Christmas   E-mail: jeast@sharprockvineyards.com
Stay Tuned: Newsletter

Sharp Rock Vineyards is located at the base of Old Rag Mountain, one of the most popular hiking destinations in Virginia, and has been a working farm since the late 1700s. Owners Jim and Kathy East first planted their vineyards in 1992 and now make twelve estate-grown wines. Tastings are held in the upper level of their restored barn. Breads and cheeses are available for purchase. There will generally be several winery dogs on hand to greet visitors. The winery is available for rental for private parties and weddings. Children and pets are welcome.

Sharp Rock also has two riverside cottages for overnight stays. Charges include a complimentary wine tasting and bottle of wine, breakfast, and snacks. The cottages are the closest accommodations available to Old Rag.

White Wines: Chardonnay, Chamois Blanc *(Chardonnay, Vidal Blanc)*, Sauvignon Blanc.

Rosé Wines: Rosé, Rosé Noir.

Red Wines: Cabernet Franc, Cabernet Sauvignon, Chamois Rouge, Malbec, Old Rag Red, Pinnacle *(Bordeaux-style blend)*, Synergy *(Petit Verdot, Malbec)*.

Price Range: $17–$30

Tastings: $3 per person.

Purchasing: Online purchasing available to AL, AK, CA, CO, CT, HI, ID, IL, IA, MN, MO, NE, NV, NM, ND, OH, OR, RI, VA, VT, WA, DC, WV, and WI.

Directions: From Sperryville, drive south on Route 231 for 8 miles. Turn right onto Sharp Rock Road (Route 601) and drive 1 mile. At the intersection with Nethers Road (Route 707), the winery will be the farm on the right.

෨෧

BORDEAUX-STYLE BLENDS

Bordeaux, Bordeaux-style, Meritage—do these terms all mean the same thing? Well, yes and no.

True Bordeaux wines are only from the area around Bordeaux, France. Specifically, the Bordeaux region encompasses vineyards along both banks of France's Gironde River, which flows through the city of Bordeaux, and its tributaries, the Garonne and Dordogne. Wine grapes have been cultivated here since at least the 1st century AD, when the Roman aristocrat and naturalist Pliny the Elder wrote about the grape-growing and wines he encountered in the area.

Also called Claret, red Bordeaux is generally a blend of Cabernet Sauvignon, Merlot, Cabernet Franc, Petit Verdot, and, to a much lesser extent, Malbec. (A sixth grape, Carmenère, is used only rarely.) The individual grape varieties are first fermented, then aged separately in oak barrels for over a year before being blended and bottled. High-quality Bordeaux wines are rich, powerful wines that age beautifully, becoming more complex and refined over time.

Wines said to be "Bordeaux-style" also are blends of two or more of the five classic Bordeaux red wine varieties. Because Bordeaux reds are considered by many to rank among the world's greatest wines, a winery's Bordeaux-style wine will often be held up as that winery's finest production. The specific grapes and proportions in the blend vary somewhat from year to year, depending on the vintage quality, and the winery may or may not reveal its specific blend.

Meritage (rhymes with "heritage") is a trademarked name for Bordeaux-style American wines. Coined in 1981, the name is a combination of "merit" to signify grape quality and "heritage" to denote the historical tradition of wine blending. To use the term Meritage on the label, the wine must be a blend of two or more of the five classic Bordeaux varieties; St. Macaire, Gros Verdot, and Carmenère grapes may also be used. No single grape variety may account for more than 90% of the blend. The winery must also join the Meritage Alliance and pay an annual licensing fee to the group.

෨෧

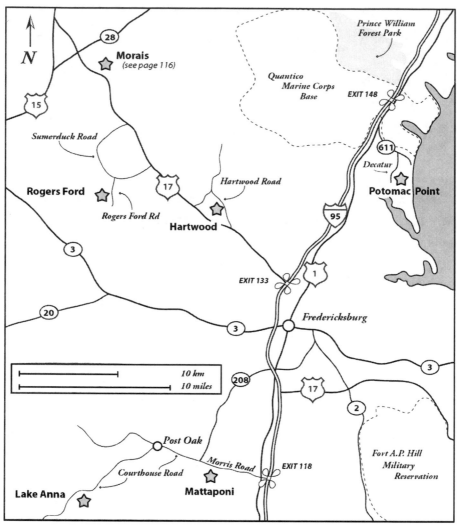

Map 4.11. Fredericksburg

FREDERICKSBURG

Hartwood Winery

345 Hartwood Road

Fredericksburg VA 22406

Hours: W–F 11:00–5:00, Sa–Su 11:00–6:00   540-752-4893

Closed New Year's, Easter, Thanksgiving, Christmas   www.hartwoodwinery.com

Stay Tuned: Facebook, Twitter, newsletter   E-mail: contact@hartwoodwinery.com

Hartwood is a small family-owned and operated winery just outside Fredericksburg. The winery has seven acres under vine on site, with twenty-five additional acres of vineyards across the state; all its wines are Virginia-grown. Opened in 1989, the winery takes its name from the surrounding Hartwood community, which is known for its large deer population. In addition to regular tastings, owner-winemakers Jim and Beverly Livingston offer private tastings and tours after hours. Hartwood also sponsors special winery events, include festivals, barrel tastings, open houses, and wine appreciation seminars. The tasting room includes a small gift shop. Children are welcome.

White Wines: Chardonnay, Deweese White *(Vidal Blanc)*, Hartwood Station White *(Chardonnay, Viognier, Rkatsiteli)*, Rappahannock White *(Seyval Blanc, Vidal Blanc)*, Sauvignon Blanc, Viognier.

Rosé Wines: Rappahannock Rose.

Red Wines: Cabernet Franc, Cabernet Sauvignon, Claret, Merlot, Rappahannock Red.

Price Range: $15–$21

Tastings: $5 per person.

Groups: Private group tastings for up to 40 ($100 per hour plus $3 per person).

Purchasing: Online ordering via VinoShipper to AK, DC, FL, ID, LA, MO, ND, NE, NH, NM, NV, OH, OR, WV, and WY.

Directions: From I-95, take Exit 133 (Warrenton) onto U.S. Route 17 North. Drive 6 miles and turn right onto Hartwood Road (Route 612). Winery will be on left in 1.5 miles.

Lake Anna Winery
5621 Courthouse Road
Spotsylvania VA 22551

Hours: W–Sa 11:00–5:00, Su 1:00–5:00   540-895-5085
Closed New Year's, Thanksgiving, Christmas   www.lawinery.com
Stay Tuned: Facebook, newsletter   E-mail: info@lawinery.com

Lake Anna Winery had its origins as a vineyard established by Bill and Ann Heidig in 1983 to sell Seyval Blanc, Cabernet Sauvignon, Chardonnay, and Merlot grapes to regional wineries. Seven years later, the Heidigs decided to produce their own wines and transformed Lake Anna into a full-fledged winery. Now under the ownership and management of sons Jeff and Eric, Lake Anna produces about seven thousand cases of wine annually under the supervision of winemaker Graham Bell, who previously worked at Horton Vineyards and Montdomaine Cellars.

Lake Anna's tasting room includes a tasting bar, tables for extra seating, and a gift shop. The winery also offers free Wi-Fi for visitors. Special events include live music, a "Wine and Whiskers" SPCA fundraiser, and annual Octoberfest. The facility may be rented for private events and weddings. Children and pets are welcome.

White Wines: Chardonnay, Lake Side White, Seyval Blanc, Totally White *(Chardonnay, Viognier, Seyval Blanc)*.

Rosé Wines: Lake Side Sunset.

Red Wines: Cabernet Franc, Enigme, Lake Side Red, Merlot, Spotsylvania Claret, Totally Red.

Sweet/Dessert Wines: Essensual *(Vidal Blanc)*.

Price Range: $12–$25

Tastings: $3 per person.

Wheelchair accessible.

Directions: From I-95, take Exit 118 (Thornburg) and turn west onto Morris Road (Route 606) which will become Courthouse Road (Route 208). At the Post Oak community, turn left to continue following Courthouse Road and drive 7.5 miles to winery entrance on left.

Mattaponi Winery
7530 Morris Road
Spotsylvania VA 22551

Hours: W–Su 11:00–6:00
Closed New Year's, Thanksgiving, Christmas

540-582-2897
www.mattaponiwinery.com
E-mail: mattaponiwinery@aol.com

Mattaponi *(matta-poe-NIGH)* Winery is a small family-operated winery that is one of only two Native American-owned wineries in the United States (North Carolina's Native Vines is the other). Owners Mike and Janette Evans got their start as home winemakers over twenty years ago before eventually deciding in 2007 to open their own winery on the grounds of their Christmas tree farm just south of Fredericksburg. The Evanses have chosen Algonquin names for several of their wines in honor of the Native Americans who originally settled Virginia. Proceeds from Mattaponi's Tibik-Kizismin blueberry wine go to support the Avon Cancer Foundation.

Fruit Wines: Kizismin *(peach)*, Makadewamin *(blackberry)*, Odeimin *(straw-berry)*, Pow Wow *(chocolate, strawberry)*, Tibik-Kizismin *(blueberry)*.

White Wines: Chardonnay, Wabamin *(Niagara)*, Riesling.

Red Wines: Cabernet Franc, Cabernet Sauvignon, Chambourcin, Freedom *(Cabernet Franc, White Moore's Diamond, Blue Concord)*, Merlot, Miskwamin *(Concord)*.

Price Range: $13–$18

Tastings: $2 per person.

Groups: Reservations required for groups of 10 or more.

Directions: From I-95, take Exit 118 (Thornburg) and turn west onto Morris Road (Route 606). Drive 4 miles to winery entrance on left and follow the gravel driveway to the tasting room entrance at the rear of the house.

Potomac Point Vineyard & Winery
275 Decatur Road
Stafford VA 22554

Hours: Su–M, W–Th, 11:00–6:00,
F 11:00–10:00, Sa 11:00–9:30
Closed New Year's, Thanksgiving, Christmas
Stay Tuned: Facebook, Twitter

540-446-2266
www.potomacpointwinery.com
E-mail: info@potomacpointwinery.com

Since opening in 2007 under the ownership of Skip and Cindi Causey, Potomac Point has become a popular venue for weekend wine tourism. The winery's tasting room opens onto an outdoor courtyard; outdoor seating is also available upstairs on a rooftop patio. Potomac Point's wines are all Virginia-grown, either from the winery's four acres or from the nearly fifty acres of leased vineyards across the state. The winery sponsors special events, including Ladies' Nights and live music on Fireside Fridays and on Sundays (with cover charge). Children are welcome to play in the "Little Buds" room. Potomac Point offers several rooms, including a ballroom, for private parties and weddings. Custom-label wines for special events, such as weddings, are also available. Pets are welcome.

White Wines: Chardonnay, Custom Label White *(Viognier, Chardonnay)*, La Belle Vie White *(Vidal Blanc, Chardonnay, Traminette, Viognier)*, Viognier.

Rosé Wines: La Belle Vie Rosé *(Syrah, Chambourcin)*.

Red Wines: Abbinato *(Sangiovese, Touriga Nacional)*, Cabernet Franc, Custom Label Red *(Bordeaux-style blend)*, Heritage *(Bordeaux-style blend)*, Merlot, Norton, Petit Verdot.

Sweet/Dessert Wines: Vin de Paille *(Petit Manseng)*.

Fortified Wines: Rabelos Port *(Touriga Nacional, Tinta Cão)*.

Price Range: $13–$33

Tastings: $5 for basic, $7 for reserve, $10 for premium (premium includes souvenir glass).

Groups: Reservations required for group tastings and tours for 10 or more; $10 for classic and $15 for premier.

Wheelchair accessible.

D'Vine Food & Wine Club, Women Wild About Wine, Amis de Barriques, and Case Club members receive wine, discounts, and member events at varying levels.

Directions: From I-95, take Exit 148 toward Quantico. Turn east onto Russell Road and then merge onto U.S. Route 1 South. Drive 1.4 miles and turn left onto Telegraph Road (Route 736). Continue another 1/2 mile and turn left onto Widewater Road (Route 611). Drive 2.8 miles and turn right onto Decatur Road. The winery driveway (portions unpaved) will be 1 mile on the left.

Rogers Ford Farm Winery
14674 Rogers Ford Road
Sumerduck VA 22742

Hours: F–M 11:00–5:00 (Mar–Dec)   540-439-3707
Closed Jan–Feb, Thanksgiving, Christmas   www.rogersfordwine.com
                                          E-mail: john@rogersfordwine.com

Rogers Ford Farm Winery is located on a fifty-five-acre property that has been a working farm since 1825. Owner-winemaker John Puckett has named several of his wines after his grandchildren and is happy to share his knowledge of the farm's Civil War history with visitors. The intimate tasting room has two small tasting bars and offers snacks for purchase. The property extends to the banks of the Rappahannock River and can be used for picnics with prior notice. Rogers Ford collaborates with a nearby equestrian center to offer wine trail rides as well as with the Inn at Kelly's Ford in nearby Remington to sponsor murder mystery dinners and wine tastings.

Sparkling Wines: Cuvée Julia *(Viognier, Chardonnay)*.

White Wines: Jacob Christopher Chardonnay, Vidal Blanc, Viognier, Virginia White.

Rosé Wines: Sumerduck Rosé.

Red Wines: Chloe Cabernet, Petit Verdot, Virginia Red.

Sweet/Dessert Wines: Brandy Station Dulce, First Frost Vidal, Petit Manseng Sweet Reserve.

Price Range: $16–$29

Tastings: $5 per person.

Groups: Please call ahead for groups of 6 to 25 (maximum size).

Purchasing: Online purchasing for VA residents or via VinoShipper to AK, CA, FL, ID, LA, MN, MO, NE, NV, NH, NM, ND, OH, OR, DC, WV, and WY.

Rogers Ford Wine Club members receive regular wine shipments and discounts.

Directions: From I-95, take Exit 133 (Warrenton) onto U.S. Route 17 North. Drive 12.5 miles and turn left onto Sumerduck Road (Route 651). Continue 3.7 miles to Rogers Ford Road. Turn left and drive 2 miles to winery on right.

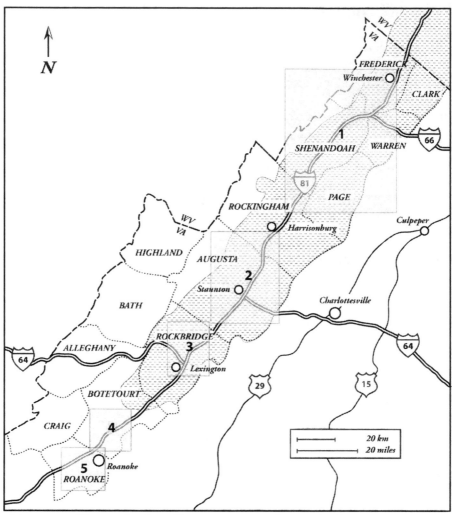

Map 5.1. Shenandoah Valley Region & Shenandoah AVA: (1) Upper Shenandoah Valley; (2) Middle Shenandoah Valley (north); (3) Middle Shenandoah Valley (south); (4) Roanoke (north); (5) Roanoke (south).

5. SHENANDOAH VALLEY REGION & AVA

The Shenandoah Valley offers visitors both rich history and stunning scenic beauty. Stretching from the Virginia-Maryland line to the city of Roanoke, it is bordered on the east by the Blue Ridge Mountains and on the west by the Alleghany and Appalachian Plateaus. Much of the region is underlain by limestone, and the Valley is pockmarked by numerous caverns. Sitting in the rain shadow of the Appalachians, summers here are drier than elsewhere in Virginia, although winters can be snowy and quite cold at times.

The Shenandoah region has about 20 farm wineries scattered the length of the valley. Large or small, all combine a serene winetasting opportunity with picturesque natural settings. The valley is bisected by I-81, a busy north-south highway that provides easy access to wineries and other sites. Visitors with more time may prefer instead to take U.S. Route 11 which parallels the interstate but is a more tranquil way to experience the small towns and scenic countryside of the Shenandoah.

<u>Things to see and do</u>: There is something for every nature lover here: caverns for exploring, trails for hiking and camping, mountains for skiing, and lakes and rivers for fishing. Visitors can explore Luray Caverns, Shenandoah Caverns, or Grand Caverns, which has been open to the public since 1806. The 50-mile-long Massanutten Mountain splits the valley from

Strasburg to Harrisonburg and offers hiking and skiing, depending on the season. Further south, visitors can admire the Natural Bridge, an ancient twenty-story-high natural arch.

The region is also rich in Civil War history. As the breadbasket of Virginia, the Shenandoah saw frequent Civil War clashes as General Thomas "Stonewall" Jackson led his troops in an extended campaign up and down the Valley. Among the battlefields are New Market, where cadets from the Virginia Military Institute (VMI) joined in the battle; Cedar Creek, near Middletown; and Kernstown, near Winchester. Self-guided driving tours allow visitors to retrace history at their own pace; downloadable brochures and maps are available at www.civilwartraveler.com/EAST/VA [case sensitive].

The town of Lexington has ties to both Stonewall Jackson and Robert E. Lee. Although Jackson was born in what is now West Virginia, he is more closely associated with Lexington, where he was on the faculty of VMI. Visitors may tour Jackson's home in downtown Lexington or visit his grave in the city cemetery.

Lexington is also home to Washington and Lee University, the ninth oldest university in the country. Originally founded in 1749 as the Augusta Academy, the institution's leaders changed its name to Washington Academy in 1796 in appreciation for George Washington's gift of stock in the James River Canal. In 1865, Robert E. Lee became president of then-Washington College, serving for five years before his death in 1870. The college then changed its name to honor Lee, who is entombed on the campus; his favorite horse, Traveller, is buried just outside the Lee Chapel.

Visitors may also experience the region's cultural history in Staunton *[STAN-ton]* at the open-air Frontier Culture Museum, a living history site that includes farmsteads from England, Germany, Ireland, and West Africa, as well as a traditional Shenandoah Valley farm. Check the website (www.frontiermuseum.org) for details on events and openings. For theater lovers, the American Shakespeare Center offers year-round performances at its Blackfriars Playhouse, a reproduction of the first indoor theater in the English-speaking world. The ASC website provides more information on performances (www.americanshakespearecenter.com).

<u>Wine Trails</u>: Three wine trails focus on Shenandoah Valley wineries: Shenandoah County Wine Trail, Shenandoah Valley Wine Country Trail, and the Wine Trail of Botetourt County. See Appendix 1 for more details.

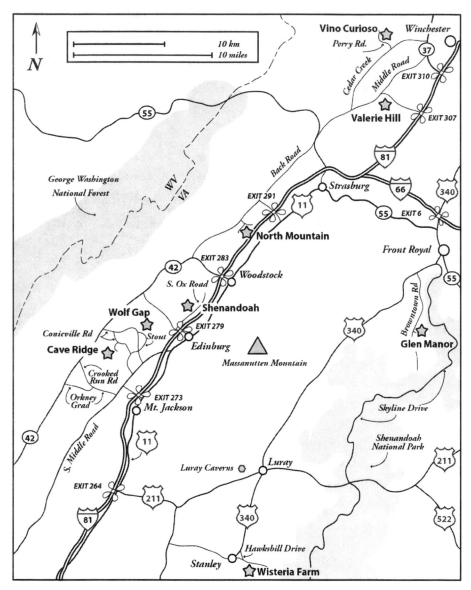

Map 5.2. Upper Shenandoah Valley

UPPER SHENANDOAH VALLEY

Cave Ridge Vineyard
1476 Conicville Road
Mt. Jackson VA 22842

Hours: M, W–Sa 11:00–5:30, Su 12:00–5:00
Closed New Year's, Thanksgiving, Christmas
Stay Tuned: Facebook, Twitter, newsletter

540-477-2585
www.caveridge.com
E-mail: caveridgewines@caveridge.com

Owner and winemaker Randy Phillips established Cave Ridge in 2000, opening the winery to the public six years later. The winery name comes from a cave on the property, and the fossil on the wine labels is a photo of a large fossil uncovered when the vines were being planted. Cave Ridge now produces about two thousand cases of estate-grown wine each year from its nine-acre vineyard. Visitors can relax on the deck or the cobblestoned courtyard outside the tasting room and may either bring their own food or purchase snacks on site. The winery's event hall may be rented for dinners, weddings, and special events. Cave Ridge sponsors occasional live music, chili Saturdays, and holiday open houses. Children and pets are welcome.

White Wines: La Petite Traminette, Riesling, Viognier.

Rosé Wines: Rambling Rose.

Red Wines: Cabernet Franc, Chambourcin, Fossil Hill Reserve, Mount Jackson Rouge, Red Silk, Syrah.

Price Range: $10–$25

Wheelchair accessible.

Fossil Hill Wine Club members receive wine shipments, discounts, and invitations to members-only events.

Directions: From I-81, take Exit 283 (Woodstock) and turn west onto Reservoir Road (Route 42). Continue for 10.4 miles and turn left onto Conicville Road. The winery's single-lane gravel drive is on the right after 1.6 miles (be careful at the semi-blind curve at the end!)

Glen Manor Vineyard
2244 Browntown Road
Front Royal VA 22630

Hours: W–Sa 11:00–5:00, Su 12:00–5:00 (Apr–Nov)   540-635-6324
F, Sa 11:00–5:00, Su 12:00–5:00 (Dec–Mar)   www.glenmanorvineyards.com
Closed Easter, Thanksgiving,   E-mail: gmvwine@glenmanorvineyards.com
Christmas through New Year's

Glen Manor Vineyards, on the western flank of the Blue Ridge Mountains, is a 212-acre working farm that has been in the same family for over one hundred years. Jeff White established Glen Manor's first vineyards in 1995 on the rocky slopes surrounding his family's farm. After working with neighboring Linden Vineyards for twelve years, he opened his own winery in 2008. Jeff's wife, Kelly, is often on hand to welcome visitors in the winery's tasting room and to talk about Glen Manor's estate-grown wines. Leashed dogs are welcome.

White Wines: Petit Manseng, Sauvignon Blanc.

Rosé Wines: Rosé.

Red Wines: Cabernet Franc, Hodder Hill *(Bordeaux-style blend)*, Petit Verdot, Vin Rouge *(Bordeaux-style blend)*.

Sweet/Dessert Wines: Rapheus *(late harvest Petit Manseng)*.

Price Range: $16–$30

Tastings: $4 to $7 per person.

Restrictions: No limos, buses, or groups over six.

Wheelchair accessible.

Wine club members receive invitations to members-only events.

Directions: From I-66, take Exit 6 (Front Royal) and turn onto U.S. Route 340 South. Continue to follow U.S. Route 340 for 4.5 miles through Front Royal. Just after passing the entrance to Skyline Drive and the Shenandoah National Park, turn left onto Browntown Road and continue 5.2 miles to the winery's gravel driveway on the left.

North Mountain Vineyard & Winery
4374 Swartz Road
Maurertown VA 22644

Hours: W–Su 11:00–5:00
Closed New Year's, Thanksgiving, Christmas

540-436-9463
www.northmountainvineyard.com
E-mail: wine@northmountainvineyard.com

North Mountain has been owned and operated since 1998 by Brad Foster and Krista Jackson-Foster, whose son, John Jackson, serves as winemaker. The tasting room includes picture windows that open onto decks, where visitors can sit and enjoy the view over a glass of wine and a snack. The winery offers barrel room tours and tastings with advance reservations. North Mountain sponsors several events, including live music on weekends, chili cook-offs, winemaker's dinners, Mother's and Father's Day events, and an annual Oktober Wein Festival. The facilities are available for weddings and private parties. Children and pets are welcome.

Fruit Wines: Apple.

Sparkling Wines: Groenendael Trocken *(Chardonnay)*, Groenendael Tervuren *(Cabernet Franc)*.

White Wines: Chardonnay, Oktoberfest, Riesling, Vidal Blanc.

Blush Wines: Mountain Sunset *(Riesling, apple)*, Sweet Caroline's Blush.

Red Wines: Cabernet Franc, Cabernet Sauvignon, Chambourcin, Claret, Mountain Midnight *(Chambourcin)*, Tom's Brook Red *(Cabernet Franc)*.

Sweet/Dessert Wines: Virginia Sweet Reserve Vidal Blanc.

Price Range: $12–$30

Tastings: Complimentary for basic tasting; $5 for 3 reserve wines.

Groups: Reservations required for groups of 8 or more ($15 per person); tasting includes a cheese and sausage platter.

Case Club members receive wine releases and purchasing discounts.

Directions: From I-81, take Exit 291 (Tom's Brook) and turn west onto Mount Olive Road. Drive 1.4 miles and turn left onto Back Road (Route 623). Continue 2 miles and turn left onto Harrisville Road (Route 655). After 0.4 miles, turn right onto Swartz Road and the winery entrance.

Shenandoah Vineyards
3659 South Ox Road
Edinburg VA 22824

Hours: Daily, 10:00–5:00
Closed New Year's, Thanksgiving, Christmas

540-984-8699
www.shentel.net/shenvine
E-mail: shenvine@shentel.net

Shenandoah Vineyards, founded in 1976, is one of the oldest Virginia wineries in operation. Owners Jim and Emma Randel's twenty-six-acre vineyard is planted to eleven varietals; all their wines are estate-grown. The tasting room is in a Civil War-era barn that offers visitors two balcony decks from which to appreciate the views of the vineyards and nearby Massanutten Mountain. Guided tours are offered on the hour. The winery sponsors special Valentine's Day tastings, wine and cheese weekends, country cookouts, an annual Harvest Festival, and a holiday open house. Children are welcome.

White Wines: Chardonnay, Johannisberg Riesling, Sauvignon Blanc, Shenandoah Blanc.

Blush Wines: Blushing Belle.

Red Wines: Cabernet Franc, Cabernet Sauvignon, Chambourcin, Rebel Red, Rhapsody in Red.

Sweet/Dessert Wines: Sweet Serenade, Fiesta, Raspberry Serenade.

Price Range: $10–$23

Tastings: $5 per person, including tour (hourly).

Wheelchair accessible.

Purchasing: Online ordering is available via VinoShipper for AK, FL, ID, LA, MN, MO, NE, NV, NH, NM, ND, OH, OR, DC, WV, and WY.

Directions: From I-81, take Exit 279 and turn west onto Stoney Creek Road. Make an immediate right onto South Ox Road. The winery will be 1.6 miles on the left.

Valerie Hill Winery
1687 Marlboro Road
Stephens City VA 22655

Hours: M–Th 11:00–6:00, F 11:00–8:00,
Sa 11:00–7:00, Su 11:00–5:00
Closed New Year's, Thanksgiving, Christmas
Stay Tuned: Facebook, Twitter

540-869-9567
www.valeriehillwinery.com
E-mail: info@valeriehillwinery.com

Valerie Hill opened to the public in 2012 on an 18-acre property just south of Winchester. The tasting room is housed in an early nineteenth-century manor house that features a stone patio and fire pit for chilly afternoons. Winemaker Justin Bogaty (Bogati Bodega, Veramar) is producing Valerie Hill's wines from all Virginia-grown grapes while the winery's own vineyard matures. A selection of cheeses, cold cuts and spreads is available for purchase. Live music is featured on select Friday evenings. Children and pets are welcome.

White Wines: Chardonnay, Manor House White, Seyval Blanc, Viognier.

Red Wines: Cabernet Franc, Stone Chimney Red.

Price Range: $12–$20

Tastings: $7 per person.

Groups: Reservations required for groups of 8 or more.

Directions: From I-81, take Exit 307 (VA Route 277) toward Stephens City/ Route 340. Turn right after 0.3 miles onto Fairfax Pike which will become Marlboro Road. Drive 3.7 miles in all to the winery entrance on the left.

Vino Curioso
1334 Perry Road
Winchester VA 22602

Hours: Sa–Su 11:00–5:00 (always call ahead)   703-447-0648
Closed New Year's, Christmas   www.vinocurioso.com
E-mail: wineguy@vinocurioso.com

Established in 2003 by Michael Matthews and Michael Sawyers, Vino Curioso has the distinction of having one of the smallest tasting rooms in Virginia. Matthews serves as the winemaker while also holding down a full-time job as a network engineer. The names of several of his wines have a special significance to the winemaker. "Franc the Tank", for instance, is named in honor of Matthews' father, Francis Matthews, and the colors of its label represent the Irish tricolor, in tribute to their Irish heritage. Snake's Den won its name because of the black snakes that populated the winery when it was first founded (the snakes have since moved on to better quarters).

The two Michaels also operate the Virginia Wine Factory, a wine tasting bar in Brambleton Town Center (22855 Brambleton Plaza, Suite 104, M–W 11:00–9:00, Th–Su 11:00–11:00), where Virginia wines may be sampled alongside wines from around the world.

White Wines: Chardonnay, Chardontage *(Chardonnays)*, Viognier.

Red Wines: Franc the Tank *(Cabernet Franc)*, Isabella's Revenge *(Merlot)*, Sangiovese, Snake's Den *(Cabernet Sauvignon)*, 954 Assemblage *(Bordeaux-style blend)*.

Price Range: $20

Tastings: $3 per person.

Directions: From I-81, take Exit 310 (Romney/Berkeley Springs) and turn onto Route 37 North. Drive 2.8 miles and take the Winchester/Opequon exit (Route 622). Turn west onto Cedar Creek Grade and drive 3.1 miles. Turn right onto Perry Road and continue 2.4 miles to winery entrance on right.

Wisteria Farm & Vineyard
1126 Marksville Road
Stanley VA 22851

Hours: Th–M 12:00–6:00 (Mar–Dec)   540-742-1489
Closed Thanksgiving, Christmas, Jan–Feb   www.wisteriavineyard.com
Stay Tuned: Facebook   E-mail: info@wisteriavineyard.com

Wisteria Vineyard is a small family-owned winery and working farm owned and operated by Sue and Moussa Ishak. The tasting room is attached to the farm's Victoria-era farmhouse and offers an outdoor deck for visitors to relax over a glass of wine. Guests may either bring their own food for a picnic or purchase cheese and snacks at the tasting room which features a mural depicting Moussa's native village in Lebanon. The winery hosts a number of special events, such as SPCA fundraisers, live bluegrass music with local performers, an annual Blessing of the Vines, and Wine & Ewe Shearing Days. Yarn and wool blankets made from wool from the farm's flock of Romney sheep are also offered for sale. Wisteria Farm is a certified Virginia Green winery. Children and dogs are welcome.

White Wines: Chardonnay, Pinot Gris, Seyval Blanc, Traminette, Viognier.

Red Wines: Adonis *(Merlot, Carmine, Traminette)*, Merlot, Norton, Velvet.

Sweet/Dessert Wines: Sweet Daisy *(Vidal Blanc)*.

Price Range: $16–$18

Tastings: $5 per person with souvenir glass.

Wheelchair accessible.

Directions: From Luray, take U.S. Route 340 South for 6 miles and bear left onto Hawksbill Road. After 1/2 mile, turn left onto Marksville Road. The winery will be on the right after about 1/4 mile.

Wolf Gap Vineyard & Winery
123 Stout Road
Edinburg VA 22824

Hours: F–Sa, M 11:00–6:00, Su 1:00–6:00
Closed Thanksgiving, Dec–Feb

540-984-3306
www.wolfgapvineyard.com
E-mail: admin@wolfgapvineyard.com

Wolf Gap Winery was founded by Will and Diane Elledge, who opened their fifty-acre property to the public in 2007. The winery is named after Wolf Gap, which is visible to the west along the Virginia-West Virginia state line. The two-story winery offers a tasting deck and events patio for warm weather seating and scenic views of the Allegheny Mountains. Private winery and vineyard tours are available with advance reservations. The facilities are available for private parties and weddings. Wolf Gap offers discounts on wine purchases for active-duty military personnel.

Fruit Wines: Blueberry Wine.

White Wines: Chardonnay, Viognier-Traminette.

Rosé Wines: Lobo Loco.

Red Wines: Cabernet Franc, Cabernet Sauvignon, Chambourcin, Chamerlot *(Chambourcin, Merlot)*, Mariage *(Cabernet Franc, Chambourcin)*, Merlot, Syrah.

Price Range: $15–$28

Tastings: $5 per person.

Groups: Please call in advance for groups of 8 or more.

Purchasing: Online purchasing available for residents of AK, FL, IA, MN, NM, NC, TX, VA, and DC.

Wolf Gap Pack Wine Club members receive discounts and special members-only events.

Directions: From I-81, take Exit 279 east onto Stoney Creek Road (Route 185). Drive about 1 mile and turn right onto South Main Street (U.S. Route 11 South). Drive 1.7 miles and turn right onto South Middle Road. Continue 2.8 miles and turn right onto Headquarters Road. After 2.4 miles, turn right onto Stout Road; the winery will be on the left.

ᘒᕤ

NORTON

One of Virginia's most noteworthy contributions to American wine was the Norton grape. Propagated by amateur horticulturist Dr. Daniel N. Norton on his farm near Richmond, the grape was first listed as Norton's Virginia Seedling in 1822 in the annual catalog of the Linnean Botanic Garden and Nurseries of Long Island, New York, perhaps the country's foremost horticultural institution at that time. The Princes' 1830 Treatise on the Vine described the grape as *Vitis nortoni* and credited the doctor with its cultivation.

It was through the efforts of German viticulturalists—George Husmann, in particular—that the Norton grape rose to prominence as a wine grape in the United States. In 1846, German settlers in the central Missouri town of Hermann planted Norton cuttings, producing the first bottle of Norton wine two years later. As the Missouri wine industry grew, becoming at one point the largest producer in the United States, so also grew the cultivation and renown of the Norton grape.

Interest in the Norton peaked in 1870, when Hermann vintner Michael Röschel and business partner John Scherer entered their Norton wine in the 1873 Universal Exhibition in Vienna, Austria. The influential English wine critic Henry Vizatelly awarded a medal of merit to the Norton, one of only three American wines to be so decorated. It was also during this time that German vineyardists in Virginia established the Monticello Wine Company whose production was based heavily on Norton grapes.

The two Virginia winemakers who have been most influential in bringing Norton back to its native state are Dennis Horton of Horton Vineyards and Jennifer McCloud of Chrysalis. A Missouri native, Horton grew up in Hermann and was introduced to Norton in his college days. He first planted Norton cuttings in his Orange County vineyard in 1988. McCloud became fascinated by the Norton grape and its history after hearing Horton speak at a conference. After establishing Chrysalis, she began planting Norton in her vineyards and now has the single largest planting of this native Virginia grape in the country.

ᘒᕤ

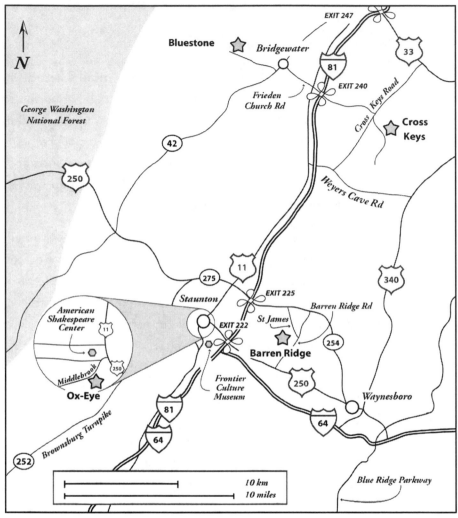

Map 5.3. Central Shenandoah Valley (northern section)

CENTRAL SHENANDOAH VALLEY

Barren Ridge Vineyards
984 Barren Ridge Road
Fishersville VA 22939

Hours: M–W 11:00–6:00, Th–Sa 11:00–9:00, Su 1:00–6:00   540-248-3300
Closed New Year's, Thanksgiving, Christmas   www.barrenridgevineyards.com
Stay Tuned: Facebook, Twitter   E-mail: info@barrenridgevineyards.com

Barren Ridge is owned by John and Shelby Higgs, who established their winery on an apple orchard and farm owned by John's family since 1934. The couple converted the property's old apple barn into the winery and tasting room, refurbishing the structure on the inside to create a welcoming space complete with fireplace and comfortable seating. Guests may purchase cheese and sausage plates to enjoy on the patio, which offers an expansive view of the vines and neighboring hills. Barren Ridge currently produces about four thousand cases annually, with the wines sourced from their own fruit and from other Shenandoah vineyards. The winery sponsors live music events on selected weekends, as well as a 5K run in the autumn. The facilities may be rented for private parties or weddings. Children and dogs are welcome.

Two of Barren Ridge's wines have labels featuring the work of local artist P. Buckley Moss; a portion of the proceeds of their sales go to benefit her Children's Education Foundation.

White Wines: Chardonnay, Harmony *(Chardonnay, Traminette, Vidal Blanc, Viognier)*, Tinkling Spring *(Viognier, Vidal Blanc, Traminette)*, Traminette, Vidal Blanc, Viognier.

Rosé Wines: Rosé *(Cabernet Franc, Merlot, Touriga Nacional, Petit Verdot)*.

Red Wines: Cabernet Franc, Meritage, Merlot, Petit Verdot, Red Barren, Touriga Nacional.

Sweet/Dessert Wines: Christof *(Viognier, Vidal Blanc)*.

Price Range: $14–$32

Tastings: $5 per person for basic tasting, $8 for reserve tasting.

Purchasing: Online purchases are available for residents of all states *except* AL, AR, DE, KY, MD, MA, MS, MT, NJ, OK, PA, SD, and UT.

Directions: From I-81, take Exit 225 onto Woodrow Wilson Parkway (Route 275) east toward Fishersville. After 1 mile, the road becomes Hermitage Road (Route 254). Continue 1.2 miles and turn right onto St. James Road. Drive 2.3 miles and turn right onto Barren Ridge Road (portions unpaved) and then to the winery entrance on the right.

Bluestone Vineyard
4828 Spring Creek Road
Bridgewater VA 22812

Hours: M–Sa 11:00–6:00, Su 1:00–6:00   540-828-0099
Closed New Year's, Thanksgiving, Christmas   www.bluestonevineyard.com
Stay Tuned: Facebook, Newsletter   E-mail: curt@bluestonevineyard.com

 Bluestone Vineyard was opened to the public in 2011 by Curt and Jackie Hartman. After Curt retired several years earlier, he began developing Bluestone's vineyard in 2002, inspired in part by his friendship with the owners of MistyRay Winery (open by appointment only). Bluestone produces all Virginia-grown wines from their twelve acres of vines. The tasting room is located in the two-story winery production building and overlooks the barrel room. Bluestone sponsors occasional live music and charity benefits.

White Wines: Beau, Chardonnay, Sauvignon Blanc, Traminette, Vidal Blanc.

Rosé Wines: Rosé.

Red Wines: Cabernet Franc, Cabernet Sauvignon, Crooked and Weedy, Merlot, Pino Noir, Quartz Hill Red.

Sweet/Dessert Wines: Blue Ice *(Traminette)*, Moscato.

Price Range: $14–$26

Tastings: $5 per person.

Wheelchair accessible.

Purchasing: Online purchases are available for residents of AK, CA, CO, FL, MO, NV, NC, PA, VA, and DC.

Directions: From I-81, take Exit 240 and turn west onto Friedens Church Road (Route 257). Drive 3.3 miles into the town of Bridgewater and turn left onto North Main Street (Route 42). After 1/2 mile, turn right onto Spring Creek Road. Continue 1.7 miles to the winery on the right.

Cross Keys Vineyards
6011 East Timber Ridge Road
Mt. Crawford VA 22841

Hours: Daily 11:00–7:00 (Apr–Oct), 11:00–5:00 (Nov–Mar)   540-234-0505
Closed New Year's, Thanksgiving, Christmas   www.crosskeysvineyards.com
Stay Tuned: Facebook, Twitter, newsletter   E-mail: info@crosskeysvineyards.com

Cross Keys was founded by Bob and Nikoo Bakhtiar, who came to the US from their native Iran as university students. They planted their first vines in 2002 and opened the winery to the public six years later. The winery's twenty-five-acre vineyard is under the supervision of winemaker Stephan Heyns from South Africa. Cross Keys offers "Grape to Glass" tours each day at 12:00, 2:00, and 4:00. The tasting room is in one wing of the winery, which features a large paved courtyard and several event rooms that can be rented for private parties or weddings. Cross Keys also hosts a variety of special events, including live music, special festivals, a holiday illumination in December, and a New Year's Eve party.

White Wines: Chardonnay, Joy White *(Vidal Blanc)*.

Red Wines: Cabernet Franc, Fiore, Joy Red *(Chambourcin)*, Meritage, Merlot, Petit Verdot, Pinot Noir.

Sweet/Dessert Wines: Ali d'Oro *(Chardonel)*.

Fortified Wines: Tavern *(Touriga Nacional)*.

Price Range: $16–$50

Tastings: $5 per person for regular or white flight, $7 for red flight, $8 for full flight.

Groups: Please call ahead for groups of 10 or more.

Wheelchair accessible.

Key Club members receive regular wine shipments, discounts, and special events.

Directions: From I-81, take Exit 240 and turn east onto Friedens Church Road (Route 682). Drive 4 miles and turn right onto Cross Keys Road (Route 276). Continue 1/2 mile to East Timber Ridge Road and turn left. The winery will be 1.2 miles on the left.

❖ ❖ ❖

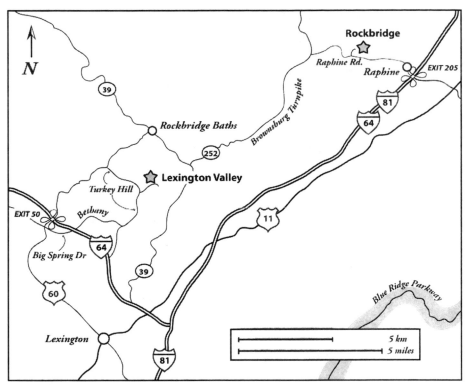

Map 5.4. Central Shenandoah Valley (southern section)

Lexington Valley Vineyard
80 Norton Way
Rockbridge Baths VA 24473

Hours: F–Su, 12:00–6:00 (May–Oct)　　　　　　　540-462-2974
Closed Nov–Apr　　　　　　　　　　　www.lexingtonvalleyvineyard.com
Stay Tuned: Facebook　　　　　　　E-mail: info@lexingtonvalleyvineyard.com

Lexington Valley Vineyard is located on sixty-seven acres just northwest of the historic town of Lexington, home of the Virginia Military Institute and Washington and Lee University, where Confederate General Robert E. Lee is buried. Owners Calvin and Janet Hale launched their vineyard with a planting of Norton in 2000 and have added to the vineyard over the years with Vignoles, Maréchal Foch, Traminette, Riesling, and Catawba.

159

In summer, the winery sponsors a "Wine and Wags" on the second Friday of every month, when guests are invited to bring a picnic and their favorite four-legged friends. Snacks are also available for purchase in the tasting room. The winery offers free Wi-Fi on the premises. Children and pets are welcome.

White Wines: Traminette, Vidal Blanc, Vignoles.

Rosé Wines: Chill *(Norton)*.

Red Wines: Cabernet Sauvignon, Maréchal Foch, Merlot, Norton.

Sweet/Dessert Wines: Kerr's Creek Catawba.

Price Range: $15–$18

Tastings: $5 per person.

Purchasing: Online purchasing is available via VinoShipper to residents of AK, FL, ID, LA, MN, MO, NE, NV, NH, NM, ND, OH, OR, DC, WV, and WY.

Directions: From I-64, take Exit 50 (Kerr's Creek) onto U.S. Route 60 East toward Lexington. Take the first left onto Big Spring Drive (Route 631) and then left again onto Bethany Road (Route 625). After about one mile, turn left onto Turkey Hill Road (Route 602) and continue 1.3 miles to the winery entrance. (GPS users: The owners recommend not entering the address until 6 to 8 miles away from the winery.)

Ox-Eye Vineyards
44 Middlebrook Avenue
Staunton VA   24401

Hours: Th 11:00–6:00, F 11:00–7:00,   540-849-7926
Sa 10:00–7:00, Su 12:00–5:00   www.oxeyevineyards.com
Closed New Year's, Thanksgiving, Christmas   E-mail: John@OxEyeVineyards.com
Stay Tuned: Facebook

Ox-Eye Vineyards was founded by John and Susan Kiers, who opened their winery to the public in 2011 after selling grapes for over a dozen years to other winemakers in the area. All of Ox-Eye's wines are estate-grown at its vineyard in nearby Swoope. The tasting room is located in Staunton in a restored railroad weigh station that is on the southern edge of Staunton's restaurant and tourism district. The name of the winery was inspired by the ox-eye daisies that proliferate in the valley where the vineyards are located.

White Wines: Chardonnay, Gewurztraminer, Gewurztraminer-Traminette, Riesling, White Ox *(Chardonnay, Riesling)*.

Red Wines: Cabernet Franc, Lemberger, Pinot Noir.

Price Range: $17–$25

Tastings: $5 per person.

Directions: From I-81, take Exit 222 onto U.S. Route 250 West. Drive about two miles into Staunton. Bear right onto Greenville Avenue, where U.S. Route 250 and U.S. Route 11 merge. Take the first left onto Commerce Road to continue following U.S. Route 250. Take the third left onto Middlebrook Avenue. The winery will be on the left in 0.1 mile; parking is available on the street or in the town parking lot across the street from the tasting room.

❖ ❖ ❖

Rockbridge Vineyard
35 Hill View Lane
Raphine VA 24472

Hours: Tu–Sa 10:00–6:00, Su–M 12:00–5:00   1-888-511-9463 (WINE)

Closed New Year's Eve & Day, Thanksgiving,   www.rockbridgevineyard.com

Christmas Eve & Day   E-mail: winery@rockbridgevineyard.com

Stay Tuned: Facebook, newsletter

Rockbridge Vineyard was established in 1992 by Shepherd Rouse and Jane Millott-Rouse. Shep, who serves as the winemaker, worked at several California wineries, including Chateau St. Jean, Schramsburg, and Carneros Creek, before returning to his native Virginia and founding his winery. Rockbridge's name comes from the county in which it is located as well as from the county's most famous natural feature, the Natural Bridge, whose depiction adorns many of the winery's labels. The DeChiel label of some of Rockbridge's wines is in honor of Shep's French Huguenot lineage. The winery and tasting room are in a large, red barn, with a small deck just outside the tasting room entrance. Light fair is available for purchase. The facility is available for rental for private parties and weddings. Rockbridge frequently sponsors live music, winemaker dinners, and harvest festivals. Children and dogs are welcome.

Fruit Wines: Vin de Pomme *(apple)*.

White Wines: Chardonnay, DeChiel Chardonnay, St. Mary's Blanc *(Vidal Blanc)*, Traminette, Tuscarora White *(Vidal Blanc)*, Vignoles, White Riesling.

Rosé Wines: Jeremiah's *(Concord)*.

Red Wines: Cabernet Franc, DeChiel Merlot, DeChiel Pinot Noir, Extra Virginia Claret Norton, Lexington & Concord *(Concord)*, Meritage, Norton, Rockbridge Pinot Noir, Syrah, Tuscarora Red.

Sweet/Dessert Wines: V d'Or *(Vidal, Riesling, Vignoles, Traminette).*

Price Range: $10–$30

Purchasing: Online purchasing is available for residents of AK, CA, CO, FL, GA, HI, IA, ID, IL, IN, KS, LA, MO, NC, NM, OR, TX, VA, WA, WI, WV, and WY.

Wine Club members receive wine shipments, discounts, and members-only events.

Directions: From I-81, take Exit 205 (Raphine) onto Route 606 West. The winery will be one mile on the right, past the village of Raphine.

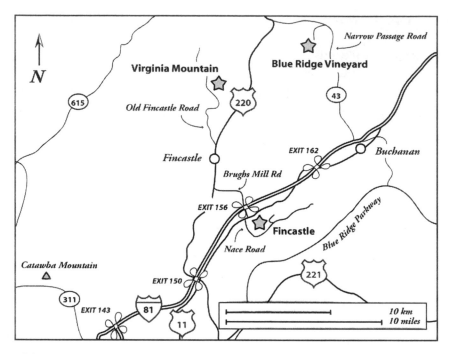

Map 5.5. Roanoke (northern section)

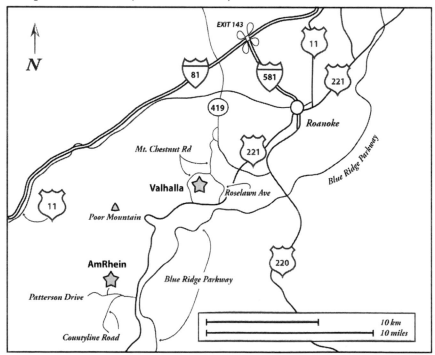

Map 5.6. Roanoke (southern section)

ROANOKE

AmRhein Wine Cellars
9243 Patterson Drive
Bent Mountain VA 24059

Hours: Th–M, 11:00–5:00 (Apr–Dec); F–Su 11:00–5:00 (Jan–Mar)   540-929-4632
Closed New Year's, Thanksgiving, Christmas   www.amrheins.com/winecellars/
Stay Tuned: Facebook, newsletter   E-mail: info@amrheins.com

Russ and Paula Amrhein have owned and operated AmRhein Wine Cellars since 1995, when they purchased forty acres on Bent Mountain. AmRhein's tasting room offers views of the surrounding hills and vineyards from the tables indoors and on the deck. Light fare is available for purchase, including wraps, cheese, and crackers; for special events, visitors may bring their own picnics. The winery hosts a range of special events, including live music on summer weekends, an annual Oktoberfest, grape stomps, and harvest soup weekends. Weather permitting, winemaker Steve Bolleter produces a true frozen-on-the-vine ice wine from the Vidal Blanc grapes in AmRhein's vineyards, which reach up to 2,500 feet in elevation. The winery is available for weddings and private events. Children are welcome.

Fruit Wines: Vin de Pêche *(peach)*.

White Wines: Petit Manseng, Pinot Grigio, Saffire *(Vidal Blanc, Viognier)*, Sauvignon Blanc, Vidal Blanc, Viognier, Traminette.

Red Wines: Aglianico, Cabernet Sauvignon, Chambourcin, Melange, Merlot, Petit Verdot, Ruby, Veranda.

Sweet/Dessert Wines: Late Harvest Vidal Blanc, Innocence *(Vidal Blanc, Viognier)*, Purity *(Sauvignon Blanc)*, Passion *(Cabernet Sauvignon, Zinfandel)*, Seduction *(Cabernet Franc, Chardonnay)*.

Price Range: $10–$45

Groups: Reservations required for groups of 8 or more.

Twisted Vines Wine Club members receive six bottles per year, discounts on wine purchases, and special members-only events.

Directions: From Roanoke, take U.S. Route 221 South and drive 13.7 miles. Turn right onto Countyline Road and continue 1.2 miles. Bear right at the fork onto Patterson Drive. The winery will be 1/2 mile on the right.

Blue Ridge Vineyard
1027 Shiloh Drive
Eagle Rock VA 24085

Hours: Daily 12:00–5:00 (Mar–Dec) 540-798-7642
Closed Thanksgiving, Christmas, Jan–Feb www.blueridgevineyard.com
Stay Tuned: Facebook, Twitter, newsletter E-mail: blueridgevines@gmail.com

Jim Holaday and Barbara Kolb first launched Blue Ridge Vineyard in 1985 and opened their winery to the public twenty-one years later. Their tasting room is housed in an old barn; in the summer and during special events, tasting tables are also set up outside. Visitors can enjoy the outstanding views of the Blue Ridge from the picnic tables or outdoor gazebo. The winery sponsors a number of live music events on weekends, ranging from bluegrass to rock to jazz, as well as special donations for the All-American Mutt Rescue. Soup 'n Sip Sundays offer live music, fresh breads, soups, and chili at no charge. Children and dogs are welcome.

White Wines: Big Bear White, Equinox, Gewurztraminer, Riesling, Sweet Shiloh, Traminette.

Red Wines: Big Bear Red, Cabernet Franc, Pinot Noir, Solstice *(Cabernet Franc)*, Sweet Shiloh.

Price Range: $14–$25

Wheelchair accessible.

Directions: From I-81, take Exit 162 toward Buchanan and turn onto U.S. Route 11 North. After 4.8 miles, turn left onto 1st Street (Route 43), which will become Narrow Passage Road, and drive for 11.4 miles. Turn left onto Shiloh Drive (portions unpaved). Winery will be on the left in 0.8 miles.

Fincastle Vineyard & Winery
203 Maple Ridge Lane
Fincastle VA 24090

Hours: Th–M 11:00–5:00

Closed Thanksgiving, Christmas

Stay Tuned: Facebook

540-591-9000

www.fincastlewine.com

E-mail: info@fincastlewine.com

Fincastle Vineyard & Winery was first opened to the public in 2003 by David and Georgia Sawyer and their son Richard Classey. Fincastle is located on an eighty-acre farm that had formerly been an apple orchard and a tomato farm at various points before the family purchased the property in 1987. The tasting room is in a small stone building attached to the main farmhouse with a stone patio for guests. The winery building is built into a hillside to allow gravity-fed processing of Fincastle's mostly estate-grown wines. Fincastle sponsors several music festivals in the summer featuring local groups and musicians; guests are welcome to bring their own picnic food to enjoy on the grounds. Dogs are welcome.

The family's renovated 1926 farmhouse is also a bed & breakfast that is perfect for nature lovers who want to explore the hiking, canoeing, and other outdoor activities in the vicinity.

White Wines: Chardonnay, Hybrid Vigor *(Traminette, Vidal Blanc, Chardonel)*, Viognier.

Rosé Wines: Rosé *(Chambourcin, Vidal Blanc)*.

Red Wines: Cabernet Franc, Cabernet Sauvignon, Knight's Tour *(Cabernet Sauvignon)*.

Sweet/Dessert Wines: Traminette.

Price Range: $12–$15

Groups: Reservations required for groups of 6 or more.

Purchasing: Online purchasing for Virginia residents only, minimum one case.

Directions: From I-81, take Exit 156 (Troutville) east onto Brughs Mill Road (Route 640). Turn right in 1/2 mile onto Lee Highway (U.S. Route 11 South). After about 1/2 mile, turn left onto Nace Road (Route 640) and continue for 1.7 miles. Make a left onto Maple Ridge Lane (portions unpaved); the winery entrance will be on the left.

Valhalla Vineyards
6500 Mt. Chestnut Road
Roanoke VA 24018

Hours: Fr 4:00–7:00 (Apr–Oct)
Sa 12:00–5:00, Su 1:00–5:00
Closed Christmas, New Year's

540-725-9463
www.valhallawines.com
E-mail: info@valhallawines.com

James and Debra Vascik established their winery and vineyard in 1994 on a two-thousand-foot mountain property overlooking the city of Roanoke. The two opera lovers named their winery after the home of the Norse gods made famous by German composer Richard Wagner. Their winemaking facility and barrel cave were built in 1996, with the barrel cave carved sixty feet underground into the mountainside. The spacious "Cellar Door" tasting room was opened to the public in 2004 and features an arched paneled ceiling and a large stone tasting bar along one wall. Light snacks are available for purchase in the tasting room. In cooler weather, visitors can warm up next to the floor-to-ceiling stone fireplace inside the tasting room or can sit near the large outdoor fireplace on the patio. Valhalla offers winemaker dinners, wine education events, and live music in summers. The facility is available for weddings, private events, and corporate events.

White Wines: Chardonnay, Rheingold Chardonnay, Row Ten *(Chardonnay, Viognier)*, Viognier.

Rosé Wines: Dry Rosé.

Red Wines: Alicante Bouschet, Cabernet Sauvignon, Cabernet/Shiraz *(Cabernet Sauvignon, Syrah)*, Cornucopia, Götterdämmerung *(Cabernet Franc, Merlot)*, Norton, Sangiovese, Syrah, Valkyrie *(Bordeaux-style blend)*.

Sweet/Dessert Wines: Late Harvest Alicante Bouschet.

Price Range: $13–$28

Purchasing: Online purchasing available for Virginia residents only.

Wine Club members receive regular shipments, discounts, members-only events.

Directions: From Roanoke, drive south on I-581 until it ends. Exit onto Franklin Road and continue through seven stoplights. Then turn left onto Brambleton Road (U.S. Route 221 South). At the third traffic light, turn right onto Roselawn Road. Continue 2.3 miles and turn left onto Mt. Chesnut Road. The winery will be one mile on the left.

Virginia Mountain Vineyards
4204 Old Fincastle Road
Fincastle VA 24090

Hours: W–Su 12:00–6:00 (mid-Mar–mid-Dec)
Closed Thanksgiving, mid-Dec–mid-Mar
Stay Tuned: Facebook, Twitter

540-473-2979
www.vmvines.com
E-mail: info@vmvines.com

David and Marie Gibbs opened Virginia Mountain to the public in 2006 after several years of selling the grapes from their ten-acre vineyard to nearby wineries. The winery hosts monthly summer music evenings with local performers, "Wine, Moon, and Stars" evenings with the Roanoke Astronomy Club, and a Holiday Open House in December. The facility may be rented for private parties or weddings. Children and pets are welcome.

White Wines: Acacia Gold, Chardonnay, Traminette.

Rosé Wines: Rosé.

Red Wines: Cabernet Franc, Merlot, Petit Verdot, Trinity *(Bordeaux-style blend)*.

Sweet/Dessert Wines: Virginia White, Virginia Red, Holiday Spice.

Price Range: $12–$20

Tastings: $3–$5 per person (amount varies depending on wines available for tasting).

Groups: Reservations required for groups of 8 or more.

Wheelchair accessible.

Purchasing: Online shipping is available for MN or VA residents, or via VinoShipper for residents of AK, CA, FL, ID, LA, MO, NE, NV, NH, NM, ND, OH, OR, DC, WV, and WY.

Directions: From I-81, take Exit 150 onto U.S. Route 220 West. Drive 10.7 miles and turn left onto Old Fincastle Road (Route 655) just past the town of Fincastle. The winery will be on the right in 4.3 miles.

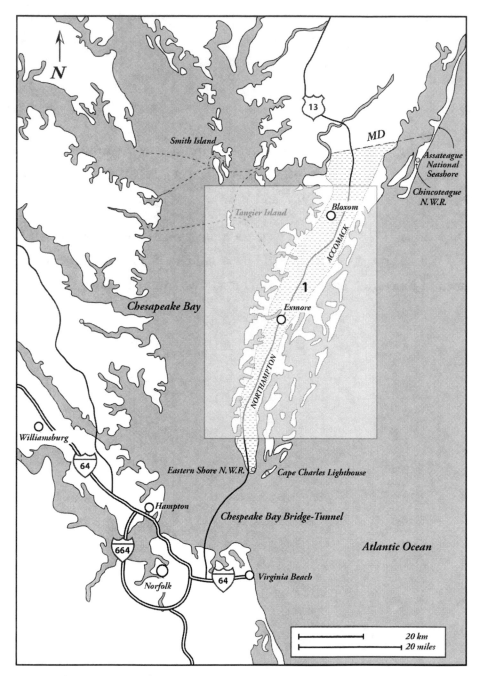

Map 6.1. Eastern Shore Region & AVA: (1) Eastern Shore

6. EASTERN SHORE REGION & AVA

The Eastern Shore of Virginia is a narrow finger of land accessible from Virginia only by way of the 17.6-mile Chesapeake Bay Bridge-Tunnel (CBBT) or by passenger ferry across the Chesapeake Bay. (For drivers with a fear of bridges, a CBBT employee can drive your car across the bridge with advance reservations.) With the Atlantic Ocean on one side and the Chesapeake Bay on the other, the region is marked by sandy, well-drained soils and a temperate climate. At its broadest point, the peninsula is only twenty-two miles wide and stretches seventy miles from the Maryland border down to its southern tip.

All three of the Eastern Shore's wineries produce AVA-designated wines, allowing wine aficionados to conduct their own horizontal tastings at home to compare the range of character and personality in wines from across Virginia.

Things to see and do: The Eastern Shore is blessed with exceptional natural beauty and offers many options for bird-watching, kayaking, boating, and fishing. Two of its national wildlife refuges (NWR)—the Eastern Shore of Virginia NWR and the Chincoteague NWR—along with the Assateague Island National Seashore and Virginia Coast Reserve translate to perhaps the longest stretch of protected coastline on the Atlantic.

The Eastern Shore NWR at the southern tip of the peninsula is well known as a waystation for migratory birds, particularly in the autumn, as well as for raptors and butterflies. Bird lovers and photographers can use the observation decks and photography blinds in the refuge to observe and photograph birds in their habitat. The refuge's visitor center at Cape Charles has various displays and exhibits to introduce visitors to the region's wildlife. A "Please Touch" table is particularly popular with children, and the summertime Butterfly Garden is a photographer's delight.

The region also offers numerous biking trails, such as a self-guided walking and biking tour on Chincoteague, several trails at Kiptopeke State Park, and the newly opened Southern Tip Bike and Hike Trail. Special bike tours include the annual Between the Waters Bike Tour, a fundraiser hosted by Citizens for a Better Eastern Shore.

In addition, Assateague is famous for its wild ponies which can be seen wandering and grazing on the island. In the Chincoteague Pony Swim in late July, about 150 ponies swim across Assateague Channel in an annual event memorialized by Marguerite Henry in her 1947 children's book, *Misty of Chincoteague*. After some of the foals are sold, the ponies then swim back to Assateague, where visitors can see them in the wild on pony-watching cruises or kayak tours.

<u>Wine Trails</u>: The Eastern Shore Wine Trail includes all three of the region's wineries. See Appendix 1 for more details.

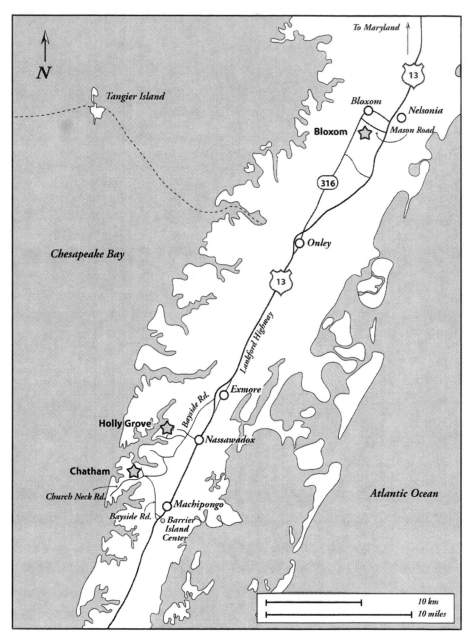

Map 6.2. Eastern Shore

EASTERN SHORE

Bloxom Vineyard
26130 Mason Road
Bloxom VA 23308

Hours: Sa only 12:00–7:00 (May);
F–Su 12:00–5:00 (Sa until 7:00) (Jun–Dec)
Closed Jan–Apr, Christmas
Stay Tuned: Facebook

757-665-5670
www.bloxomwinery.com
E-mail: bloxomwine@verizon.net

Robert and Francesca Giardina founded Bloxom Vineyard in 2000 after moving to the Eastern Shore from New York City, where Robert had been in the construction business and Francesca worked as a pastry chef. The two Morocco natives opened their winery to the public in 2004 and now make over nine hundred cases of estate-grown wine each year from their six-acre vineyard. In the summer, the winery offers fresh pizza baked in the wood-fired oven on the winery's trellised patio. The winery also sponsors Bloxomfest each year, featuring live music, a grape stomp, and local artist displays. The Mediterranean-style tasting room, designed and built by Robert, also has light fare for purchase. Children are welcome.

White Wines: Chardonnay.

Blush Wines: Some Like It Blush.

Red Wines: Cabernet Franc, Merlot, Red Kiss *(Cabernet Sauvignon, Merlot)*.

Price Range: $13–$15

Tastings: $.50 per taste.

Wheelchair accessible.

Directions: From U.S. Route 13 on the Eastern Shore, turn west onto Mason Road (Route 681). Drive 2 miles and turn left into the winery's gravel driveway.

Chatham Vineyards & Winery
9232 Chatham Road
Machipongo VA 23405

Hours: Th–Sa, M 10:00–5:00, Su 12:00–5:00   757-678-5588
Closed major holidays   http://chathamvineyards.net
Stay Tuned: Facebook, Twitter, newsletter   E-mail: info@chathamvineyards.net

Chatham Vineyards is owned and operated by Jon Wehner on the historic Chatham Farm. The farm's manor house, built in 1818, was named for William Pitt, Earl of Chatham. Jon is a second-generation vineyard owner, having worked in his parents' Great Falls Vineyard while growing up in northern Virginia's Fairfax County. Wine tastings are held in the wine-making facilities while the family restores an old farmhouse for use as an expanded tasting room. The wines are all bottled under the Church Creek label, named for the stream that flows next to the farm. Chatham Vineyards hosts several special winery events, including kayak tours and "Girls Days Out." The winery may be rented for private parties and weddings. Children and pets are welcome.

White Wines: Chardonnay.

Rosé Wines: Rosé *(Merlot)*.

Red Wines: Cabernet Franc, Merlot, Vintner's Blend *(Bordeaux-style blend)*.

Sweet/Dessert Wines: Late Harvest Dessert Wine *(Cabernet Franc, Merlot)*.

Price Range: $14–$24

Wheelchair accessible.

Purchasing: Online sales are available for residents of MD, NY, VA, and DC.

Directions: From U.S. Route 13 on the Eastern Shore, turn west at the Barrier Islands Center just south of the town of Machipongo onto Young Street (Route 627). Turn right onto Bayside Road (Route 618) and drive 3 miles. Turn left onto Church Neck Road and make an immediate right onto Chatham Road. The winery will be on the left.

Holly Grove Vineyards
6404 Holly Bluff Drive
Franktown VA 23354

Hours: Daily 12:00–5:00 (summer only);
Sa–Su 12:00–5:00 (fall–spring)
Closed Thanksgiving, Christmas–early Jan
Stay Tuned: Facebook, Twitter

757-442-2844
www.hollygrovevineyards.com
E-mail: holly.grove@verizon.net

Holly Grove was established in 2003 by Jonathan Bess after he retired from his career as a naval officer. Jonathan bottled his first wines four years later, producing them either from estate-grown vines or from vineyards that he leases. Holly Grove is on the shore of an arm of the Chespeake Bay, and visitors can enjoy the view from the grounds or can take a closer look by renting a kayak from the winery. Holly Grove's Genesis wine is named in honor of the Mid-Atlantic Regional Spaceport (MARS); Jonathan donates 10 percent of the proceeds from its sales to a scholarship fund at the Virginia Space Flight Academy.

White Wines: Celebration *(Petit Manseng)*, Chardonnay, Coastal Trio, High Tide Traminette.

Rosé Wines: Sunset Rosé *(Merlot)*.

Red Wines: Genesis *(Bordeaux-style blend)*, Merlot, Petit Verdot.

Price Range: $18–$22

Tastings: $1 per taste.

Wheelchair accessible.

Purchasing: Online purchasing for VA residents only.

Directions: From U.S. Route 13, turn west at the town of Nassawadox onto Rogers Drive. Turn left onto Bayside Drive and take the first right onto Wellington Neck Road. Follow Wellington Neck Road for 1.4 miles and turn right onto Holly Bluff Road. The winery will be on the left.

SPARKLING WINES

Few things add a more festive and elegant touch to any celebration than sparkling wine. Sparkling wine as we know it originated and was perfected in France's Champagne region by, as tradition has it, the Benedictine monk Dom Perignon.

Only sparkling wines made in Champagne may be called by that name; all others are more correctly termed "sparkling" wines although they may indicate on their labels if they were made using the *méthode champenoise*, or champagne method. (The official term in Europe is now traditional or classic method, the European Union bureaucracy having banned the phrase "champagne method.")

In this champagne method, sparkling wine gets its bubbles through a second fermentation in the bottle. After the grapes have been pressed and the base wine fermented and blended, a sugar-yeast mixture is added to the wine, which is then put into the familiar thick, dark bottles we see on wine store sheles. After this second fermentation has been completed, the yeast sediments are frozen and removed through a process called disgorgement, and the bottles are then corked and sealed.

While sparkling wine may be made from a range of different grapes, the classic varieties used in the Champagne region are Chardonnay, Pinot Noir, and Meunier (also called Pinot Meunier). Classic champagne is often a blend of wines from two or more of these grapes. However, if the label includes the phrase "blanc de blancs" (French for "white from white"), the wine was made solely from Chardonnay grapes. If the label indicates "blanc de noirs" ("white from black") then only Pinot Noir was used.

181

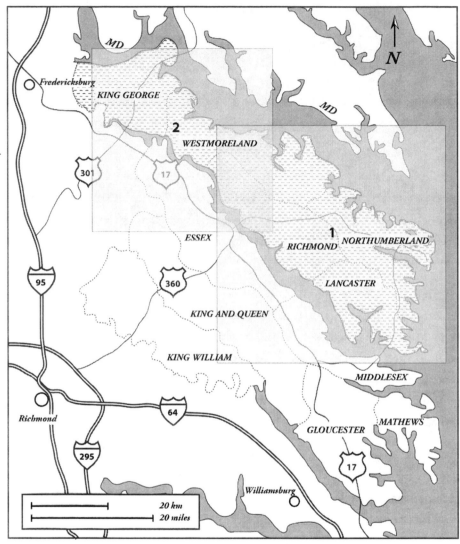

Map 7.1. Chesapeake Bay Region & Northern Neck-George Washington Birthplace AVA: (1) Northern Neck (southern section); (2) Northern Neck (northern section)

7. CHESAPEAKE BAY REGION & NORTHERN NECK-GEORGE WASHINGTON BIRTHPLACE AVA

Virginia's three long peninsulas jutting into the Chesapeake Bay were the first to be colonized by the English in the seventeenth century. The northernmost of these, the Northern Neck, is bounded on the north by the Potomac River and on the south by the Rappahannock. The Middle Peninsula is next, bounded by the Rappahannock to the north and the York River to the south.

The name of the AVA is generally given simply as Northern Neck, the original longer title having been a compromise between the two names originally proposed. The AVA is characterized by relatively flat terrain and light, sandy, well-drained soils. It has a comparatively mild climate, especially during winter: the moderating influence of the Chesapeake Bay keeps frost days at a minimum, and river breezes help temper summertime heat and humidity.

The region's wineries produce the full range of wine types, from sparkling to dessert and even fortified. For their largely estate-grown production, Northern Neck wineries use varietals that are also grown elsewhere in Virginia, but the nature and essence of their wines will be distinctly different precisely because of the AVA's unique climate and soil combinations. Reds, in particular, can be lighter than those from central Virginia, for instance.

Things to See and Do: The Chesapeake Bay region was first explored by a European in 1608 when Captain John Smith led two expeditions from Jamestown northward to map the Chesapeake and its native American settlements. The region's agricultural and fishing resources attracted a growing number of planters and colonists from England who settled in the area.

A number of these families rose to prominence during the American War of Independence. Presidents George Washington, James Madison, and James Monroe were born on the Northern Neck, as were Francis Lightfoot Lee and Richard Henry Lee, signers of the Declaration of Independence. The Lee brothers' cousin, Henry Lee, was the grandfather of General Robert E. Lee, commander of the South's Army of Northern Virginia, who was born at Stratford Hall, the family plantation on the banks of the Potomac.

The Northern Neck boasts a rich variety of outdoor activities for nature lovers to enjoy, including boating, camping, and hiking trails. Northern Neck wetlands welcome over 200 species of migratory birds each year and are home to one of the largest populations of bald eagles on the eastern U.S. coast, making the region a bird-watcher's paradise.

Wine Trails: The Chesapeake Bay Wine Trail includes the wineries in the Northern Neck, as well as two in the Hampton Roads region (New Kent and Saudé Creek). Please see Appendix 1 for more details.

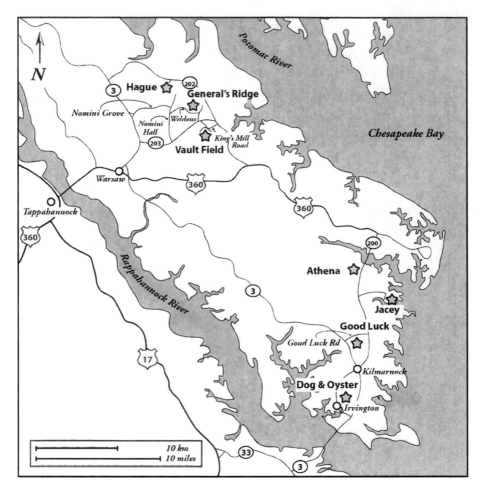

Map 7.2. Northern Neck (southern section)

NORTHERN NECK

Athena Vineyards & Winery

3138 Jesse Dupont Memorial Highway

Heathsville VA 22473

Hours: 12:00–6:00 W–Su (May–Dec) 804-580-4944

12:00–5:00 Sa only (Jan–May) www.athenavineyards.com

Closed Thanksgiving, Christmas, New Year's E-mail: winery@athenavineyards.com

Longtime friends Carol Spengler, Ada Jacox, and Ruth Harris founded Athena Vineyards in 2002 on a large riverfront site they had originally purchased as an investment property. From the beginning, the three nurses have run virtually all aspects of the winery, from planting vines to pruning and picking grapes to marketing their wines. Working with renowned Virginia winemaker, the late Jacques Recht, they planted over twenty varieties of grapes on fifteen acres overlooking the scenic Great Wicomico River. Named for the ancient Greek goddess of wisdom, Athena features a wraparound porch with ample seating, picnic tables on the lawn, and a small gift shop and free Wi-Fi inside the tasting room. A vineyard trail offers visitors the chance to explore the vines on a self-guided tour. The winery may be rented for private events. Children and pets are welcome.

White Wines: Athena's White *(Vidal Blanc, Seyval Blanc)*, Chardonnay, Nightingale Chardonnay, Pinot Grigio.

Rosé Wines: Athena's Rosé.

Red Wines: Athena's Holiday Gift *(Cabernet Sauvignon, Merlot)*, Cabernet Franc, Cabernet Sauvignon, Galleon Treasure Red *(Chambourcin, Cabernet Franc)*, Meritage, Nightingale Red *(Chambourcin)*.

Sweet/Dessert Wines: Athena's Sweet White, Sweet Notes Red.

Fortified Wines: Mellow Notes *(Vignoles)*, Safe Harbor *(Chambourcin)*.

Price Range: $12–$40

Tastings: $3 per person.

Groups: Reservations required for groups of 10 or more.

Purchasing: Online ordering available to AK, CA, CO, FL, MI, MN, MO, NH, NM, NC, VA, and WA, or via VinoShipper to ID, NE, NV, ND, OH, OR, Dc, WV, and WY.

Directions: From U.S. Route 17, turn onto U.S. Route 360 East (Queen Street) at the town of Tappahannock. Cross the Rappahannock River and drive for 33.5 miles. Turn right onto Jesse Ball Dupont Memorial Highway (Route 200). The winery is 3.4 miles on the right, after crossing the Wicomico River.

Belle Mount Vineyards
2570 Newland Road
Warsaw VA 22572

Hours: W–Su 11:00–5:00 (15 Mar–20 Dec)   804-333-4700
Closed 21 Dec to 14 Mar   www.bellemount.com
Stay Tuned: Facebook, Twitter, newsletter   E-mail: winery@bellemount.com

Located on the 243-acre Belle Mount estate, Belle Mount Vineyards is in the Heritage Park Resort, which offers a range of outdoor activities for nature-lovers, including campgrounds, hiking trails, and fishing holes in addition to an outdoor swimming pool. The winery was founded in 2002 by Ray and Catherine Petrie, who also serve as the winemakers and vineyard managers. The winery can host a variety of special events and also offers five cabins for overnight stays. Children and pets are welcome.

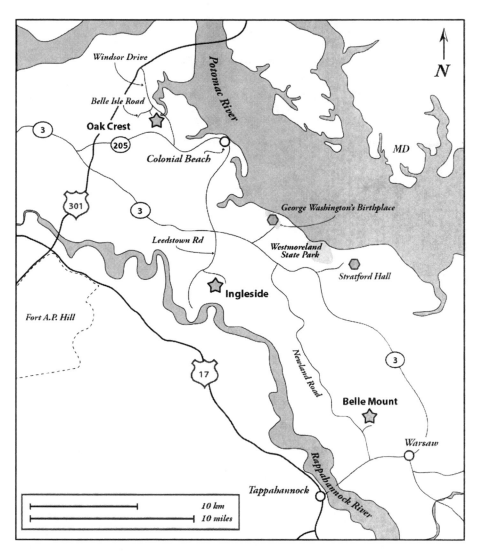

Map 7.3. Northern Neck (northern section)

White Wines: Chardonnay, Vidal Blanc.

Red Wines: Cabernet Franc, Lighthouse Rouge, Merlot, Norton.

Sweet/Dessert Wines: Sweet Breeze, Workboat Red *(Chambourcin)*.

Price Range: $10–$22

Groups: Reservations required for groups of 10 or more.

Purchasing: Online purchases are available for residents of Virginia.

Directions: From U.S. Route 17, take U.S. Route 360 East at the town of Tappahannock and cross the Rappahannock River. After four miles, turn left onto Newland Road. The winery entrance is 2.7 miles on the right.

The Dog and Oyster Vineyards
170 White Fences Drive
Irvington VA 22480

Hours: W-M 11:00–6:00 (mid-Mar–mid-Nov)   804-438-5559
F-Su11:00–5:00(mid-Nov–mid-Mar)   www.hopeandglory.com/thevineyard/winery.html
E-mail: dudley@hopeandglory.com

Formerly known as White Fences Vineyard, the Dog and Oyster was bought in 2011 by Doug and Peggy Patterson, who named the winery after the dogs who shoo deer away from the vines and the oysters of the Chesapeake Bay. The winery is easily recognizable from the road by the pair of giant corkscrews on either side of the drive leading to the six-acre vineyard. The small tasting room includes both a covered patio with several chairs and tables, as well as an interior room with a tasting bar and small shop. The winery's production under its new label will be available in 2012.

Guests may stay at the Pattersons' Hope and Glory Inn in Irvington, which includes the Tents at Vineyard Grove, a row of cottages immediately adjacent to the Dog and Oyster Vineyard itself.

Tastings: $6 per person.

Groups: Call ahead for groups over six.

Wheelchair accessible.

Directions: From U.S. Route 17, take U.S. Route 360 East into the town of Tappahannock. Cross the Rappahannock River and turn right onto Route 3 at the town of Warsaw. Drive 29.6 miles and turn right onto Route 200 (Irvington Road). Drive 4 miles and turn left into White Fences Lane.

General's Ridge Vineyard & Winery
1618 Weldons Drive
Hague VA 22469

Hours: Th, Su 12:00–5:00, F 12:00–7:00, Sa 12:00–6:00   804-472-3172
Closed New Year's, Thanksgiving, Christmas   http://generalsridgevineyard.com
Stay Tuned: Facebook, Twitter, newsletter   E-mail: info@generalsridgevineyard.com

Founded by retired General Rick Phillips and his wife, Linda, General's Ridge began operations ten years ago as a vineyard selling its production to nearby wineries. The Phillipses decided to start their own winery and to the public in 2011. They currently have about thirty acres under vine and work with Michael Shaps of Virginia Wineworks, which handles their production. Snacks and light food may be purchased in the tasting room. General's Ridge offers various events, including wine pairings and dinners.

General's Ridge also offers two guest houses for overnight stays, private parties, and weddings. The Manor House is a restored, two-story, nineteenth-century house; the smaller Carriage House can hold small conferences or wedding receptions.

White Wines: Chardonnay, GRV White, Traminette, Viognier, Vidal Blanc.

Rosé Wines: Rosé.

Red Wines: GRV Red, Merlot, Petit Verdot, Pinot Noir, Westmoreland Red.

Price Range: $11–$20

Tastings: $5 per person with souvenir glass.

Directions: From U.S. Route 17, turn onto U.S. Route 360 East at the town of Tappahannock. Drive 6.6 miles and turn left onto Route 3 at the town of Warsaw. Continue following Route 3 for 6 miles. Turn right onto Nomini Grove Road (Route 621, which will become Route 600). Drive 3.7 miles until Nomini Grove Road until it ends at Nomini Hall Road and turn right. Take the second left onto Weldons Drive. The winery entrance will be about a mile on the left.

Good Luck Cellars
1025 Good Luck Road
Kilmarnock VA 22482

Hours: Th–Sa 11:00–6:00 (F to 8:00, Su 12:00–5:00   804-435-1416
Closed January, Thanksgiving, Christmas   www.goodluckcellars.com
Stay Tuned: Facebook, Twitter   E-mail: info@goodluckcellars.com

Good Luck Cellars was established by Paul and Katie Krop, longtime wine enthusiasts and home winemakers from Virginia Beach. The Krops spent several years restoring the property on the site of a former sand and gravel pit, and then planting a twelve-acre vineyard. The winery opened to the public in 2011 and includes a tasting room with both indoor and outdoor seating, including a wrap-around veranda where visitors can sit over a glass or bottle of wine.

White Wines: Chardonel, Chardonnay, Four Blonds, Vidal Blanc, Vignoles, Viognier.

Rosé Wines: Rip Rap Rosé *(Vidal Blanc, Chambourcin).*

Red Wines: Cabernet Franc, Cabernet Sauvignon, Inheritage *(Bordeaux-style blend)*, Petit Verdot, Radiant Red *(Chambourcin).*

Price Range: $14–$22

Wheelchair accessible.

Directions: From U.S. Route 17, turn east onto Route 33 and drive 7 miles. Turn left onto Greys Point Road (Route 3) and cross the Rappahannock River. Follow Route 3 for 14 miles and turn right onto Good Luck Road. The winery will be about one mile on the right.

The Hague Winery
8268 Cople Highway
Hague VA 22469

Hours: Daily 11:00–5:00 (Apr–Nov)   804-472-5283
Closed Dec–Mar   www.thehaguewinery.com
Stay Tuned: Newsletter   E-mail: cmadey@thehaguewinery.com

Stephen and Cynthia Madey purchased the historic Buena Vista plantation, which dates to 1835, just outside the hamlet of Hague, Virginia, and established their five-acre vineyard soon afterward. The first vines were planted in 2005, and the first wines released in 2009. The Madeys work under the guidance of Lucie Morton, one of Virginia's pioneering viticulturists, in producing their estate-grown wines; they currently make their wines at Virginia Wineworks, a custom-crush facility owned by Michael Shaps. The Hague's tasting room is in a renovated barn with several tables and chairs indoors as well as a covered patio outside where guests may enjoy light snacks over a glass or bottle of wine.

White Wines: Chardonel.

Rosé Wines: Rosé.

Red Wines: Cabernet Franc, Meritage, Merlot, Petit Verdot.

Dessert Wines: Cynthia *(Muscat Ottonel)*.

Price Range: $14–$29

Tastings: $4 per person.

Groups: Reservations encouraged for groups of 8 or more.

Restrictions: No children or pets.

Purchasing: Online purchases are available for Virginia residents only.

Wine Club members receive quarterly shipments and discounts on purchases.

Directions: From U.S. Route 17, turn onto U.S. Route 340 East at the town of Tappahannock. Drive 6.6 miles and turn left onto Route 3 at the town of Warsaw. Continue following Route 3 for 3.3 miles and turn right onto Oldhams Road (Route 203). Drive 7.5 miles and turn left onto Cople Highway (Route 202). Drive 4.6 miles to the winery entrance on left.

Ingleside Vineyards
5872 Leedstown Road
Oak Grove VA 22443

Hours: M–Sa 10:00–5:00, Su 12:00–5:00
(Memorial Day to Labor Day, open until 6:00)
Closed New Year's, Easter,
Thanksgiving, Christmas
Stay Tuned: Facebook, Twitter, newsletter

804-224-8687
www.inglesidevineyards.com
E-mail: info@inglesidevineyards.com

One of Virginia's earliest wineries, Ingleside Vineyards is also one of the largest in terms of acreage, with about 60 acres under vine. Ingleside's largely estate-grown wines are produced under the supervision of winemaker Bill Swain, who joined Ingleside after working at wineries in California, Oregon, and Venezuela. The winery sponsors a range of special events, including live music, barrel tastings, and harvest festivals, and can host private parties or weddings for up to 150 guests on the grounds. The tasting room is in an old dairy barn and includes a patio with tables and chairs where visitors may enjoy a picnic lunch. Children will find a small natural history museum at one end of the patio. Pets are welcome.

Sparkling Wines: Virginia Brut *(Chardonnay)*.

White Wines: Blue Crab Blanc, Chardonnay, Chesapeake Chardonnay, Colonial White *(Viognier, Albariño, Petit Manseng)*, Pinot Grigio.

Rosé Wines: Blue Crab Blush, Rosato di Sangiovese, Sweet Virginia Rosé.

Red Wines: Blue Crab Red, Cabernet Franc, Cabernet Merlot, Cabernet Sauvignon, Merlot, Petit Verdot, Sangiovese, Syrah.

Dessert Wines: October Harvest *(Petit Manseng, Riesling)*, Virginia Gold.

Price Range: $11–$33

Tastings: $3 per person for basic; $7 per person for reserve (with souvenir glass); $10 per person for full tasting (with souvenir glass).

Groups: Reservations are encouraged for groups of 8 or more.

Wheelchair accessible.

Purchasing: Online purchasing is available *except* for residents of MD, MA, MO, and NJ.

Directions: From U.S. Route 301, turn south onto Route 3. Drive 10 miles and turn right onto Leedstown Road (Route 638). Drive 2.2 miles to the winery's gravel driveway on the left.

Jacey Vineyards
619 Train Lane
Heathsville VA 22579

Hours: Th, Su 10:00–5:00, F–Sa 10:00–7:00   804-580-4053
Closed New Year's, Easter, Thanksgiving, Christmas   http://jaceyvineyards.com
Stay Tuned: Facebook, Newsletter   E-mail: info@jaceyvineyards.com

Robert and Tammie Jacey founded Jacey Vineyards in 2004 when they first planted their eight-acre vineyard on a 150-acre farm. Their first vintage was in 2010, produced under the guidance of winemaker Delaina Cooper. Jacey Vineyards is located on Mill Creek, with a dock for those who wish to arrive by boat. Tastings are currently held in the winery's Vineyard Restaurant, which features seafood from the Chesapeake Bay.

White Wines: Vidal Blanc.

Red Wines: Malbec, Norton, Petit Verdot, Zinfandel.

Price Range: $13–$22

Tastings: $5 per person with souvenir glass.

Groups: Reservations requested for groups of 8 or more.

Directions: From U.S. Route 17, take U.S. Route 360 East into the town of Tappahannock. Cross the Rappahannock River and turn right onto Route 3 at the town of Warsaw. Drive 29.6 miles and turn left onto Route 200. Drive 7.6 miles and turn right onto Remo Road. Drive 2.2 miles and turn right onto Mill Point Road. After 0.2 miles, turn left onto Train Lane. The winery will be 0.5 mile on the left

Oak Crest Vineyard & Winery
8215 Oak Crest Drive
King George VA 22485

Hours: W–Sa, M holidays 10:00–5:00, Su 11:00–5:00   540-663-2813

Closed Easter, Thanksgiving, 23 Dec through Feb   www.oakcrestwinery.com

Stay Tuned: Newsletter   E-mail: winery@oakcrestwinery.com

Oak Crest Vineyard & Winery was opened in 2002 by Conrad and Dorothy Brandt. The Brandts use the Symphony grape for most of their white wines, which vary in taste depending on the specific yeasts used in production. The tasting room and winery are built into the side of a hill, with the barrel room literally carved into the ground. Guests may purchase snacks in the tasting room or bring their own picnics to enjoy on the decks and patio that adjoin the tasting room. The winery may be rented for private parties and weddings. Children and pets are welcome.

White Wines: Moonlight Sonata *(Symphony)*, Symphony, Viognier.

Rosé Wines: Summer Rose *(Cabernet Franc)*.

Red Wines: Cabernet Franc, Cabernet Sauvignon, Merlot, Sunset Serenade *(Bordeaux-style blend)*.

Sweet/Dessert Wines: Finale *(Symphony)*, Sunset Medley *(Symphony, strawberries)*, Symphony (sweet).

Fortified Wines: Ruby *(Cabernet Sauvignon, Cabernet Franc, Merlot)*.

Other: Hot Jazz *(Symphony, jalapeño peppers)*.

Price Range: $13–$22

Groups: Reservations requested for groups of 8 or more.

Restrictions: Reservations required for buses and limos (parking lot is very small).

Purchasing: E-mail purchases for residents of Virginia only.

Directions: From U.S. Route 301 North, turn south onto Windsor Drive (Route 218). Drive 2.5 miles and turn right onto Belle Isle Road. Make an immediate left onto Oak Crest Drive and the winery's gravel driveway.

Vault Field Vineyards
2952 Kings Mill Road
Kinsale VA 22488

Hours: Th–Sa, 11:00–5:00, Su 12:00–6:00 (May–Dec) 804-472-4430
Sa 11:00–5:00, Su 12:00–4:00 Jan–May (call ahead to confirm) www.vaultfield.com
Closed Thanksgiving, mid-Dec to New Year's E-mail: info@vaultfield.com
Stay Tuned: Twitter

After a career in the insurance industry, Keith and Joanne Meenan decided to purchase the historic Vault Field Farm and start a vineyard and winery. The Meenans and their son Dan manage all operations on the vineyard, with Keith also serving as winemaker. The tasting room is inside the winery building. The winery sponsors fall barrel tastings and a spring open house featuring music and light food; proceeds from the events are donated to the local volunteer fire department. Vault Field offers private tastings by appointment.

White Wines: Chardonnay, Conundrum *(Chardonnay, Vidal Blanc, Chardonel)*, Vidal Blanc.

Rosé Wines: Rosé.

Red Wines: Merlot, Red *(Merlot, Cabernet Sauvignon, Chambourcin)*, Syrah.

Price Range: $15–$22

Tastings: $3 per person.

Wheelchair accessible.

Purchasing: Online purchasing is available *except* for residents of AL, AK, AR, DE, HI, MA, MT, NJ, NM, OK, PA, SD, and UT.

Directions: From U.S. Route 17, turn onto U.S. Route 340 East at the town of Tappahannock. Drive 6.6 miles and turn left onto Route 3 at the town of Warsaw. Continue following Route 3 for 3.3 miles and turn right onto Oldhams Road (Route 203). Drive 7.5 miles and turn right onto Cople Highway (Route 202). Take the first right onto Kings Mill Road. The winery driveway will be about 1 mile on the right.

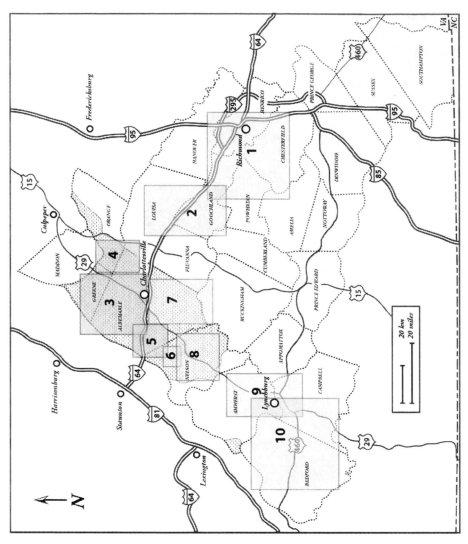

Map 8.1. Central Virginia Region & Monticello AVA: (1) Richmond; (2) Louisa; (3) Upper Monticello (western section); (4) Upper Monticello (eastern section); (5) Afton-Crozet; (6) Rockfish Gap; (7) South Monticello (eastern section); (8) South Monticello (western section); (9) Lynchburg (northern section); (10) Lynchburg (southern section).

8. CENTRAL VIRGINIA REGION & MONTICELLO AVA

Bounded by the Blue Ridge on the west and Tidewater on the east, the Central Virginia Region is rich in history and natural attractions. The topography of this region varies considerably, rising from the flat terrain of the fall line at Richmond to the Blue Ridge Mountains. The Monticello AVA is centered around Charlottesville in the western part of the larger region. While summers throughout Central Virginia are warm, the Blue Ridge helps moderate winter temperatures in the AVA, protecting it from the lower temperatures that can sometimes occur in the Shenandoah Valley immediately to the west.

The Central Virginia region is second only to Northern Virginia in the number of wineries, with about four dozen that are regularly open to the public. Roughly two-thirds of these are in the Monticello AVA, whose vineyards produce twenty-four separate varieties of grapes, including less commonly known ones such as Rkatsiteli, Touriga Nacional, and Pinotage. As of 2010, 144 wines were labeled with the Monticello AVA designation, which means that 85 percent of the grapes used to produce them originated in the AVA. Soils here are generally clay underlain by granite and can produce quite full-bodied wines.

<u>Things to see and do</u>: There are numerous historical attractions spread throughout the region, ranging from homes of the founding fathers

(Thomas Jefferson's Monticello and James Monroe's Ash Lawn) to the National D-Day Memorial at Bedford, the American town with the highest per capita losses at that pivotal event in World War II.

Virginia's capital of Richmond offers a number of interesting sites for visitors. The Church Hill district, located immediately to the east of the downtown area, is a colonial-era neighborhood that includes the historic St. John's Church, where Patrick Henry gave his famous "Give me liberty or give me death!" speech in 1775. The Virginia state capitol building was designed by Thomas Jefferson, who used the Roman-era Maison Carrée in Nîmes, France, as his architectural inspiration.

The entire region is particularly rich in Civil War history. The Richmond area includes, among other sites, the Museum of the Civil War Soldier, located near Petersburg on the battlefield where General Ulysses S. Grant's forces shattered General Robert E. Lee's lines in April, 1865. The Sailor's Creek battlefield, just east of Farmville, was the last major battle of the Civil War in the Virginia theater. Three days after losing 7,700 men in combat there against Union forces, General Lee surrendered to General Grant at Appomattox Court House 46 miles to the west. The Lee's Retreat Trail is a self-guided driving tour that traces Lee's last moves in retreating from Petersburg to Appomattox (www.varetreat.com/lee.asp).

The region also includes part of Virginia's Civil Rights in Education Heritage Trail (www.varetreat.com/CivilRights.asp), a self-guided driving tour of key sites in the struggle of African-Americans, Native Americans, and women to attain greater access and rights to educational resources.

<u>Wine Trails</u>: There are several wine trails for Central Virginia wineries, including The Appellation Trail, Heart of Virginia Wine Trail, the Monticello Wine Trail, and Nelson 151. More details are available in Appendix 1.

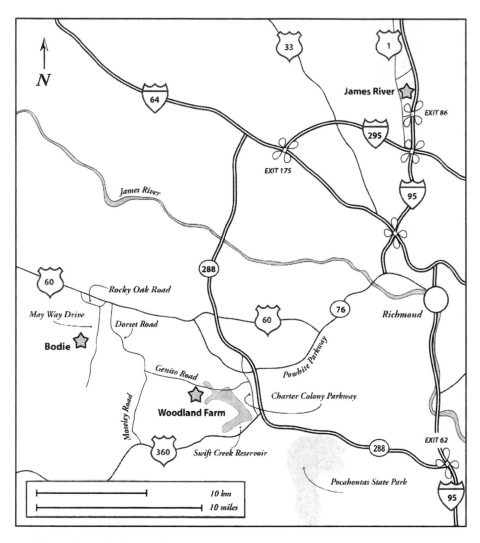

Map 8.2. Richmond

RICHMOND

Bodie Vineyards
1809 May Way Drive
Powhatan VA 23139

Hours: M–Sa 1:00–5:00 (until 6:00 in summer)   804-598-2625
Closed New Year's, Thanksgiving, Christmas   www.bodievineyards.com
Stay Tuned: Facebook   E-mail: bodievineyards@rocketmail.com

Clyde and Mary Bodie are longtime home winemakers who established their small farm winery in 2008, opening it to the public two years later. The facilities include an outdoor pavilion and picnic tables, where guests are welcome to enjoy a picnic from home. The winery sponsors annual harvest festivals that welcome volunteers to help bring in the grapes. The facilities are available for private parties and events. Children and dogs are welcome.

White Wines: Michaux Blanc *(Cayuga).*

Red Wines: Rochette Rouge *(Buffalo).*

Price Range: $15

Directions: From Route 288, turn west onto U.S. Route 60. Drive 8 miles and turn south onto Rocky Oak Road. After about half a mile, turn left onto May Way Drive. The winery driveway will be 1/3 mile on the right.

James River Cellars
11008 Washington Highway
Glen Allen VA 23059

Hours: Su–Th 11:00–5:00, F–Su 10:00–6:00   804-550-7516
Closed New Year's, Thanksgiving, Christmas   www.jamesrivercellars.com
Stay Tuned: Facebook, Twitter   E-mail: winecellars@jrgm.com

James River was founded by Ray Lazarchic in 2001 and is now owned by James and Mitzi Batterson; James also serves as winemaker, assisted by Sebastian Nagy, a native of Hungary. James River offers a picnic area and patio just outside the tasting room, where it hosts Fridays on the Patio on the fourth Friday of every month, as well as a harvest wine festival. Dogs are welcome to both for a two-dollar charge that is donated to the Richmond SPCA, which attends the events with animals ready for adoption. The facility can be rented for weddings and private events. A portion of the proceeds of the sale of Rad Red are contributed to cancer research, and the winery's Party with a Purpose is a benefit event for the American Cancer Society. Children and leashed dogs are welcome.

White Wines: Chardonel, Chardonnay, Gewurztraminer, Vidal Blanc.

Red Wines: Cabernet Franc, Chambourcin, Colonial Red, Hanover *(Cabernet Franc, Chancellor)*, Meritage, Merlot, Petit Verdot, Rad Red.

Sweet/Dessert Wines: Divino *(Vidal Blanc, Traminette)*, Hanover White *(Chardonnay, Chardonel, Muscat)*, Montpelier Blush.

Price Range: $10–$35

Tastings: $5 per person.

Groups: Please call ahead for groups of 8 or more; pricing varies according to group size.

Wheelchair accessible.

Purchasing: Online ordering available to CA, FL, MO, NC, VA, and DC.

Directions: From I-95, take Exit 86B (Elmont) and drive west on Sliding Hill Road. Turn right at the second traffic light onto Washington Highway (U.S. Route 1 North). The winery will be on the right in about 1 mile.

Woodland Vineyard Farm Winery
15501 Genito Road
Midlothian VA 23112

Hours: Sa-Su 1:00–5:00 (mid-Mar to early Dec)   804-739-2774
Closed early Dec to mid-Mar   www.woodlandvineyard.com
Stay Tuned: Newsletter   E-mail: info@woodlandvineyard.com

One of Virginia's smallest farm wineries, Woodland Vineyard Farm produces about two hundred cases of wine annually from its two small vineyards. The winery was established in 1997 by Eric Gretenhart and Melissa Jeltema on a half-acre plot on their farm southwest of Richmond. After opening their doors to the public seven years later, the couple has now expanded their operations to a second vineyard in Amelia County. Woodland Vineyard Farm sponsors harvest parties, Mother's and Father's Day weekends, and a holiday open house. The winery is available for private parties, with seating available both inside the tasting room and outside on the patio. Children and pets are welcome.

White Wines: Chardonnay, Muscat, Vidal Blanc, Viognier, Woodland White *(Chardonnay, Vidal Blanc).*

Rosé Wines: White Merlot.

Red Wines: Cabernet Franc, Cabernet Sauvignon, Merlot, Woodland Red *(White Merlot, Cabernet Sauvignon).*

Price Range: $14–$20

Tastings: $2 per person.

Directions: From Powhite Parkway, turn south onto Charter Colony Parkway. Drive 1.4 miles and make a sharp right onto Genito Road. The winery will be on the left after 3 miles.

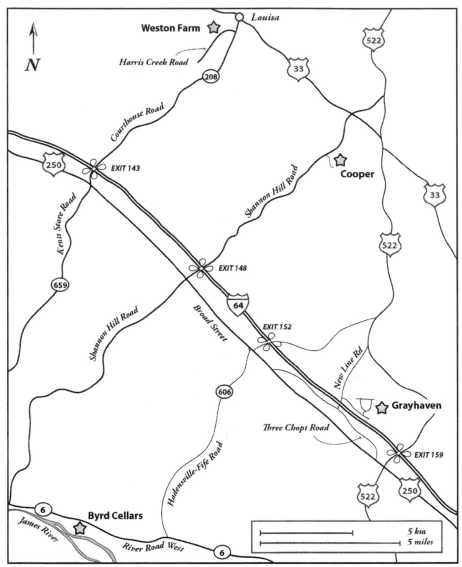

Map 8.3. Louisa

LOUISA

Byrd Cellars
5847 River Road West
Goochland VA 23063

Hours: Sa–Su 1:00–5:00

Closed New Year's, Christmas

Stay Tuned: Facebook, Twitter

804-652-5663

www.byrdcellars.com

E-mail: info@ByrdCellars.com

Byrd Cellars was established in 2008 as a collaborative venture by three Goochland County vineyard owners. The tasting room offer visitors a light-filled space with scenic views of the James River. Byrd Cellars wines are all from Virginia-grown grapes, including from their own fifteen acres of vines. Guests are welcome to sit indoors or outside with a glass or bottle of wine. The facilities are available for small private events and parties. Children and pets are welcome.

Fruit Wines: Apple-Concord, Dry Apple, Leonora's Meadowsweet, Sweet Apple.

White Wines: Chardonnay, Sauvignon Blanc.

Orange Wines: Muscat.

Rosé Wines: Vin Rosé *(Cabernet Franc, Viognier)*.

Red Wines: Dahlgren's Raid *(Bordeaux-style blend)*, Merlot, Norton, Petit Verdot, Raven Red *(Cabernet Sauvignon, Merlot, Syrah, Norton)*, Syrah.

Sweet/Dessert Wines: Muscat.

Price Range: $8–$18

Tastings: $5 per person.

Byrd Club members can purchase limited release wines and receive discounts on events.

Directions: From I-64, take Exit 152 south onto Old Fredericksburg Road toward Hadensville. Turn right onto U.S. Route 250 West (Broad Street Road) and then make an immediate left onto Hadensville-Fife Road (Route 606). Drive nine miles and turn right onto River Road West (Route 6). The winery entrance will be 2.7 miles on the left.

Cooper Vineyards
13372 Shannon Hill Road
Louisa VA 23093

Hours: Daily 11:00–5:00   540-894-5474
Closed New Year's, Thanksgiving, Christmas   www.coopervineyards.com
Stay Tuned: Facebook, Twitter, newsletter   E-mail: info@coopervineyards.com

Geoffrey Cooper and Jacque Hogge established their family-owned and operated winery in scenic Louisa County. Working with winemaker Graham Bell, the winery produces a range of wines including their Noche dessert wine, a blend of Norton and chocolate, and two ice wines. Cooper sponsors an annual mini-Cooper rally, fundraisers for the local SPCA, "Jazz and Chocolate" festivals, and a holiday open house, among other activities. Visitors are welcome to bring their own picnic food to enjoy on the grounds. Cooper's two-story, LEED-certified tasting facilities opened in 2011 and include an outdoor tasting area, weather permitting. Guests are welcome to sit on the veranda overlooking the vines. The facilities are available for private events and parties. Children and pets are welcome.

White Wines: Chardonel, Chardonnay, Coopertage Blanc *(Viognier, Chardonnay)*, Viognier.

Rosé Wines: St. Stephen's Rosé.

Red Wines: Cabernet Franc, Chambourcin, Coopertage *(Bordeaux-style blend)*, Norton, Petit Verdot.

Sweet/Dessert Wines: Noche *(Norton, chocolate)*, Rhapsody *(Vidal Blanc, Chardonel, Viognier)*, Soleil *(Viognier)*, Sweet Louisa *(Norton, Concord, Merlot)*, Vida *(Vidal Blanc)*.

Price Range: $15–$30

Tastings: $5 per person.

Purchasing: Online purchasing is available for AK, CA, FL, NC, MD, MN, MO, NM, VA, and DC residents.

Directions: From I-64, take Exit 148 (Shannon Hill Road). Drive north on Shannon Hill Road (Route 605) about 8 miles to the winery's gravel driveway on right.

Grayhaven Winery
4675 E. Grey Fox Circle
Gum Spring VA 23065

Hours: M, Th–F, Su 11:00–5:00, Sa 11:00–6:00   804-556-3917
Closed New Year's, Thanksgiving, Christmas   www.grayhavenwinery.com
Stay Tuned: Facebook, newsletter   E-mail: max@grayhavenwinery.com

Established by Chuck and Lyn Peple and their daughters, Max and Mallory, Grayhaven was named after the Elvish port of Gray Havens in J.R.R. Tolkien's *Lord of the Rings* trilogy. The winery opened to the public in 1995 and offers a range of estate-grown wines. As a small-lot producer, the variety of Grayhaven wines available for tasting may vary significantly from month to month, depending on which wines have been released or are still available. Visitors are welcome to linger over a glass or bottle after their tastings to enjoy the grounds, either from the patio or small deck overlooking a koi pond. The winery hosts occasional special tastings, including a South Africa tasting weekend, and live music. The facilities may be rented for weddings and other special events for up to two hundred people. Children and dogs are welcome.

White Wines: Chardonnay Fumé Blanc, Moonlight White, Riesling, Sauvignon Blanc, Seyval Blanc, Voyager.

Blush Wines: Eventide.

Red Wines: Cabernet Franc, Cabernet Sauvignon, Pinotage, Rendezvous, Touriga, Trekker, Sojourn.

Price Range: $15–$35

Tastings: $4 per person.

Groups: Reservations required for groups of 8 or more, and for all bus tours.

Wheelchair accessible.

Directions: From I-64, take Exit 159 (Gum Spring) and turn south onto Cross County Road (Route 522). Turn right onto Broad Street (U.S. Route 250 West) and make the first right onto Three Chopt Road (Route 700). Drive 2.3 miles and turn right onto New Line Road (Route 619). Take the first right onto Sheppard Spring Road and then turn left onto Fox Chase Run. Turn right onto East Grey Fox Circle. The winery entrance will be on the right.

❖ ❖ ❖

Weston Farm Vineyard & Winery
206 Harris Creek Road
Louisa VA 23093

Hours: Daily 11:00–5:30
Closed New Year's, Thanksgiving,
Christmas

540-967-4647
www.westonfarmvineyardandwinery.com
E-mail: pennymlouisa@aol.com

Bobby and Penny Martin opened Weston Farm Vineyard to the public in 2010. Working with Virginia vintner Gabriele Rausse, the Martins began making wine in 2009 after planting their vineyard four years earlier. Visitors are welcome to bring a picnic lunch to enjoy on the grounds after their tastings. Weston Farm is an animal lover's delight, with winery dogs Charlie and Suzie often on hand to greet visitors to the tasting room, and rescue horses, miniature donkeys, and cows on the farm. The winery sponsors live music and fundraisers on selected weekends. Children and pets are welcome.

Fruit Wines: Peach, Raspberry.

White Wines: Chardonnay.

Rosé Wines: Rosé *(Cabernet Franc)*.

Red Wines: Cabernet Franc, Meritage, Norton, Rosso *(Rosé, Norton)*.

Price Range: $12–$18

Tastings: $5 per person.

Directions: From I-64, take Exit 143 onto Courthouse Road (Route 208) north toward Louisa. Drive 8 miles and turn left onto Harris Creek Road (Route 630). The winery entrance will be on the right.

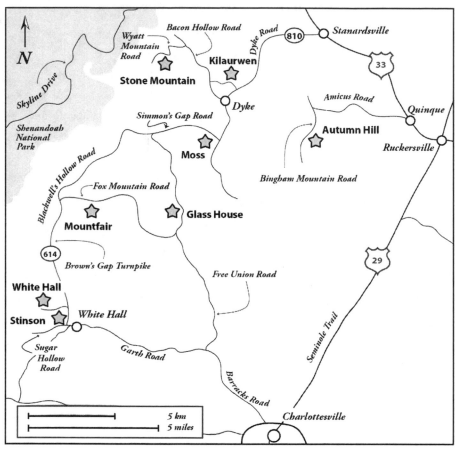

Map 8.4. Upper Monticello (western section)

UPPER MONTICELLO

Autumn Hill Vineyards & Blue Ridge Winery
301 River Drive
Stanardsville VA 22973

Hours: Open to the public 4 weekends per year   434-985-6100
(Check website or call for specific dates)   www.autumnhillwine.com
E-mail: autumnhillwine@gmail.com

Autumn Hill was established in 1979 by Ed and Avra Schwab in the foothills of the Blue Ridge Mountains. The Schwabs focus their estate-grown production on all dry wines, with the reds bottled unfined and unfiltered. Autumn Hill is open to the public each year for their Spring Harvest Barrel Tasting (two weekends) and the Autumn Barrel Tasting (two weekends). Both feature food, barrel samples, cellar tours, and vertical tastings of Autumn Hill wines. Children are welcome.

White Wines: Chardonnay, Chardonnay Vintner's Reserve, Viognier.

Red Wines: Cabernet Franc, Cabernet Sauvignon, Horizon Rouge *(Bordeaux-style blend)*, Merlot, Petit Verdot/Merlot.

Price Range: $14–$24

Tastings: $7 per person with souvenir glass.

Vintage Wine Club members receive wine shipments, discounts, and members-only events.

Purchasing: Online ordering available for VA, NC, and DC residents only.

Directions: From U.S. Route 29, turn onto U.S. Route 33 West at Ruckersville and drive 2 miles. At the village of Quinque, turn left onto Amicus Road (Route 633) and continue 6.5 miles to the end of the road. Turn left onto Bingham Mountain Road (Route 603) and continue about one mile. The winery entrance will be on the left.

Barboursville Vineyards
17655 Winery Road
Barboursville VA 22923

Hours: M–Sa 10:00–5:00, Su 11:00–5:00   540-832-3824
Closed New Year's, Thanksgiving, Christmas   www.barboursvillewine.net/winery
Stay Tuned: Facebook, Twitter, e-newsletter   E-mail: bvvy@barboursvillewine.com

Barboursville Vineyards is one of the largest and oldest farm wineries in Virginia. Owned by Gianni and Silvana Zonin, who purchased the historic nine-hundred-acre Barboursville estate in 1976, Barboursville produces over thirty thousand bottles of wine annually from its 140-acre vineyard and is a very popular stop on the weekend winery trail. The tasting room overlooks the octagonal ruins of the Barbour family mansion designed by Thomas Jefferson and destroyed by fire on Christmas Day 1884. The ruins are featured on the label of the winery's flagship Octagon wine and also serve as a backdrop for the annual Shakespeare in the Ruins in August. Free tours are offered on Saturday and Sunday from noon to 4:00 p.m. or by appointment. The facilities may be rented for private events and weddings. Children are welcome.

The winery's Palladio Restaurant is open for lunch Wednesday to Sunday (reservations recommended) and dinner Friday and Saturday (reservations required). The winery grounds also include two restored buildings—the 1804 Inn and Vineyard Cottage—that are available for overnight stays.

Sparkling Wines: Barboursville Brut *(Chardonnay, Pinot Noir).*

White Wines: Chardonnay, Pinot Grigio, Sauvignon Blanc, Vermentino, Viognier.

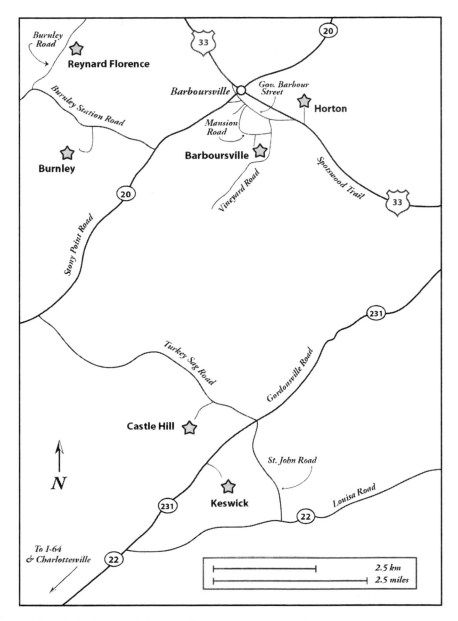

Map 8.5. Upper Monticello (eastern section)

Rosé Wines: Vintage Rosé.

Red Wines: Barbera, Cabernet Franc, Cabernet Sauvignon, Merlot, Nebbiolo, Octagon *(Bordeaux-style blend)*, Petit Verdot, Sangiovese.

Sweet/Dessert Wines: Malvaxio Passito *(Moscato Ottonel, Vidal)*, Philéo *(Moscato Ottonel, Traminer Aromatico)*.

Price Range: $12–$50

Tastings: $5 per person with souvenir glass.

Groups: Reservations required for group tour buses and limos.

Wheelchair accessible.

Purchasing: Online purchasing available for CA, FL, IL, MD, MI, MN, NC, NM, NH, SC, VA, WA, and DC.

Directions: From U.S. Route 33, turn south onto Route 20 (Constitution Highway). Make an immediate left onto Governor Barbour Street. Take the third right onto Mansion Road. After 3/4 mile, turn right onto Winery Road and the winery parking lot.

Burnley Vineyards
4500 Winery Lane
Barboursville VA 22923

Hours: Daily, 11:00–5:00 (Apr–Dec) 540-832-2828
F–M 11:00–5:00 (Jan–Mar) www.burnleywines.com
Closed: New Year's, Thanksgiving, E-mail: bvwinery@gmx.com
Christmas Eve & Day

Burnley Vineyard was opened to the public in 1984 by the Reeder family, who first planted their vineyard in 1977. Visitors may purchase snacks, bread, and cheese to enjoy with a glass or bottle of one of Burnley's estate-grown wines. Burnley hosts a number of special winery events, including wine and cheese weekends, an annual Thanksgiving Open House (Friday–

Sunday), a holiday open house in December, and special vertical tastings. The facility may be rented for private parties. Children are welcome.

Burnley also offers overnight stays at its Fernando's Hideaway, a furnished guest house with room for four.

Fruit Wines: Peach Fuzz, Spicy Rivanna.

White Wines: Barrel Fermented Chardonnay, Chardonnay, Rivanna White *(Vidal Blanc)*, Riesling.

Blush Wines: Rivanna Sunset *(Chambourcin)*.

Red Wines: Barbera, Cabernet Sauvignon, Chambourcin, Dog Gone Red, Norton, Rivanna Red *(Chambourcin, Norton, Cabernet Sauvignon)*, Zinfandel.

Sweet/Dessert Wines: Aurora *(red wine with chocolate, raspberries)*, Somerset *(Chardonnay, Vidal Blanc, Riesling, Norton, Chambourcin, Cabernet Sauvignon)*.

Fortified Wines: Rubix *(Norton port-style)*.

Price Range: $12–$18

Tastings: $3 per person.

Wheelchair accessible.

Purchasing: Online ordering for Virginia residents only.

Directions: From U.S. Route 33, turn south onto Route 20 (Constitution Highway) and drive 2 miles. Turn right onto Burnley Station Road (Route 641). The winery entrance will be 1/3 mile on the left.

Castle Hill Cider
6065 Turkey Sag Road
Keswick VA 22947

Hours: Tu–Su 11:00–5:30 (Apr–Nov), W–Su 11:00–5:00 (Dec–Mar) 434-296-0047
Closed New Year's, Thanksgiving, Christmas www.castlehillcider.com
Stay Tuned: Facebook, Twitter E-mail: events@castlehillcider.com

Castle Hill Cider opened to the public in 2011 on the grounds of the historic Castle Hill estate. The estate's manor house was built in 1764 as the home of Colonel Thomas Walker, who was appointed as Thomas Jefferson's guardian after his father's death. The cidery is housed in a barn that includes the cidery's tasting and tank rooms, and an events facility. Cidermaker Stuart Madany is using kvevri terracotta vessels to make Castle Hill's Levity cider; kvevri originated over eight thousand years ago in the Republic of Georgia, where they are still used in traditional wine production. Castle Hill's grounds and events room may be rented for weddings, private parties, and dinners.

Ciders:

Celestial is a blend of Ellis Bitter and Albemarle Pippin apples.

Terrestrial is a dry crisp cider made from a blend of Winesap and Albemarle Pippin apples.

Levity is a rich cider produced from Albemarle Pippins.

Gravity is a blend of Grimes Golden, Pink Lady, Ellis Bitter, Dabinette, Yerlington Mill, and English bittersweet apples.

Price Range: $17–$23

Tastings: $5 per person.

Groups: Reservations requested for groups of 10 or more.

Wheelchair accessible.

Directions: From I-64, take Exit 124 onto U.S. Route 250 East (Shadwell). Drive 1.9 miles and turn onto Route 22 East. After 5.4 miles, stay straight to go onto Gordonsville Road (Route 231). Continue 3.3 miles and turn left onto Turkey Sag Road (Route 640). Drive 3/4 mile and turn left into the cidery driveway between the white stone posts.

Glass House Winery
5898 Free Union Road
Free Union VA 22940

Hours: Th–Su 12:00–5:30 (F til 9:00)   434-975-0094
Closed New Year's, Thanksgiving, Christmas   www.glasshousewinery.com
Stay Tuned: Facebook, newsletter   E-mail: michelle@glasshousewinery.com

Glass House Winery was established by Jeff and Michelle Sanders who moved to Virginia after having spent five years in Honduras where Jeff operated a plant nursery. The Sanders bought a twenty-two-acre farm and established a six-acre vineyard currently planted with eight varieties of grapes. Production is mostly estate-grown, supplemented by grapes from other Virginia vineyards. The winery features a glass-enclosed tropical greenhouse that is available for rental for weddings and private events. Michelle also makes hand-crafted gourmet chocolates that are on sale in the tasting room. The winery hosts various special events, including live music on select weekends.

Glass House operates a four-bedroom bed-and-breakfast inn on the property for visitors.

White Wines: Pinot Gris, Viognier, Vino Signora *(Traminette)*.

Rosé Wines: Eville Pink Drink.

Red Wines: Barbera, C-Villian *(Chambourcin, Cabernet Franc, Merlot)*, Merlot, Twenty-First *(Bordeaux-style blend)*.

Sweet/Dessert Wines: Meglio Del Sesso.

Price Range: $15–$24

Tastings: $5 per person with souvenir glass.

Purchasing: Online ordering available to AK, FL, MN, VA, and DC residents.

Wine Club members receive regular wine shipments, discounts on purchases, complimentary tastings, and members-only events.

Directions: From Charlottesville and U.S. Route 29 North, take Barracks Road West and drive about 4 miles; the road will become Garth Road. Turn right onto Free Union Road (Route 601) at the Hunt Country Market. Continue following Free Union Road for 7.9 miles and turn left onto the winery's drive.

Horton Vineyards
6399 Spotswood Trail
Gordonsville VA 22942

Hours: Daily 10:00–5:00

Closed New Year's, Thanksgiving, Christmas

Stay Tuned: Facebook, Twitter, newsletter

800-829-4633

www.hortonwine.com

E-mail: vawinee@aol.com

Horton Vineyards had its origins in a home vineyard started in 1983 by owner and winemaker Dennis Horton that culminated in his 1988 purchase of a fifty-five-acre property in Orange County. Horton was a pioneer in bringing to Virginia the Viognier grape, which he discovered in an early trip to France to research grape varieties. A native of Missouri, he also has been particularly interested in the Norton grape, which was first cultivated in Virginia and rose to prominence in Horton's home town of Hermann, Missouri. Horton probably plants the widest range of grape varieties in the state, ranging from the familiar Chardonnay to lesser-known varieties such as Rkatsiteli and Pinotage. Horton Vineyards also bottles a wide variety of fruit wines under the Chateau le Cabin label that honors Dennis Horton's early home winemaking days in his Aroda, Virginia cabin.

Horton sponsors a wide range of events, including a Mardi Gras festival, barrel and vertical tastings, annual pig roasts, and a Thanksgiving weekend open house. While tastings are normally complimentary, there is an entrance fee for special events.

Fruit Wines: Blackberry *(blackberry, Petit Verdot)*, Blueberry *(blueberry, Petit Verdot)*, Cranberry *(cranberry, Cabernet Franc)*, Peach *(peach, Viognier)*, Pear *(pear, Viognier)*, Plum *(plum, Cabernet Franc)*, Pomegranate *(pomegranate, Syrah)*, Raspberry *(raspberry, Cabernet Franc)*, Strawberry *(strawberry, Grenache)*.

Sparkling Wines: Viognier.

White Wines: Black Cat Chardonnay, Blue Run Chardonnay, Petit Manseng, Roussanne, Rkatsiteli, Stonecastle White, Vidal Blanc, Viognier.

Blush Wines: Stonecastle Blush.

Red Wines: Cabernet Franc, Côtes d'Orange *(Rhone-style blend)*, Iberia *(Tempranillo, Graciano, Touriga Nacional, Tinta Cão)*, Malbec, Mourvedre, Nebbiolo, Norton, Pinotage, Route 33 Red, Stonecastle Red, Syrah, Tannat, Touriga Nacional.

Sweet/Dessert Wines: Açai, Eden *(apple)*, Eclipse Red, Eclipse White, Late Harvest Viognier, Niagara, Rkatsiteli, Sweet Concord, Blanco XOCO *(chocolate, Rkatsiteli, Vidal Blanc)*, Rojo XOCO *(Chocolate, Touriga Nacional)*.

Fortified Wines: Courage, Pear Port, Vintage Port.

Price Range: $9–$35

Wheelchair accessible

Directions: From U.S. Route 29, turn east onto U.S. Route 33 East at Ruckersville. Drive 8 miles to the winery entrance on the left.

Keswick Vineyards
1575 Keswick Winery Drive
Keswick VA 22947

Hours: Daily 9:00–5:00 (F til 6:00 in summer)
Closed New Year's, Thanksgiving, Christmas
Stay Tuned: Facebook, Twitter

434-244-3341
www.keswickvineyards.com
E-mail: info@keswickvineyards.com

Al and Cindy Schornberg have owned Keswick Vineyards, located at the historic Edgewood estate just outside Charlottesville, since 2000. South African native Stephen Barnard serves as winemaker and concentrates on small-batch production; as a result, the specific wines available for tastings may vary considerably from one visit to the next. The winery's tasting room offers good views of the vineyard from its front windows and porch, which has several tables for visitors. Cheese, bread, salsa, and chips are available for purchase. Keswick sponsors special events such as the Sunday afternoon Yappy Hour for dogs, SPCA fundraisers, and book signings. The facility is available for weddings and private events. Children and pets are welcome.

White Wines: Chardonnay, Les Vents d'Anges Viognier, Pinot Gris, Verdejo, Viognier.

Rosé Wines: Rosé.

Red Wines: Cabernet Franc, Cabernet Sauvignon, Chambourcin, Consensus, Heritage *(Cabernet Sauvignon, Merlot)*, Merlot, Norton, Petit Verdot, Syrah, Touriga Nacional, Trevillian *(Bordeaux-style blend)*.

Sweet/Dessert Wines: Nektar *(Viognier)*.

Price Range: $18–$60

Tastings: $5 per person for regular tasting.

Groups: Reservations required for groups of 10 or more, with a sliding fee schedule depending on group size; please contact winery for specifics.

Restrictions: Limos and bus groups Sa–Su from 9:00–2:00 only.

Wheelchair accessible

Purchasing: Online purchasing for residents of AK, CA, CO, FL, IL, MI, MN, MO, NH, NY, NC, OH, SC, TX, VA, WA, and DC.

Wine Club members receive discounts and invitations to special events at various levels.

Directions: From I-64, take Exit 124 onto U.S. Route 250 East (Shadwell). Drive 2 miles and turn onto Louisa Road (Route 22 East). After 5.4 miles, stay straight to go onto Gordonsville Road (Route 231). Continue 2.2 miles to Keswick Winery Drive and the winery on the right.

Kilaurwen Vineyards
1543 Evergreen Church Road
Stanardsville VA 22973

Hours: F–Su, holiday M 12:00–5:00 (Apr–Nov)   434-985-2535
Closed Dec–Mar   www.kilaurwenwinery.com
Stay Tuned: Facebook, newsletter   E-mail: kilaurwen@gmail.com

Bob and Dorien Steeves founded Kilaurwen Winery in 2009 and opened their tasting room to the public two years later. The Steeves decided to open their winery after spending a number of years growing and furnishing grapes to various Virginia wineries. The winery is named after their three daughters, Kimberlee, Laura, and Wendy, who are actively engaged in winery operations. Light snacks are available in the tasting room. Children and leashed pets are welcome.

White Wines: Fiesta White, Kilaurwen White, Riesling.

Red Wines: Cabernet Franc, Cabernet Sauvignon, Fiesta Red.

Price Range: $14–$20

Tastings: $5 per person.

Directions: Take U.S. Route 29 to Ruckersville and turn onto U.S. 33 West to Stanardsville. Turn left onto Dyke Road (Route 810) and drive 5.1 miles. Turn right onto Evergreen Church Road. The winery entrance will be 1/3 mile on the right.

Moss Vineyards
1849 Simmons Gap Road
Nortonsville VA 22935

Hours: F–Su 11:00–5:00 (Mar–mid-Nov)
Closed mid-Nov–Feb
Stay Tuned: Facebook, Twitter

434-990-0111
www.mossvineyards.net
E-mail: mossvineyards@gmail.com

Barry Moss opened Moss Vineyards to the public in 2012, three years after first planting the winery's vineyards. Visitors can enjoy scenic views of the winery's vineyards and the hills beyond from the tasting room, which was designed by Barry, an architect in the Norfolk area. A fireplace inside helps warm chilly autumn afternoons, and the tasting room deck offers ample outdoor seating. Moss Vineyards hosts occasional special events and live music. Children and leashed dogs are welcome.

White Wines: Viognier.

Rosé Wines: Rosé.

Red Wines: Archittetura, Cabernet Franc, Vino Rosso *(Bordeaux-style blend)*.

Price Range: $10–$48

Tastings: $5 per person.

Directions: Take U.S. Route 29 to Ruckersville and turn onto U.S. 33 West to Stanardsville. Turn left onto Dyke Road (Route 810) and drive 8 miles. Turn right onto Simmons Gap Road. The winery entrance will be about 1/3 mile on the left.

Mountfair Vineyards
4875 Fox Mountain Road
Mountfair VA 22932

Hours: F–Su 12:00–6:00 (Mar–Nov)   434-823-7605
Closed Dec–Apr   www.mountfair.com
Stay Tuned: Facebook, newsletter   E-mail: info@mountfair.com

Located on the eastern slope of the Blue Ridge Mountains just west of Charlottesville, Mountfair Vineyards opened to the public in 2008 with a focus on small-batch production of Bordeaux-style blends. The winery currently produces about five hundred cases of wine annually; as a small-lot producer, the specific wines available for tasting and sale may vary considerably from month to month. Mountfair hosts quarterly parties at which the winery introduces its newest vintages. The winery is available for weddings and private events. Pets are welcome.

Red Wines: Belated, Cabernet Franc, Composition, Engagement, Indigenous, Merlot, Wooloomooloo.

Price Range: $25

Groups: Please call ahead for groups of 6 or more.

Purchasing: Online ordering available to CA, CO, FL, NC, NY, VA, and WA

Wine Club members receive regular wine shipments, discounts on purchases, and first call on all new wine vintages.

Directions: From Charlottesville and U.S. Route 29 North, take Barracks Road West, which becomes Garth Road. Continue to the village of White Hall, where the road curves to the right at the Piedmont Store and becomes Browns Gap Turnpike (Route 614). Follow Browns Gap Turnpike for 4 miles. Turn right onto Fox Mountain Road (portions unpaved) and cross the Doyles River bridge. The winery entrance will be on the right in 1/3 mile. (Note: Some map websites and GPS units may not recognize Mountfair as a town; use Crozet instead.)

Reynard Florence Vineyard
16109 Burnley Road
Barboursville VA   22973

Hours: Sa–Su 11:00–5:00   540-832-3895
Closed New Year's, Christmas   www.reynardflorence.com
Stay Tuned: Facebook, Twitter   E-mail: info@reynardflorence.com

Reynard Florence was established by Roe and Dee Allison, who planted their first vines in 2006 and produced their first vintage three years later, working with Michael Shaps. The winery's name combines the old French spelling for "fox" (Reynard) with Dee's first name (Florence). The Allisons' flagship white variety is Petit Manseng, which they use both as a pure varietal and in blending with other grapes. The tasting room overlooks the production facility, which Roe often uses for informal jam sessions with friends on weekends. Children and pets are welcome.

White Wines: Petit Manseng, Reynard Blanc.

Red Wines: Cabernet Franc, Grenache, Merlot.

Price Range: $18–$32

Tastings: $5 per person.

Directions: From U.S. Route 29, take U.S. Route 33 East at Ruckersville. Continue 3.6 miles and turn right onto Burnley Road. The winery entrance will be 1.6 miles on the left.

Stinson Vineyards
4744 Sugar Hollow Road
Crozet VA   22932

Hours: Th–Su 11:00–5:00   434-823-7300
Closed New Year's, Thanksgiving, Christmas   www.stinsonvineyards.com
Stay Tuned: Facebook, Twitter, newsletter   E-mail: info@stinsonvineyards.com

Scott and Martha Stinson opened Stinson Vineyards in 2011 on the grounds of the historic Piedmont House, which dates from 1796. Scott is an architect who purchased the property with the intent of renovating it and became intrigued at the idea of making wine when he discovered an abandoned vineyard on the grounds. The tasting room offers sandwiches and food platters for purchase, or guests may bring their own for a picnic on the patio.

White Wines: Chardonnay, Sauvignon Blanc, Sugar Hollow White.

Rosé Wines: Rosé.

Red Wines: Cabernet Franc, Sugar Hollow Red.

Sweet/Dessert Wines: Petit Manseng Dessert.

Fortified Wines: Imperialis *(port-style)*.

Price Range: $16–$29

Tastings: $5 per person.

Directions: From Charlottesville and U.S. Route 29 North, take Barracks Road West, which becomes Garth Road. Continue through the village of White Hall; stay straight in order to go onto Sugar Hollow Road when the main road bends to the right. The winery will be immediately on the right.

Stone Mountain Vineyards
1376 Wyatt Mountain Road
Dyke VA 22935

Hours: F–Su, M holidays 11:00–5:00, Mar– mid-Dec   434-990-9463 (WINE)
Closed Easter, mid-Dec–Feb   www.stonemountainvineyards.com
Stay Tuned: Newsletter   E-mail: info@stonemountainvineyards.com

Stone Mountain was founded in 1986 by Al Breiner after a vacation to Germany's Rhine Valley. The winery has now expanded to twenty acres under the guidance of Al's son Chris, who also serves as winemaker and works with noted Virginia vintner Gabriele Rausse. The tasting room includes an observation deck that offers sweeping views of the valley beneath its 1,700-foot elevation. Visitors are welcome to picnic on the grounds, either with snacks purchased at the winery or their own picnic lunches from home. The winery offers sunset dinners and open houses.

Stone Mountain also has a two-bedroom guesthouse on the winery grounds that is available for rent.

White Wines: Bacon Hollow Revenuer's Select *(Chardonnay, Pinot Grigio)*, Chardonnay, Pinot Grigio, Viognier.

Rosé Wines: Maquillage *(Cabernet Sauvignon, Sangiovese, Cabernet Franc, Chardonnay).*

Red Wines: Bacon Hollow Sunset *(Cabernet Franc)*, Cabernet Franc, Cabernet Sauvignon, Malbec, Merlot, Petit Verdot, Twelve Barrels Meritage.

Price Range: $12–$26

Purchasing: Online purchasing available via VinoShipper for AK, FL, ID, LA, MO, NE, NV, NH, NM, ND, OH, OR, DC, WV, and WY.

Directions: Take U.S. Route 29 to Ruckersville and turn onto U.S. Route 33 West to Stanardsville. Turn left onto Dyke Road (Route 810) to the village of Dyke, and turn right onto Bacon Hollow Road (Route 627). Drive 3.6 miles and turn left onto Wyatt Mountain Road (Route 632) (unpaved). Drive up the winding and narrow gravel mountain road 2 miles to the winery entrance on left. (Winery advises not using a GPS unit.)

White Hall Vineyards
5184 Sugar Ridge Road
White Hall VA 22987

Hours: W–Su 11:00–5:00

434-823-8615

Closed New Year's, Easter, Thanksgiving,

www.whitehallvineyards.com

Christmas Eve & Day

E-mail: tastingroom@whitehallvineyards.com

Stay Tuned: Facebook, Twitter, newsletter

Tony and Edie Champ established White Hall in 1992 with the planting of their six-acre vineyard. Now expanded to forty-five acres, White

Hall's production is supervised by winemaker Michael Panczak, who got his start in the California wine industry. The winery tasting room includes ample seating and a large fireplace that invite visitors to linger after their tastings. The facilities include a large banquet room on the second floor with expansive views of the Blue Ridge that is available for private parties or weddings. Children are welcome.

White Wines: Chardonnay, Gewurztraminer, Petit Manseng, Pinot Gris, Sugar Ridge White, Viognier.

Rosé Wines: Vin Gris.

Red Wines: Breakheart Red, Cabernet Franc, Cabernet Sauvignon, Cuvée des Champs *(Bordeaux-style blend)*, Merlot, Petit Verdot, Syrah, White Hall Red.

Sweet/Dessert Wines: Edichi *(Touriga Nacional, Petit Verdot)*, Soliterre.

Price Range: $10–$30

Tastings: $5 per person.

Wheelchair accessible.

Purchasing: Online purchasing available for AK, CA, DC, FL, IA, MN, NM, OH, and VA residents.

Wine Club members receive regular shipments, discounts on purchases, and invitations to special events.

Directions: From Charlottesville and U.S. Route 29 North, take Barracks Road West, which becomes Garth Road. Continue to the village of White Hall, where the road curves to the right at the Piedmont Store and becomes Browns Gap Turnpike (Route 614). Take the first left onto Sugar Ridge Road (portions unpaved). The winery will be 1.5 miles on the right.

SWEET WINES

Sweet wines can range widely from lightly sweet, or "off dry," wines—enjoyed on their own or with food—to rich, almost voluptuous wines that are an exquisite finish to a fine meal.

While the sweetness of a wine is technically defined by its residual sugar (the percentage of sugar per liter of liquid), a wine's perceived sweetness depends on its acidity, tannins, alcohol strength, and serving temperature. This means that wines with as little as 1.5% residual sugar can taste quite sweet.

Sweet wines are made by stopping fermentation before all the natural sugars have been consumed, by adding grape sugar (called "sweet reserve") after fermentation, or by concentrating the grapes' sweetness before fermentation.

While the first two methods are done after the process of making wine from grapes has begun, concentrating the fruit's natural sweetness takes place in advance. The three main ways of concentrating sweetness are by freezing the grapes, drying the grapes, or delaying harvest.

Ice wines are just what they sound like. Grapes are either allowed to freeze on the vine or are frozen through mechanical means after being harvested. Depending on the altitude of a vineyard and the climate of a given year, some Virginia wineries are occasionally able to make true "frozen on the vine" ice wines.

Sweet wine may be made from grapes that have been spread on trays or mats and allowed to dry or "raisin" before the winemaking process begins. Potomac Point Winery, for instance, offers a Vin de Paille as part of its selection of wines; *paille* means "straw" in French and refers to the straw mats traditionally used to dry grapes.

Late-harvest wines use grapes that have been left on the vine to the point of ultraripeness or even raisining before they are harvested. This concentrates the natural sugars of the grapes and gives their juice an added richness of flavor.

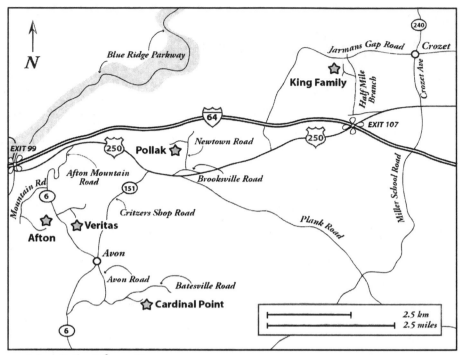

Map 8.6. Afton-Crozet

AFTON-CROZET

Afton Mountain Vineyards
234 Vineyard Lane
Afton VA 22920

Hours: W–M 11:00–6:00 (Mar–Dec),
F–M 11:00–5:00 (Dec–Feb)
Closed New Year's, Easter,
Thanksgiving, Christmas
Stay Tuned: Facebook, Twitter, newsletter

540-456-8667
www.aftonmountainvineyards.com
E-mail: finewines@aftonmountainvineyards.com

Nestled at the base of its namesake mountain, Afton Mountain Vineyards is located on the site of the former Bacchanal Vineyards, one of the pioneer vineyards of Virginia. Owned and operated by Tony and Elizabeth Smith since 2009, Afton Mountain produces a dozen wines—from a sparkling méthode champenoise to an ice wine—under the guidance of winemaker Lucien Dimani. Afton's picnic area offers a lovely view of the Virginia countryside and of Afton Mountain itself. Picnic foods are available from the tasting room. The winery is available for weddings. Dogs are welcome.

Sparkling Wines: Tête de Cuvée.

White Wines: Chardonnay, Gewurtztraminer, Mountain White *(Chardonnay, Riesling, Vidal Blanc)*, Riesling.

Rosé Wines: Mountain Rosé.

Red Wines: Cabernet Franc, Cabernet Sauvignon, Festa di Bacco *(Super Tuscan-style)*, Merlot, Mountain Red *(Sangiovese, Cabernet Franc)*, Petit Verdot, Pinot Noir.

Sweet/Dessert Wines: Pentola d'Oro *(Gewurztraminer, Muscat)*.

Price Range: $14–$42

Tastings: $5 per person for regular, $8 per person for reserve.

Groups: Reservations required 24 hours in advance for group of 6 to 15 and one week in advance for groups of 15 to 35; $10 per person fee. Reservations required for buses, campers, and RVs.

Wheelchair accessible.

Wine Club members receive wine shipments, discounts, and special events.

Directions: **From I-64 Westbound,** take Exit 107 onto U.S. Route 250 West; drive 6.7 miles and turn left onto Afton Mountain Road (Route 6). **From I-64 Eastbound,** take Exit 99 onto U.S. Route 250 East; drive 1.9 miles and turn right onto Afton Mountain Road (Route 6). Descend 1.6 miles and turn right onto Mountain Road (Route 631). Drive 1.2 miles to the winery's long driveway on the left.

Cardinal Point Vineyard & Winery
9423 Batesville Road
Afton VA 22920

Hours: Daily 11:00–5:30   540-456-8400
Closed New Year's, Easter, Thanksgiving, Christmas   www.cardinalpointwinery.com
Stay Tuned: Facebook, Twitter, newsletter   E-mail: info@cardinalpointwinery.com

Cardinal Point was founded by Paul and Ruth Gorman, whose son Tim now serves as the vineyard manager and winemaker. Cardinal Point offers visitors a video tour of the winemaking process from the tasting room, which also includes a small gift area. The winery sponsors a number of special events, including an annual oyster roast and live music, and may be rented for private events. Children and pets are welcome.

White Wines: A6 *(Viognier, Chardonnay)*, Chardonnay, Quattro *(Riesling, Gewurztraminer, Viognier, Traminette)*, Riesling+Gewurztraminer, Viognier.

Rosé Wines: Rosé *(Cabernet Franc).*

Red Wines: Cabernet Franc, Cabernet Franc+Viognier, Cabernet Sauvignon+Petit Verdot+Cabernet Franc, Rockfish Red *(Cabernet Franc).*

Sweet/Dessert Wines: Tess *(Riesling).*

Price Range: $15–$22

Tastings: $5 per person; fee waived for teachers and military personnel with valid ID.

Groups: Reservations required for groups of 10 or more.

Wheelchair accessible

Purchasing: Online purchasing is available for residents of FL, MD, MN, NC, VA, and DC.

Case Club members receive discounts on purchases, free tastings, and invitations to members-only events.

Directions: **From I-64 Eastbound,** take Exit 99 onto U.S. Route 250 East, and drive 3.8 miles to a right onto Critzers Shop Road (Route 151). **From I-64 Westbound,** take Exit 107 onto U.S. Route 250 West; drive 4.8 miles and make a left onto Critzers Shop Road (Route 151). Once on Route 151, drive 2.5 miles and make a left onto Avon Road. Drive one mile and turn left onto Batesville Road. The winery will be 1/2 mile on the right.

King Family Vineyards & Roseland Polo Farm
6550 Roseland Farm
Crozet VA 22932

Hours: Daily 10::00–5:30

Closed New Year's Eve & Day, Easter,

Thanksgiving, Christmas Eve & Day

Stay Tuned: Facebook, Twitter, newsletter

434-823-7800

www.kingfamilyvineyards.com

E-mail: info@kingfamilyvineyards.com

King Family Vineyards was founded in 1998 by Texas natives David and Ellen King. The winery's tasting room features a fireplace and a number of small tables at which visitors may sit after over a glass or bottle of wine. The covered veranda and grassy lawn in front of the tasting room offer a spot to relax over a picnic lunch which may be brought from home or purchased at the winery. King Family hosts a range of special events, including Sunday afternoon polo matches (summers only), harvest dinners, and exhibits by local artists. The facility may also be rented for private events, parties, and weddings. Mathieu Finot, a native of Crozes-Hermitage in France's Rhone Valley, serves as the winemaker. Chocolates, cheeses, salamis, spreads, and French bread are available for purchase at the winery. Children and pets are welcome.

Sparkling Wines: Brut.

White Wines: Chardonnay, Roseland *(Chardonnay, Viognier)*, Viognier.

Rosé Wines: Crosé *(Merlot)*.

Red Wines: Cabernet Franc, Meritage, Merlot, Petit Verdot.

Sweet/Dessert Wines: Loreley 'Late Harvest' *(Viognier, Petit Manseng)*.

Fortified Wines: Seven *(Merlot, aged in bourbon barrels)*.

Price Range: $17–$35

Tastings: $5 per person with souvenir glass.

Groups: Reservations required for groups of 8 or more; $10 per person fee for tasting and tour, with $80 reservation charge.

Wheelchair accessible

Wine Club members receive regular shipments, discounts on purchases, and invitations to special events.

Directions: From I-64, take Exit 107 (Crozet) and turn onto U.S. Route 250 East. Drive 1/2 mile and make a left onto Hillsboro Lane (Route 797).

Make the first right onto Half Mile Branch (Route 684) and drive one mile to the winery entrance on left.

Pollak Vineyards
330 Newtown Road
Greenwood VA 22943

Hours: Daily 11:00–5:00, Apr–Oct, W–Su 11:00–5:00, Nov–Mar   540-456-8844

Closed New Year's, Thanksgiving, Christmas   www.pollakvineyards.com

Stay Tuned: Facebook, newsletter   E-mail: info@pollakvineyards.com

Pollak was founded in 2003 by Margo and David Pollak, who came to Virginia from Cincinnati. David spent a number of years in wineries in California's Russian River and Carneros wine regions before establishing his own winery. The ninety-eight-acre farm produces about four thousand cases of estate-grown wine each year, with twenty-five acres currently under vine. The tasting room opened in 2008 and offers visitors scenic views of the vineyards, pond, and adjacent hills from its veranda and tasting area. Hot baguettes and cheese plates are available for purchase to enjoy over a glass or bottle of wine. The winery may be rented for private events, dinners, and weddings. Pets are welcome.

White Wines: Chardonnay, Durant White *(Chardonnay, Viognier, Pinot Gris)*, Pinot Gris, Viognier.

Rosé Wines: Rosé.

Red Wines: Cabernet Franc, Cabernet Sauvignon, Durant Red *(Merlot, Cabernet Franc)*, Meritage, Merlot, Petit Verdot.

Fortified Wine: Mille Fleurs (Viognier, eau-de-vie).

Price Range: $16–$30

Tastings: $5 per person.

Groups: Reservations required for groups of 8 or more and for tour buses and limos.

Wheelchair accessible.

Purchasing: Online ordering available for AK, FL, ID, LA, MO, NE, ND, NH, NM, OH, OR, VA, WV, WY, and DC residents.

Case Club members receive free tastings, invitations to special events.

Directions: From I-64, take Exit 107 (Crozet) and turn onto U.S. Route 250 West. Drive about 3 miles. Just past Ridgeley Estate, turn right onto Brooksville Road (Route 796) and drive 1/2 mile. Turn right again onto Newtown Road. The winery drive will be 1/2 mile on left.

Veritas Vineyards & Winery
151 Veritas Lane
(GPS address: 145 Saddleback Farm)
Afton VA 22920

Hours: M–F 9:30–5:30, Sa–Su 11:00–5:00   540-456-8000
Closed New Year's, Thanksgiving, Christmas   www.veritaswines.com
Stay Tuned: Facebook, Twitter, newsletter   E-mail: contact@veritaswines.com

Veritas is owned by Andrew and Patricia Hodson, who opened the winery to the public in 2002; daughter Emily serves as the winemaker. The spacious tasting room has a long tasting bar as well as armchairs and small sofas for visitors. The veranda offers a view of Veritas's vineyards as well as the Blue Ridge beyond. The facility is available for private events and weddings, and sponsors a variety of special events, including summertime "Starry Nights" and winter winemaker's dinners and festivities. Light fare is available for purchase; picnic foods brought by customers must be consumed outside. Children and pets are welcome, although no pets are allowed for "Starry Nights."

Guests may stay overnight in one of the six suites at The Farmhouse, a restored farmstead originally built in 1836.

Sparkling Wines: Scintilla *(Chardonnay)*, Mousseux *(Merlot)*.

White Wines: Chardonnay, Sauvignon Blanc, Viognier, White Star.

Rosé Wines: Rosé *(Cabernet Franc, Merlot)*.

Red Wines: Cabernet Franc, Claret, Merlot, Red Star *(Cabernet Franc, Merlot, Chambourcin)*, Vintner's Reserve *(Bordeaux-style blend)*.

Sweet/Dessert Wines: Kenmar, Petit Manseng.

Fortified Wines: Othello *(Tannat, Touriga Nacional, Petit Verdot)*.

Price Range: $15–$35

Tastings: $5 per person for flight of white wines, $5 per person for flight of red wines (can vary depending on number of wines available).

Groups: Reservations required for groups of 8 or more. Cellar tours are offered on weekends at 11:00, 12:00, 1:00 and 2:00.

Wheelchair accessible.

Wine Club members receive quarterly shipments, discounts, and members-only events.

Directions: From I-64 Westbound, take Exit 107 onto U.S. Route 250 West; drive 6.7 miles and turn left onto Afton Mountain Road (Route 6). From I-64 Eastbound, take Exit 99 onto U.S. Route 250 East; drive 1.9 miles and turn right onto Afton Mountain Road (Route 6). Descend down the mountain for 2 miles and turn left onto Saddleback Trail. Veritas Lane and the winery parking lot will be on the right.

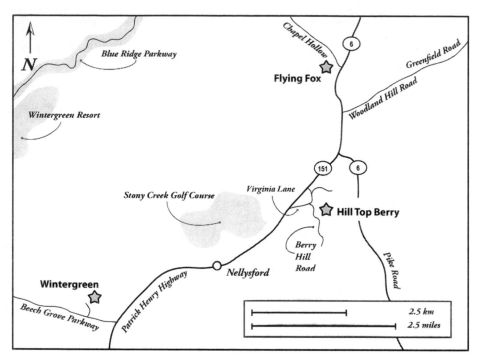

Map 8.7. Rockfish Valley

ROCKFISH VALLEY

Flying Fox Vineyard
27 Chapel Hollow Road
Afton VA 22920

Hours: F–Su 11:00–5:00 (til 6:00 in summer)   434-361-1692
Closed January–February   www.flyingfoxvineyard.com
Stay Tuned: Facebook, newsletter   E-mail: info@flyingfoxvineyard.com

Flying Fox Vineyard is a small family-run winery located in the heart of scenic Nelson County. Owners Rich Evans and Lynn Davis planted the first vines in 2000 and produced their first vintage six years later. Most of the winery's production is estate-grown; Flying Fox supplements its own grape production from nearby vineyards, including Ridge Run Vineyard owned by Lynn's sister and brother-in-law. The tasting room is located next to the Bleu Ridge Bed and Breakfast and is housed in the former stable of this 1840-era inn. The building has a wood-burning fireplace for chilly autumn days and a small pet-friendly picnic area. The tasting room includes art and photography exhibits by local artists. Pets are welcome

White Wines: Chardonnay, Fox White, Pinot Gris, Viognier.

Rosé Wines: Rosé.

Red Wines: Cabernet Franc, Fox Red *(Cabernet Franc, Merlot)*, Merlot, Petit Verdot, Trio *(Bordeaux-style blend)*.

Price Range: $16–$23

Tastings: $5 per person.

Purchasing: Online ordering is available for FL, MD, MN, NC, VA, and DC.

Directions: From I-64 Eastbound, take Exit 99 onto U.S. Route 250 East; drive 3.8 miles and turn right onto Critzers Shop Road (Route 151). From I-64 Westbound, take Exit 107 onto U.S. Route 250 West; drive 4.8 miles and turn left onto Critzers Shop Road (Route 151). Once on Route 151, continue 7 miles to Chapel Hollow Road and the winery on right.

Hill Top Berry Farm & Winery
2800 Berry Hill Road
Nellysford VA 22958

Hours: W–Su 11:00–5:00
Closed New Year's, Easter, Thanksgiving,
Christmas Eve & Day
Stay Tuned: Facebook

434-361-1266
www.hilltopberrywine.com
E-mail: hilltop1@ntelos.net

Hill Top Berry has its roots in a pick-your-own blackberry farm begun by Marlyn and Sue Allen. Over the years, their interest in winemaking grew, with a special focus on "true to the fruit" wines and meads. The winery is now owned and operated by the Allens' daughters, Kimberly Allen Pugh, Crystal Allen Brennan, and Marlo Gayle Allen. Because Hill Top's production is seasonal, offerings in the tasting room vary. The winery offers a covered deck with a view of the farm and Rockfish Valley. Special events include a May Day celebration, a blackberry harvest festival, a fall foliage open house, and a holiday open house. Children and dogs are welcome.

Fruit Wines: Blackberry Delight, Blue Heeler *(blueberry)*, Cranberry, Little Heeler *(blueberry)*, Mountain Apple, Peach, Pear, Three Sisters Elderberry, Virginia Blackberry, Virginia Plum, Virginia Raspberry, Sweet Cherry, Sweet Vixen *(strawberry)*.

Meads: Blue Ridge Mountain Mead Pyment *(concord grapes, honey)*, Dragon's Blood *(pomegranate, honey)*, Perry *(pear, honey)*, Pyment, Rockfish River

Cyser, Lavender Metheglin, Blueberry Melomel, Hunter's Moon Melomel *(pumpkin)*, Nectarine Melomel, Pounding Branch Persimmon Melomel, Raspberry Melomel, Strawberry Melomel.

Price Range: $10–$20

Tastings: $3 per person.

Groups: Please call ahead for groups of 6 or more.

Directions: From I-64 Eastbound, take Exit 99 onto U.S. Route 250 East; drive 3.8 miles and turn right onto Critzers Shop Road (Route 151). From I-64 Westbound, take Exit 107 onto U.S. Route 250 West; drive 4.8 miles and turn left onto Critzers Shop Road (Route 151). Once on Route 151, continue 10 miles and turn left onto Virginia Lane (Route 612). After 0.4 miles, turn right onto Berry Hill Road. Continue 1/3 mile across the bridge and up the hill to the winery on left.

Wintergreen Winery
462 Winery Lane
Nellysford VA 22958

Hours: Daily 10:00–6:00 (Apr–Oct); 10:00–5:00 (Nov–Mar) 434-361-2519
Closed New Year's, Thanksgiving, Christmas www.wintergreenwinery.com
Stay Tuned: Facebook, Twitter, newsletter E-mail: info@wintergreenwinery.com

Originally founded in the late 1980s, Wintergreen Winery has been owned and operated by Jeff and Tamara Stone since 1998. Located near the Wintergreen Resort, the winery houses its tasting room in a restored nineteenth-century carriage house. Wintergreen offers a range of special events throughout the year, including live music, picnics, and wine and cheese pairings. The facility may be rented for weddings and private parties. Children and pets are welcome.

Fruit Wines: Mill Hill Apple, Raspberry.

White Wines: Black Rock Chardonnay, Three Ridges White, Thomas Nelson White, Viognier.

Red Wines: Black Rock Red, Brent's Mountain Merlot, Raven's Roost Cabernet Franc, Three Ridges Red.

Price Range: $12–$24

Tastings: $5 per person with souvenir glass.

Groups: Reservations required for groups of 10 or more; fee will vary depending on size of group.

Wheelchair accessible.

Purchasing: E-mail ordering for residents of Virginia and Washington D.C.

Directions: From I-64 Eastbound, take Exit 99 onto U.S. Route 250 East; drive 3.8 miles and turn right onto Critzers Shop Road (Route 151). From I-64 Westbound, take Exit 107 onto U.S. Route 250 West; drive 4.8 miles and turn left onto Critzers Shop Road (Route 151). Once on Route 151, drive 14 miles and turn right onto Beech Grove Parkway (Route 664). The winery driveway will be 1/2 mile on right.

FORTIFIED WINES

Fortified wines, quite simply, are wines whose alcohol strength has been raised by adding some form of grape spirit, such as brandy. During fermentation, the grape juice's natural sugar is converted into alcohol through the action of yeasts. If left uninterrupted, this process will continue until all the sugar has been consumed. In fortified wine production, extra alcohol is added before, during, or after fermentation.

The most well-known fortified wines are from the Iberian peninsula and the Portuguese island of Madeira.

Sherry originated in southwest Spain in the area around the city of Jerez, from which it draws its name. Made from the Palomino, Pedro Ximénez, and Muscat of Alexandria grapes, sherry is fortified after fermentation has occurred. Classic Spanish sherries are dry and range from the light and elegant Fino to the more concentrated Oloroso.

Port wines take their name from the Portuguese city of Oporto in the Douro region. Grape varieties traditionally used for port include Touriga Nacional, Touriga Francesa, Tinta Cão, Tinta Barroca, and Tinta Roriz. Because port wine is fortified during the fermentation process, the result is a sweet and strong wine.

Madeira is from the island of the same name. It originated by chance in the seventeenth century when merchants discovered that wine transported by ship across the tropics was transformed into a rich, sweet wine with an exceptional shelf life. Madeiras now are fortified during fermentation and then heated to caramelize the sugars. Madeira was very popular among American colonists in the seventeenth and eighteenth centuries. Indeed, patriots at the Second Continental Congress toasted the signing of the Declaration of Independence in 1776 with glasses of madeira.

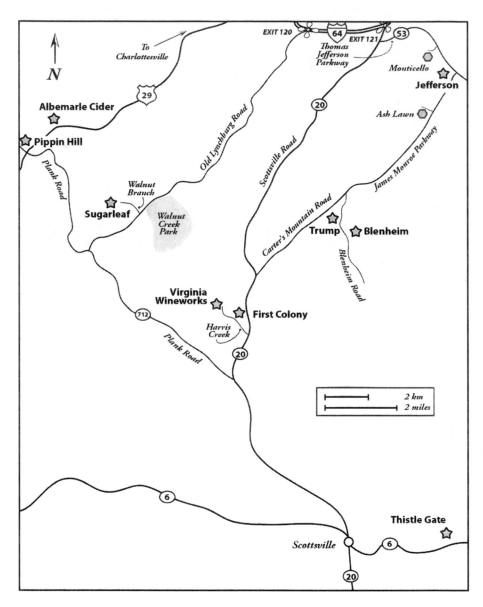

Map 8.8. Lower Monticello (eastern section)

LOWER MONTICELLO

Albemarle Cider Works
2545 Rural Ridge Lane
North Garden VA 22959

Hours: W–Su 11:00–5:00
Closed New Year's, Thanksgiving, Christmas
Stay Tuned: Facebook, Twitter

434-297-2326
www.vintagevirginiaapples.com
E-mail: fruit@vintagevirginiaapples.com

Chuck and Charlotte Shelton opened Albemarle Cider Works in 2009 as a collateral line to their family's Rural Ridge Orchard, which specializes in heirloom apples. The cidery offers an apple festival as well as various workshops on apple growing and cider making throughout the year. Live music is featured on summertime Second Sunday Ciders, when guests are invited to come picnic on the grounds. Guests are welcome to stay overnight in the cidery's Rural Ridge Cottage, which can be booked through the Crossroads Inn website.

Ciders:

Jupiter's Legacy is a dry sparkling cider made from the classic cider apple varieties of Harrison, Yates, Hyslop, and Virginia Crab.

Royal Pippin is a dry, champagne-like cider produced from Albemarle Pippins.

Ragged Mountain is a semi-dry cider pressed from a blend of Albemarle Pippin, Winesap, Black Twig, Grimes Golden, and Smyrna apples.

Old Virginia Winesap is a spicy, tart cider made from Winesap apples.

Price Range: $16

Tastings: $3 per person.

Directions: From I-64, take Exit 118 and turn onto U.S. Route 29 South. Drive 8 miles and turn right onto Rural Ridge Lane at the Rural Ridge Orchard.

Blenheim Vineyards
31 Blenheim Farm
Charlottesville VA 22902

Hours: Daily 11:00–5:30
Closed New Year's Eve & Day, Thanksgiving,
Christmas Eve & Day
Stay Tuned: Facebook, Twitter

434-293-5366
www.blenheimvineyards.com
E-mail: info@blenheimvineyards.com

Blenheim Vineyards was established in 2000 by Dave Matthews on the historic Blenheim estate that dates to a 1730 land grant to John Carter, son of Robert "King" Carter and is named after a key battle won by England's Duke of Marlborough, an ancestor of Winston Churchill. Blenheim's winery and tasting room are in one building, with the tasting area on the top floor and the winemaking facilities located below and visible through paneled glass floors. A deck and outdoor tables are also available for spending time over a glass of wine and the various cheeses and snacks that are available for sale. The winery is available for rental for private events. Children are welcome.

White Wines: Chardonnay, Painted White, Viognier, White Table Wine.

Rosé Wines: Rosé.

Red Wines: Cabernet Franc, Cabernet Sauvignon, Painted Red *(Bordeaux-style blend)*, Petit Verdot, Red Table Wine, Seven Oaks Merlot, Syrah.

Price Range: $14–$30

Tastings: $5 per person.

Groups: Reservations required for groups of 8 or more; cellar tastings available for groups of 20 or more, $10 per person fee; private tour and tasting available with reservations, $25 per person fee.

Restrictions: No dogs.

Purchasing: Online purchases are available for residents of AZ, CA, CO, FL, GA, ID, IL, IN, IA, KS, ME, MD, MI, MN, MO, NE, ND, NM, NV, NH, NY, NC, OH, OR, SC, TN, TX, VA, VT, WA, DC, WI, WV, and WY.

Wine Club members receive regular wine shipments, free tastings, discounts on wine purchase and special winery events.

Directions: From I-64 East, take Exit 121A (Scottsville) onto Route 20 South. Drive 1/2 mile and turn left onto Thomas Jefferson Parkway (Route 53). After 3.2 miles, make a slight right onto the James Monroe Parkway, which becomes Carters Mountain Road after 2.6 miles. Drive another 2.2 miles and turn left onto Blenheim Road. The winery entrance will be 1/2 mile on the right.

DelFosse Vineyards & Winery
500 DelFosse Winery Lane
(GPS: 4649 Old Roberts Mountain Road)
Faber VA 22938

Hours: W–Su 11:00–5:00
Closed Thanksgiving, Christmas
Stay Tuned: Facebook, Twitter

434-263-6100
www.delfossewine.com
E-mail: finewines@delfossewine.com

Claude and Geneviève DelFosse founded their winery and vineyard in 2000 about thirty minutes south of Charlottesville. The light-filled

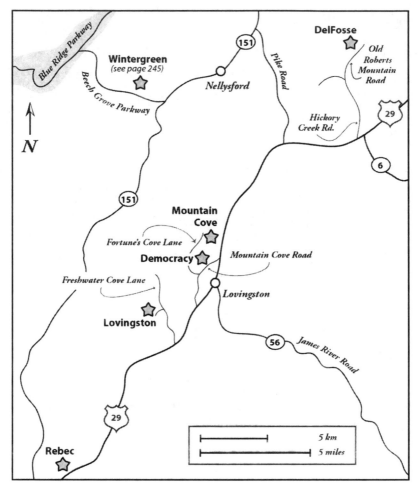

Map 8.9. Lower Monticello (western section)

tasting room offers tables overlooking the terraced vineyards and nearby lake. Visitors are welcome to stay over a glass of wine and a cheese platter purchased at the winery. DelFosse sponsors a range of events, including a Labor Day weekend barbecue, French crêpe days, wine and food pairings, and a New Year's Day brunch. The facilities are available for rental for private parties and weddings. Children and pets are welcome.

A restored century-old cabin that once served as the original tasting room is available for overnight stays (two-night minimum). DelFosse's grounds also include 5.5 miles of trails for visitors to explore.

White Wines: Chardonnay, Deer Rock Farm White, Petit Manseng, Réserve d'Oriane, Sauvignon Blanc, Viognier.

Rosé Wines: Rosé.

Red Wines: Cabernet Franc, Cabernet Sauvignon, Cuvée Laurent, Deer Rock Red, Grand Cru Olivier, Malbec, Merlot, Meritage, Petit Verdot.

Sweet/Dessert Wines: Ambrosia *(Petit Manseng, Vidal Blanc).*

Fortified Wines: Meditation *(port-style).*

Price Range: $16–$29

Tastings: $5 per person, $10 for reserve tasting.

Groups: Please call ahead for groups of 8 or more.

Wheelchair accessible.

Wine Club members receive wine shipments, discounts on purchases.

Directions: From I-64, take Exit 118 onto U.S. Route 29 South toward Lovingston and drive 18.4 miles. Turn right onto Hickory Creek Road (Route 616) and drive 2.3 miles. Turn right onto Old Roberts Mountain Road and drive 0.8 miles to the entrance on left.

Democracy Vineyards
585 Mountain Cove Road
Lovingston VA   22949

Hours: Sa 11:00–5:00, Su 1:00–5:00, M holidays 12:00–5:00   434-263-8463
Closed Easter, late Nov–Mar   www.democracyvineyards.com
Stay Tuned: Newsletter   E-mail: info@democracyvineyards.com

Susan Prokop and Jim Turpin founded their winery in 2009 on the grounds of an old apple orchard and opened their tasting room to the public three years later. The couple has a long background in politics, a professional interest that is reflected in the choice of names for their wines as well as in the political memorabilia that decorates the tasting room. Winemaker Michael Shaps uses all Virginia grapes for the wines, either from Democracy's own vines or other Virginia vineyards.

Fruit Wines: Village View Gold *(apple)*.

White Wines: Declaration, Republic, Unum.

Red Wines: Campaign, Emancipation *(Merlot)*, Suffrage *(Chambourcin)*.

Sweet/Dessert Wines: Alabaster.

Price Range: $14–$19

Tastings: $5 per person.

Purchasing: Online purchasing is available for AK, AR, AZ, CA, CO, CT, DC, FL, GA, HI, ID, IL, IN, IA, KS, LA, ME, MD, MI, MN, MO, NE, NV, NH, NM, NY, NC, ND, OH, OR, PA, SC, TN, TX, VA, WA, DC, WV, WI, and WY.

Directions: From I-64, take Exit 118 onto U.S. Route 29 South and drive 28 miles. Turn right onto Mountain Cove Road (Route 718) and drive one mile to the winery on the right.

First Colony Winery
1650 Harris Creek Road
Charlottesville VA 22902

Hours: M–F 10:00–5:00, Sa 11:00–6:00, Su 11:00–5:00   434-979-7105

Closed New Year's, Thanksgiving, Christmas   www.firstcolonywinery.com

Stay Tuned: Facebook, newsletter   E-mail: info@firstcolonywinery.com

Founded in 2000 by Randy McElroy, First Colony Winery is now owned by Bruce and Heather Spiess and Jeff Miller, who work with wine-maker Jason Hayman. The tasting room offers seating at several small tables indoors, as well as outdoor decks under the trees that surround the building. Guests may purchase crackers and cheese for a snack on the grounds; groups under 10 may also bring their own food from home for a picnic. First Colony also sponsors a number of events and may be rented for private events, parties, and weddings. Children and pets are welcome.

White Wines: Chardonnay, Seyval Blanc, Sweet Shanando *(Vidal Blanc)*, Viognier, Zephyr *(Vidal Blanc, Petit Manseng)*.

Rosé Wines: Rosé.

Red Wines: Cabernet Franc, Cabernet Sauvignon, Claret *(Cabernet Sauvignon, Cabernet Franc, Touriga Nacional, Petit Verdot)*, Meritage, Merlot, Petit Verdot, Tannat.

Sweet/Dessert Wines: Late Harvest *(Traminette)*.

Price Range: $15–$25

Tastings: $5 per person.

Groups: Reservations required for groups of 10 or more.

Purchasing: Online purchasing is available for AK, AL, AR, AZ, CA, CO, CT, DC, DE, FL, GA, HI, ID, IL, IN, IA, LA, ME, MI, MN, MO,

NE, NH, NM, NV, NY, NC, ND, OH, OR, RI, SC, SD, TX, VA, VT, WA, WV, WI, and WY.

Directions: From I-64, take Exit 121A and merge onto Route 20 South. Drive 10.4 miles and turn right onto Harris Creek Road (portions unpaved). Winery will be on right in 3/4 mile.

Jefferson Vineyards
1353 Thomas Jefferson Parkway
Charlottesville VA 22902

Hours: Daily 10:00–6:00 (Apr–Nov), 9:00–5:00 (Dec–Mar)   434-977-3042
Closed Easter, Thanksgiving, Christmas   www.jeffersonvineyards.com
Stay Tuned: Facebook, Twitter   E-mail: info@jeffersonvineyards.com

Jefferson Vineyards is located midway between Thomas Jefferson's Monticello and James Monroe's Ash Lawn on the site of the vineyard originally planted by Filippo Mazzei for Jefferson. Owner Stanley Woodward decided in 1981 to resurrect the vineyard which now includes twenty acres of vines replanted under the guidance of Gabriele Rausse. While there is no seating in the tasting room itself, guests may relax on the deck between the tasting room and the winery building. All the winery's production is from Virginia-grown grapes. Jefferson Vineyards occasionally hosts formal winemaker dinners, including an annual Fête de la Bastille (14 July).

White Wines: Chardonnay, Pinot Gris, Riesling, Vin Blanc *(Traminette, Petit Manseng)*, Vin de Trois *(Viognier, Traminette, Petit Manseng)*, Viognier.

Rosé Wines: Rosé.

Red Wines: Cabernet Franc, Estate Reserve, Meritage, Merlot, Petit Verdot, Vin Rouge *(Chambourcin)*.

Price Range: $16–$30

Tastings: $10 per person, with souvenir glass.

Groups: Reservations required for groups of 10 or more, $10 fee per person.

Wheelchair accessible.

Restrictions: No tour buses.

Connoisseur's Club members receive regular shipments, discounts.

Directions: From I-64, take Exit 121A and turn onto Route 20 South. After 1/2 mile, turn left at the traffic light onto Thomas Jefferson Parkway (Route 53) and drive 3.3 miles to the winery entrance on the right.

Lovingston Winery
885 Freshwater Cove Lane
Lovingston VA 22949

Hours: W–F 10:00–4:00, Sa–Su 11:00–5:00 (Apr–Nov)   434-263-8467
Closed Thanksgiving, Dec–Mar   www.lovingstonwinery.com
Stay Tuned: Facebook, Twitter   E-mail: info@lovingstonwinery.com

Lovingston Winery, located just south of Charlottesville, was opened to the public in 2010 by owners Ed and Janet Puckett. The Pucketts had cultivated a vineyard in Georgia for several years before moving to Virginia when their daughter enrolled at the University of Virginia. Their tasting room is housed on the ground floor in the winery itself, allowing visitors a good view of the winemaking process in action from the second-floor tasting room. Winemaker Riaan Rossouw, a South African native, currently oversees Lovingston's 8.5 acres of vines and wine production.

White Wines: Chardonnay, Petit Manseng, Wahoo White.

Rosé Wines: Rosé.

Red Wines: Cabernet Franc, Estate Reserve, Lovwine *(Merlot, Petit Verdot)*, Merlot, Pinotage, Rotunda Red *(Bordeaux-style blend)*.

Price Range: $15–$27

Purchasing: Online shipping available to AK, CA, FL, GA, MI, MN, NY, NC, TX, VA, and DC.

Directions: From I-64, take Exit 118 onto U.S. Route 29 South. Drive 32.6 miles and turn right onto Freshwater Cove Lane (Route 653). The winery entrance will be on the left in 1 mile.

Mountain Cove Vineyards
1362 Fortune's Cove Lane
Lovingston VA 22949

Hours: W–Su 12:00–5:00 (Mar–Dec)   434-263-5392
Closed Thanksgiving, Christmas, Jan–Feb   www.mountaincovevineyards.com
                                                E-mail: aweed1@juno.com

Founded in 1973 by Al and Emily Weed, Mountain Cove is the oldest winery still operating in Virginia. The vineyards and winery are located in the heart of Nelson County in a scenic valley next to Fortune's Cove, a Nature Conservancy property with numerous hiking trails. As a small family-operated winery, one of the owners is likely to be on hand to greet visitors. Mountain Cove's wines are all vegan and, with the exception of its Chardonnay, all estate grown. While the tasting room has no indoor seating, the winery grounds include a pavilion. The facilities may be rented for private events and weddings.

Fruit Wines: Apple, Blackberry, Peach.

White Wines: Chardonnay, Skyline White *(Villard Blanc, Vidal Blanc)*, Traminette, Vidal Blanc.

Rosé Wines: Skyline Rosé.

Red Wines: Cabernet Franc, Cabernet Sauvignon, Chambourcin, Tinto *(Norton, Chambourcin, Cabernet Franc)*.

Price Range: $12–$15

Wheelchair accessible.

Directions: From I-64, take Exit 118 onto U.S. Route 29 South and drive 28 miles. Turn right onto Mountain Cove Road (Route 718) and drive 1.6 miles. Turn right onto Fortune's Cove Lane. The winery will be 1.4 miles on the right.

Pippin Hill Farm & Vineyards
5022 Plank Road
North Garden VA 22959

Hours: Tu–Su 11:00–5:00   434-202-8063
Closed Thanksgiving, Christmas Eve & Day, 1–15 Jan   www.pippinhillfarm.com/winery
Stay Tuned: Facebook   E-mail: info@pippinhillfarm.com

Lynn and Dean Andrews opened Pippin Hill Farm to the public in 2011. Their focus is on sustainable agriculture and eco-friendly practices. Light fare is available for purchase in the tasting room. While Pippin Hill's own vineyards are maturing, the winery is leasing vineyards from elsewhere in the Monticello region for its production. The winery is available for rental for private parties and weddings. Children and pets are welcome.

Sparkling Wines: Blanc de Blanc *(Chardonnay)*.

White Wines: Chardonnay, Viognier.

Rosé Wines: Summer Farm Rosé *(Cabernet Franc)*.

Red Wines: Cabernet Franc, Cabernet Sauvignon, Merlot, Winemaker's Select Red *(Cabernet Franc, Chambourcin)*.

Sweet/Dessert Wines: Vin Doux Naturale *(Petit Manseng)*.

Price Range: $19–$30

Tastings: $6 for tastes of four wines.

Groups: Please call ahead for groups of 10 or more.

Directions: From I-64, take Exit 118 and turn onto U.S. Route 29 South. Drive 9 miles and turn right onto Plank Road. The winery entrance will be on the right in 1/4 mile.

Rebec Vineyards
2229 North Amherst Highway
Amherst VA 24521

Hours: Daily 10:00–5:00

Closed New Year's, Thanksgiving, Christmas

Stay Tuned: Facebook, Twitter, newsletter

434-946-5168

www.rebecwinery.com

E-mail: winery@rebecwinery.com

Richard and Lynn Hanson founded Rebec on their seventy-acre farm at the edge of the Blue Ridge and began selling wines to the public in 1988. The winery was designed and built by Richard and son-in-law Mark Magruder, who used wood salvaged from old outbuildings on the property, including a two-hundred-year-old tobacco barn. Owner/winemaker Svetlozar Kanev has included a Bulgarian-style herbal sweet wine, Sweet

Sofia, in honor of his Bulgarian roots. Visitors are welcome to picnic on the grounds or sit on the deck behind the tasting room.

On the second weekend in October, Rebec hosts the annual Virginia Wine and Garlic Festival. The winery also sponsors a Summer Cooler festival (proceeds are donated to the American Cancer Society) and Third Thursday live music performances. Children and pets are welcome.

White Wines: Chardonnay, Gewurztraminer, Landmark White, Riesling, Viognier.

Red Wines: Cabernet Franc, Cabernet Sauvignon, Landmark *(Tannat, Touriga Nacional)*, Merlot, Pinot Noir.

Sweet/Dessert Wines: Autumn Glow, Landmark, Landmark Dessert, Sweet Briar, Sweet Sofia.

Price Range: $10–$25

Tastings: $5 per person for basic tasting.

Groups: Please call ahead for groups of 8 or more.

Directions: From I-64, take Exit 118 onto U.S. Route 29 South and drive 40.3 miles to the winery entrance on the right. From the town of Amherst, drive 5 miles north on U.S. Route 29 to the winery on the left of the highway.

Thistle Gate Winery
3613 Walnut Branch Lane
North Garden VA 22959

Hours: F–Su 1:00–5:30 (Apr–Dec), Sa 12:00–6:00 (Jan–Feb)   434-979-7105
Closed New Year's, March, Thanksgiving, Christmas   wwww.thistlegatevineyard.com
Stay Tuned: Facebook. newsletter   E-mail: george@caiweb.com

Owned by George and Leslie Cushnie, Thistle Gate opened its tasting room to the public in 2012 after growing their own grapes for six years. Working with winemaker Kirsty Harman (Blenheim Vineyards), the Cushnies are producing all Virginia-grown wines from their own fruit or from grapes from other nearby vineyards. The tasting room includes several tables for indoor seating, as well as outdoor spaces on the veranda and wraparound deck. Children and leashed dogs are welcome.

White Wines: Chardonnay, Thistle White *(Seyval Blanc, Viognier)*.

Rosé Wines: Thistle Blush *(Cabernet Franc, Viognier)*.

Red Wines: Batteau Red, Cabernet Franc, St. George Chambourcin, Thistle Red.

Fortified Wines: Highland *(port-style)*.

Price Range: $14–$27

Tastings: $5 per person.

Wine Club members receive regular wine shipments, purchasing discounts.

Directions: From Charlottesville, take Route 20 south and drive 19 miles. At Scottsville, turn west onto Main Street (VA 6) and drive 1/2 mile. Turn left onto Fluvanna Street to continue following VA 6. Drive 5 miles and turn into the winery entrance on the left..

Trump Winery
3550 Blenheim Road
Charlottesville VA   22902

Hours: Su–F 11:00–6:00, Sa 11:00–8:00

434-984-4855

Closed Thanksgiving, Christmas

www.trumpwinery.com

Stay Tuned: Facebook, Twitter

E-mail: cstrong@trumpwinery.com

Trump Winery is located on the slopes of Carter's Mountain in the Blue Ridge. Light fare is available for purchase and enjoyment on site. The facilities are available for rental for special events, weddings, and dinners. While Trump Winery's own production is being vinted, visitors may purchase Kluge label wines; a sampling of Kluge wines is listed below. The winery is particularly well known for its range of sparkling wines made in the classic méthode champenoise. Last pours for tastings begin thirty minutes before closing.

Sparkling Wines: Kluge Estate Blanc de Blancs *(Chardonnay)*, Kluge Estate Rosé *(Chardonnay, Pinot Noir)*.

White Wines: Albemarle Sauvignon Blanc.

Rosé Wines: Albemarle Rosé.

Red Wines: Albemarle Simply Red, Kluge Estate New World Red *(Bordeaux-style blend)*.

Fortified Wines: Kluge Estate CRU *(Chardonnay, brandy)*.

Price Range: $14–$35

Tastings: $8–$18, depending on flight of wines tasted.

Directions: From I-64 East, take Exit 121A (Scottsville) onto Route 20 South. Drive 1/2 mile and turn left onto Thomas Jefferson Parkway (Route 53). After 3.2 miles, make a slight right onto the James Monroe Parkway, which becomes Carters Mountain Road after 2.6 miles. Drive another 2.2 miles and turn left onto Blenheim Road. The winery entrance will be 1/4 mile on the right.

Virginia Wineworks
1781 Harris Creek Way
Charlottesville VA 22902

Hours: Daily 11:00–5:00

Closed New Year's, Christmas

434-296-3438

www.virginiawineworks.com

E-mail: info@virginiawineworks.com

Virginia Wineworks was established by Virginia vintner Michael Shaps and partner Philip Stafford in 2007. Located in the former Montdomaine winery, Virginia Wineworks produces its wine under two labels. Both make wines sourced from a variety of Virginia vineyards, with the Michael Shaps line using grapes only from vineyards that are leased and managed by Shaps and Stafford themselves. The winery also provides custom crush production for individuals and wineries, both new start-ups and already-established smaller wineries. About twenty Virginia wineries are among Wineworks' customers.

White Wines: Wineworks Chardonnay, Wineworks Viognier, Wineworks White *(Viognier, Vidal Blanc)*, Michael Shaps Chardonnay, Michael Shaps Viognier.

Rosé Wines: Wineworks Rosé.

Red Wines: Wineworks Cabernet Franc, Wineworks Red, Michael Shaps Cabernet Franc, Michael Shaps Merlot, Michael Shaps Meritage, Michael Shaps Petit Verdot.

Sweet/Dessert Wines: Michael Shaps "Raisin d'Être" Late Harvest.

Price Range: $12–$32

Tastings: $5 per person.

Groups: Please call ahead for groups of 8 or more.

Directions: From I-64, take Exit 121A and merge onto Route 20 South. Drive 10.4 miles and turn right onto Harris Creek Road (portions unpaved). The winery will be straight ahead in 1 mile.

Wonder Oak Winery
3613 Walnut Branch Lane
North Garden VA 22959

Hours: Th–Su, holiday M 12:00–6:00 (Mar–Dec)   434-984-4272
Sa-Su 11:00–6:00 (Jan–Feb)   www.sugarleafvineyards.com
Closed New Year's, Thanksgiving, Christmas   E-mail: info@sugarleafvineyards.com

Wonder Oak Winery, formerly known as Sugarleaf Vineyards, is owned and operated by Jerry Bias on a farm he had originally purchased as a getaway. The tasting room offers visitors a good vantage point for appreciating the surrounding hills, as do the winery's patio and grounds. The winery is available for rental for private parties and weddings. Children are welcome.

White Wines: Chardonnay, Petit Manseng, Vidal Blanc, Viognier.

Red Wines: Cabernet Franc, Cabernet Sauvignon, Cuvée Neubia *(Cabernet Sauvignon)*, Petit Verdot.

Sweet/Dessert Wines: Neubia Nectar *(Petit Manseng, Vidal Blanc)*.

Price Range: $17–$42

Tastings: $7 per person.

Groups: Reservations required for groups of 8 or more, $10 per person fee.

Purchasing: Online purchasing is available for residents of CA, DC, FL, IL, MN, NM, NY, OH, and VA.

Wine Club members receive regular wine shipments, discounts on purchases, and member-only events.

Directions: From I-64, take Exit 120 and turn onto Fifth Street Southwest, which eventually becomes Old Lynchburg Road. Continue on Old Lynchburg Road for about 7.5 miles. Turn right onto Walnut Branch Lane (narrow, portions unpaved) and drive 1.5 miles to the winery.

FRUIT WINES, CIDERS, AND MEADS

While most wine is made from grapes, wine can also be made from many types of fruits, most often from apples, berries, and stone fruits such as pears or peaches. These wines may be made entirely from fruit or may contain a mixture of grape-based wine along with the fruit wine. Because many fruits lack enough natural sugars for fermentation to occur, the winemaker often must add sugar to the juice, and fruit wines can be slightly sweet as a result.

Like apple wine, hard cider is fermented apple juice but is lower in total alcohol strength than wine. Ciders range from 2% to 8.5% alcohol strength, while apple wines are higher in alcohol. Ciders may be either still or sparkling, depending on the cidermaker's wish. Cidermaking was brought to the United States by colonists from England, where hard cider is a traditional brew. Hard cider is considered to have been the most popular alcoholic beverage available in colonial America into the nineteenth-century and was consumed by people from all levels of society. Presidents John Adams and Thomas Jefferson, for instance, both regularly drank and served cider.

Mead is a fermented beverage made from honey and has been produced since ancient times in Europe, the Middle East, Africa, and parts of Asia. Mead is often associated with the history of old Germany and Scandinavia, where it was often drunk from horns. Key scenes in the great Anglo-Saxon epic *Beowulf* are set in the king's mead-hall, a large public room in the palace where warriors met to drink their mead in the evenings. Meads made solely from honey may also be called hydromels, the name by which mead is known in France. Meads blended with fruit juice are known as melomels, while metheglin is mead flavored with herbs or spices.

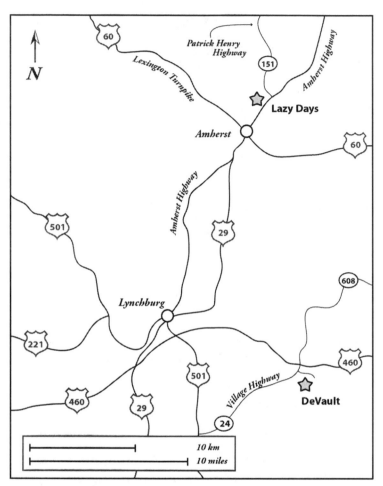

Map 8.10. Lynchburg (northern section)

LYNCHBURG

DeVault Family Vineyards
247 Station Lane
Concord VA 24538

Hours: M–Sa 11:00–6:00
Closed January, Thanksgiving, Christmas

434-993-0561
www.devaultvineyards.com
E-mail: devaultvineyards@hotmail.com

The DeVault family opened their small family winery to the public in 2010. DeVault is located on a thirty-two-acre farm midway between Appomattox Court House and Lynchburg, with the wood-panelled tasting room housed in a restored barn. The winery sponsors an annual holiday open house in December as well as live music and special events throughout the year. In addition to wine tastings, DeVault offers visitors a tennis court, basketball goal, stocked pond for fishing, and an indoor pool. The facilities may be rented for parties and weddings. Children and pets are welcome.

Fruit Wines: Old Time Watermelon.

White Wines: Chardonel, Niagara, Sweet Autumn Mist.

Blush Wines: Lover's Blush.

Red Wines: Darien's Reserve *(Norton)*, Merlot, Mr. D's Blend, Norton.

Price Range: $15–$24

Tastings: $3 per person.

Wheelchair accessible.

Directions: From Lynchburg, take U.S. Route 460 East for about 10 miles. Turn right onto Village Highway (Route 24). Take the second left onto Station Lane (Route 741). Drive 1/3 mile and bear right to stay on Station Road. The winery entrance will be 0.2 miles on the right.

Hickory Hill Vineyards & Winery
1722 Hickory Cove Lane
Moneta VA 24121

Hours: Th–M 11:00–5:00 (Apr–Nov);   540-296-1393

Sa 11:00–5:00 (20 Dec–31 Mar)   www.smlwine.com

Closed 25 Dec–1 Jan, Easter, Thanksgiving   E-mail: info@hickoryhillvineyards.com

Stay Tuned: Facebook, Twitter, newsletter

Hickory Hill Vineyard was established by Roger and Judy Furrow, longtime home winemakers who opened their doors to the public in 2001. Hickory Hill is located on scenic Smith Mountain Lake, best known for standing in for Lake Winnipesaukee in the 1991 movie, *What About Bob?* The tasting room is located in a renovated 1923 farmhouse next to the winery where Hickory Hill's mostly estate-grown wines are produced. The winery does not sell food, but guests are welcome to bring their own for picnics on the grounds. The winery includes a small gift shop with crafts from local artisans. Sunset Saturdays offer live music performances. Tours are offered as time and operations permit. Children and dogs are welcome.

White Wines: Chardonnay, Vidal Blanc, Lake Chardonnay, Smith Mountain Lake Mist *(Vidal Blanc, Chardonnay)*, Vidal Blanc.

Red Wines: Cabernet Franc, Cabernet Sauvignon, Merlot, Smith Mountain Lake Country Red.

Sweet/Dessert Wines: Smith Mountain Lake Redbud *(Cabernet Sauvignon, Chardonnay, Vidal Blanc)*, Smith Mountain Lake Sunset *(Chardonnay, Vidal Blanc)*, Sweet Red Sail *(Cabernet Franc, Cabernet Sauvignon)*.

Price Range: $10–$20

Groups: Reservations required for groups of 10 or more.

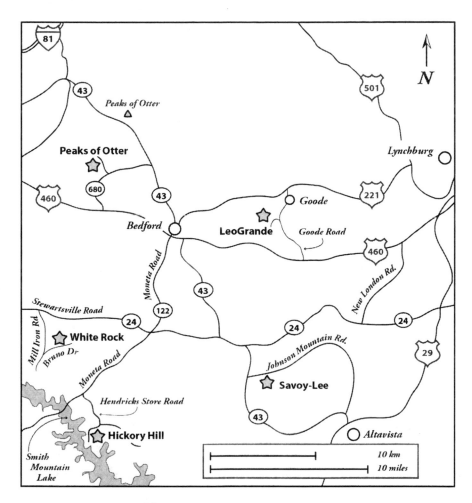

Map 8.11. Lynchburg (western section)

Wheelchair accessible.

Purchasing: Online shipping is available for VA residents; online purchasing available via VinoShipper for AK, FL, ID, LA, MO, NE, NV, NH, NM, ND, OH, OR, DC, WV, and WY.

Harvesters' Club members receive discounts in exchange for assisting at harvests, bottling, or wine festivals.

Directions: From U.S. Route 460, take the Route 122 ramp at Bedford and turn south onto Burks Hill Road (Route 122), which will become Moneta

Road, and drive 14.4 miles. Turn left onto Hendricks Store Road. Drive 2 miles and turn right onto Hickory Cove Lane. The winery drive will be about one mile on left.

Lazy Days Winery
1351 North Amherst Highway
Amherst VA 24521

Hours: W–Su, 11:00–5:00

Closed New Year's, Thanksgiving, Christmas

Stay Tuned: Facebook

434-381-6088

www.lazydayswinery.com

E-mail: john@lazydayswinery.com

Bill and Marianne Fitzhugh established Lazy Days in 2007 when they planted the first vines in their three-acre vineyard; the winery opened to the public in 2010. The tasting room is a renovated livestock pavilion, which offers views of the vineyard from its covered patio. Visitors are welcome to bring a picnic lunch to enjoy on the grounds. Lazy Days sponsors several special events throughout the year, including a summer solstice festival and live music on selected weekends. The facilities are available for private events and weddings. Children and pets are welcome.

White Wines: Capuchin White *(Petit Manseng)*, Petit Manseng *(Vidal Blanc, Chardonnay)*, Sweet Lazy Days, Viognier.

Red Wines: Malbec, Merlot, Petit Verdot.

Sweet/Dessert Wines: Sweet Lazy Days Red, Sweet Nights.

Price Range: $16–$20

Directions: From Lynchburg, take U.S. Route 29 North toward Charlottesville. Drive 5 miles and make a U-turn at Route 151 North. The winery will be on the right.

LeoGrande Vineyards & Winery
1343 Wingfield Drive
Goode VA 24556

Hours: W–Su 11:00–6:00 (May–Dec) 540-586-4066
Closed Jan–Apr, Thanksgiving, Christmas www.leograndewinery.com
Stay Tuned: Facebook E-mail: info@leograndewinery.com

Norman LeoGrande launched his small boutique winery on his four-hundred-acre working farm, where he also raises Black Angus cattle and American Saddlebred horses. A renovated farmhouse serves as the tasting room, which also includes a porch from which to appreciate the view of the winery's vines and a splendid view of the surrounding mountains. The winery dogs may be on hand to greet you, or you may spot them on patrol, walking through the vines. Nearly all LeoGrande's wines are estate-grown; as a small-lot producer, the specific wines available for tasting may vary greatly from month to month. Children and pets are welcome.

White Wines: Chardonnay, Roaring White *(Niagara, Sauvignon Blanc)*, Sauvignon Blanc.

Rosé Wines: Roaring Rosé.

Red Wines: Barbera, Nebbiolo, Roaring Red *(Sangiovese)*, Sangiovese, Syrah.

Sweet/Dessert Wines: Autumn Kiss *(Sangiovese, Barbera ice wine)*.

Price Range: $10–$25

Tastings: $4 per person with souvenir glass.

Groups: Please call ahead for groups of 6 or more.

Purchasing: Online purchasing is available via VinoShipper for AK, FL, ID, LA, MO, NE, NV, NH, NM, ND, OH, OR, DC, WV, and WY.

Directions: From Lynchburg, take U.S. Route 221 South about 9 miles. Turn left onto Goode Station Road (Route 668) into the town of Goode. Turn right onto Goode Road and drive 1.3 miles. Make another right onto Wingfield Drive. The winery will be on the right in 1/2 mile.

Peaks of Otter Winery & Orchards
2122 Sheep Creek Road
Bedford VA 24523

Hours: Daily 12:00–5:00 (Apr–Dec),
Sa–Su 12:00–5:00 (Jan–Mar)
Closed New Year's, Thanksgiving, Christmas
Stay Tuned: Facebook, Twitter

540-586-3707
www.peaksofotterwinery.com
E-mail: appleseed@earthlink.net

Peaks of Otter Winery is owned and operated by Danny and Nancy Johnson, who opened the winery in 1995 on the grounds of their fifth-generation apple orchard. Their specialty is fruit wines in an amazing range of flavors. The winery has two tasting rooms: a summer tasting facility in the orchard packing house and a winter room attached to the Johnsons' home. Both offer a wide range of jams and jellies, relishes, sauces, many produced by Johnson's Orchard.

Two of the winery's most unusual wines are made with peppers. Chili Dawg features apple and chili pepper and won third place in the 2009 Scovie Awards; the winery pairs it with Cheez Whiz for tasting. Trying the winery's Kiss The Devil wine, made from 30 different types of chili peppers, will win an "I kissed the devil" sticker. Facebook fans receive a 5% discount on purchases. Children and dogs are welcome.

The Johnsons also have a four-bedroom guest house, Elmo's Rest, that is available for rent by the week.

Fruit Wines: Apple Truffle, Beale's Treasure Sweet Apple, Blackberry Cobbler, Blackberry Jammed, Blueberry Muffin, Café Vino *(apple, coffee)*, Cherry Cheese Cake, Cinfulicious *(apple, cinnamon)*, Light Pear, Mango Tango, Peach of Otter, Plumlicious Sweet Plum, Puff *(apple, dragonfruit)*, Pumpkin Pie, Pure Passion, Ras Ma Tas Raspberry, Salty Frog Margarita *(apple)*, Strawberry Shortcake, Sweetheart *(apple, pomegranate)*, Vino Colado, Virginia Apple Lovers Dry Apple.

Grape Wines: Blue Ridge Mountain Grape *(Concord)*, Frosty Morn, Sangria, Sheep Creek Ruby *(Cabernet Franc)*.

Other: Chili Dawg *(apple, chili pepper)*, Kiss The Devil *(30 chili peppers)*.

Price Range: $10–$25 ($30 for specialty bottles)

Wheelchair accessible.

Purchasing: Online purchasing available for VA residents, via VinoShipper for AK, FL, ID, LA, MN, MO, NE, NV, NH, NM ND, OH, OR, DC, WV, and WY.

Directions: From U.S. Route 460, go north onto Patterson Mill Road, which becomes Sheep Creek Road (Route 680). Drive 5.5 miles to winery entrance on left.

Savoy-Lee Winery
5800 Johnson Mountain Road
Huddleston VA 24104

Hours: F–M 12:00–6:00
Closed New Year's, Christmas
Stay Tuned: Facebook, Twitter, newsletter

540-297-9275
www.savoy-lee.com
E-mail: David@savoy-lee.com

Owner-winemaker David Wood established his vineyard in 2001, with the winery and tasting room opening in 2004. Savoy-Lee hosts occasional live music events featuring local entertainers as well as special fundraisers, including one for the All-American Mutt Rescue. The winery may be rented for private events and parties. Children are welcome.

White Wines: Chardonnay, Johnson Mountain Picnic White, Riesling, Seyval Blanc, Vidal Blanc.

Blush Wines: Johnson Mountain Picnic Blush.

Red Wines: Cabernet Franc, Cabernet Sauvignon, Echo Forest Red, Johnson Mountain Picnic Red.

Price Range: $15–$22

Wheelchair accessible.

Purchasing: Online purchases are available for residents of AR, CA, FL, ID, LA, MO, NE, NV, NH, NM, ND, OH, OR, VA, DC, and WV.

Directions: From Lynchburg, take U.S. Route 460 West. Turn left at the Sheetz station onto New London Road. Drive 2 miles and turn right onto Colonial Highway (Route 24). After 5 miles, turn left onto Route 43. Drive 2.5 miles and turn left onto Johnson Mountain Road (Route 626). Drive 2.4 miles to the winery on the right.

White Rock Vineyards & Winery
2117 Bruno Drive
Goodview VA 24095

Hours: Th–M 12:00–5:00 (Apr–Nov)   540-890-3359
Closed Thanksgiving   www.whiterockwines.com
Stay Tuned: Facebook, Twitter   E-mail: whiterockwines@gmail.com

Fred and Drema Sylvester planted their first vines in 2000, opening to the public five years later. Their certified Virginia Green winery and tasting room offers a covered veranda where visitors may sit and enjoy the view of the vineyards over a glass or bottle of White Rock's estate-grown wines. The winery sponsors occasional festivals and special events, including a West Virginia Heritage Festival in the fall and a Fork and Cork festival in the spring.

White Wines: Chardonnay, Moon Glow, White Mojo *(Pinot Gris).*

Red Wines: Cabernet Franc, Cabernet Sauvignon, Merlot, Scarlet Sunrise, Velvet Sky.

Price Range: $12–$16

Directions: From U.S. Route 460, take the Route 122 ramp at Bedford and turn south onto Burks Hill Road (Route 122), which becomes Moneta Road, and drive 7 miles. Turn right onto Stewartsville Road (Route 24) and drive 9 miles. Turn left onto Mill Iron Road (Route 653). After 2 miles, turn left on Bruno Drive. The winery is 1 mile on the left.

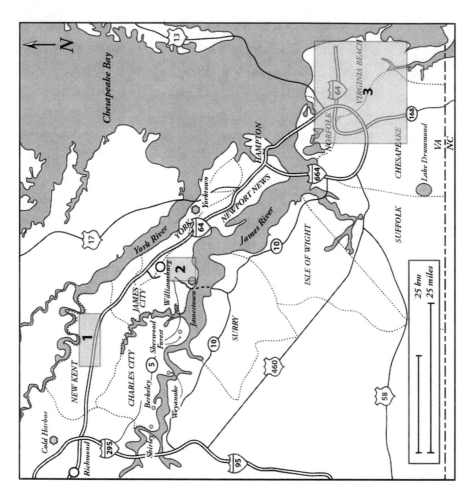

Map 9.1. Hampton Roads Region: (1) New Kent-Saudé Creek; (2) Williamsburg, (3) Norfolk-Virginia Beach.

9. HAMPTON ROADS REGION

Located in the Tidewater of Virginia, this region is one of gentle, low hills and terrain crisscrossed with small creeks that flow into the James and York Rivers. The climate on the Virginia Peninsula and southeastern Virginia is the warmest in the state. Summers are hot and humid, while temperatures rarely dip below freezing in the winter. Soils in the region range from rich and loamy to downright swampy; indeed, the region is home to the Great Dismal Swamp which straddles the Virginia-North Carolina line. It also is the site of Lake Drummond, one of Virginia's only two natural lakes.

<u>Things to see and do</u>: Virginia's Hampton Roads Region is, in many ways, the heart of historic Virginia. It was here that English colonists first settled in 1607 at Jamestown and, after a shaky start, gradually began expanding their presence further into Virginia. This is also where Virginia's four original counties as an English colony were established in 1617: Henrico, James City, Bermuda Hundred, and Kecoughtan (the latter two no longer exist). Williamsburg was the colonial capital of Virginia from 1704 until 1799 and is just northwest of the site of the decisive Revolutionary War battle at Yorktown, where American forces defeated British troops and won America's struggle for independence.

Just across the James River from Williamsburg and Jamestown is Bacon's Castle, built in 1665 by Arthur Allen. The property is best known for its role in Bacon's Rebellion, a 1676 uprising led by Nathaniel Bacon against Royal Governor William Berkeley.

The John Tyler Memorial Highway (Route 5) is a scenic road that winds along the James River from Williamsburg to Richmond. There are a number of historic homes along its path for visitors to explore, including President John Tyler's Sherwood Forest, the Harrison family's Berkeley Plantation, and the Carter family's Shirley Plantation. More details are available at the James River Plantation website (http://www.jamesriverplantations.org).

Civil War history abounds here as well. McClellan's peninsula campaign of 1862 started at Fort Monroe, at the tip of Hampton Roads, and the army moved up the peninsula toward Richmond, where the Seven Days' Battles occurred. In 1864, General Ulysses Grant moved down from Spotsylvania in pursuit of General Robert E. Lee. The battlefield at Cold Harbor, where Grant's army launched a headlong assault on Lee's fortified position, offers a vivid and moving glimpse into what soldiers faced on the field of war. Grant then moved his army across the James at Weyanoke, starting the final campaign that ultimately ended in Lee's surrender at Appomattox Court House in 1865.

The Virginia Beach-Hampton Roads area offers numerous attractions for visitors, including the Virginia Aquarium and Marine Science Center, the Mariner's Museum, and Nauticus. Those interested in spending time on the beach and boardwalk will find ample opportunity for food and fun at Virginia Beach.

Wine Trails: Two of the Hampton Roads Region wineries—New Kent and Saudé Creek—are included in the Chesapeake Bay Wine Trail.

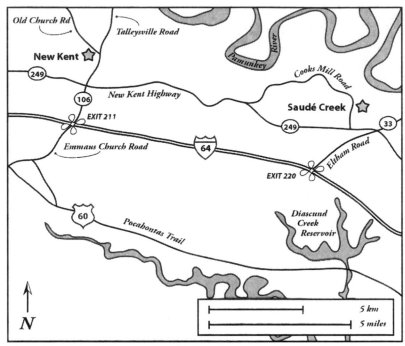

Map 9.2. New Kent & Saudé Creek

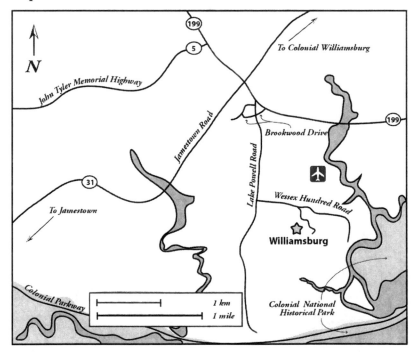

Map 9.3. Williamsburg

HAMPTON ROADS

Mermaid Winery
330 West 22nd Street, #106
Norfolk VA 23517

Hours: Daily 11:00–midnight
Closed Thanksgiving, Christmas, New Year's
Stay Tuned: Facebook

757-233-4155
www.mermaidwinery.com
E-mail: info@mermaidwinery.com

Mermaid Winery is owned by Jennifer Doumar, who opened her urban winery in 2012 in Norfolk's Ghent neighborhood. The wines are currently made by Dean Gruenburg (Prince Michel, Castle Gruen). Most of the wines are sourced from Virginia vineyards, supplemented by grapes from other regions. The winery hosts various events and offers eleven other flights of wines for tasting, in addition to its own production. Mermaid offers appetizers and light dishes to enjoy, as well as a list of 150 different wines by the bottle.

Fruit Wines: Elizabeth River (Cabernet Franc, raspberry), East Beach (Viognier, peach).

White Wines: Chardonnay, Siren's White (Viognier, Petit Manseng, Roussanne).

Red Wines: Cabernet Franc, Poseidon's Red (Pinotage, Syrah, Tannat).

Price Range: $15–$30

Tastings: $6.50 per person.

Groups: Reservations required for groups of 10 or more.

Wheelchair accessible.

Atlantis Wine Club members receive wine shipments, discounts, and invitations to special events.

Directions: From I-264, take Exit 9 (Waterside Drive/St. Paul's Boulevard) onto St. Paul's Boulevard (U.S. Route 460 Alt East). Drive 1.5 miles and turn left onto East Princess Anne Road. Take the third right onto Llewellyn Avenue. After 1/2 mile, turn left onto 22nd Avenue. The winery is 3/4 mile on the right at the Palace Station Shops.

New Kent Winery
8400 Old Church Road
New Kent VA 23124

Hours: Tu–Su 10:00–5:00 (6:00 in summer)   804-932-8240
Closed Thanksgiving, Christmas, New Year's   www.newkentwinery.com
Stay Tuned: Facebook, newsletter   E-mail: info@newkentwinery.com

New Kent Winery opened in 2008 on the grounds at the Viniterra community, just east of Richmond. Winemaker Tom Payette oversees the production of New Kent's mostly estate-grown wines at the 17,000-square-foot winery, which is owned by the Kitty Hawk Land Corporation and other investors. The winery sponsors a range of special events in the two-story tasting room. The facilities may be rented for private parties and weddings.

White Wines: Chardonnay, Vidal Blanc.

Rosé Wines: White Merlot, White Norton.

Red Wines: Merlot, Meritage.

Price Range: $15–$24

Tastings: $8 per person, with souvenir glass.

Groups: Reservations required for groups of 10 or more.

Wheelchair accessible.

Wine Club members receive shipments, discounts, and special events.

Directions: From I-64, take Exit 211 (Talleysville/Roxbury) north onto Emmaus Church Road (Route 106 North). Continue through two round-abouts. At the third roundabout, take the second exit onto Old Church Road. The winery will be 1/3 mile on the left.

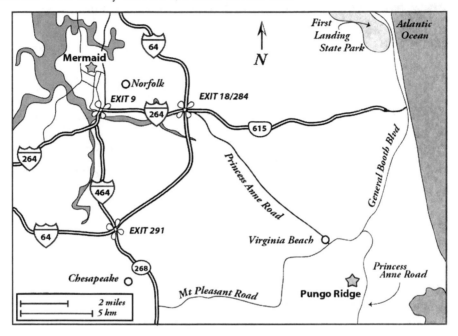

Map 9.4. Norfolk-Virginia Beach

Pungo Ridge Winery
1665 Princess Anne Road
Virginia Beach VA 23456

Hours: F–Su 12:00–4:30 (Jun–Nov)
Closed Dec–May
Stay Tuned: Facebook, newsletter

757-426-1665
www.pungoridgewinery.com
E-mail: fred@fredhavens.com

Retired photographer Fred Havens opened Pungo Ridge Winery in 2011 after making fruit wine as a hobby for some years. Fred and his brother Eugene run the winery and produce their wines using much of their own fruit grown on their five-acre farm in the Pungo region of Virginia Beach with the balance coming from other Virginia farms. The brothers are expanding Pungo Ridge's production to a range of fruit wines and meads.

Fruit Wines: Apple, Blackberry, Blueberry-Honey, Pear, Plum.

Meads: Strawberry Mead.

Price Range: $15

Tastings: $5 per person.

Directions: From I-64, take Exit 286B onto Indian River Road East. Continue following Indian River Road for 12.5 miles and turn right onto Princess Anne Road (VA Route 615). Drive 3/4 mile to the winery on the right.

Saudé Creek Vineyards
16230 Cooks Mill Road
Lanexa VA 23089

Hours: W–M 11:00–5:00 (6:00 in summer)   804-966-5896
Closed New Year's, Thanksgiving, Christmas   www.saudecreek.com
Stay Tuned: Facebook   E-mail: catherinestanley@saudecreek.com

Jason Knight and John Britt opened Saudé [*SAW-dee*] Creek Vineyards in 2011 after selling their wines for several years at wine festivals and other events. The winery is located on the grounds of Frank's Tavern, a colonial-era inn (now no longer standing) that counted George Washington and French General Rochambeau among its clientele; the winery's name is from a creek that ran behind the Alabama home of Jason's grandmother. The wines are all from Virginia-grown fruit, either from the owners' forty-acre vineyard in Halifax County or from other Virginia producers. Saudé Creek offers ample seating indoors in its spacious two-story tasting room as well as outside on the decks and covered porches, which provide a scenic view of the grounds and the Pamunkey. The winery sponsors live music on selected weekends. The facilities are available for private parties or events.

Fruit Wines: Saudé Creek White.

White Wines: Chardonnay, Pamunkey Fall, Tavern White.

Rosé Wines: Saudé Creek Blush *(Chambourcin)*.

Red Wines: Cabernet Franc, Chambourcin, Meritage, Merlot, Saudé Creek Red, Tavern Red.

Price Range: $12–$18

Tastings: $7 per person, with souvenir glass.

Groups: Reservations required for groups of 8 or more, $10 per person fee.

Wheelchair accessible.

Directions: From I-64 East, take Exit 220 and turn onto Eltham Road (Route 33 East). Drive 2.9 miles and turn left onto New Kent Highway (Route 249). After a mile, turn right onto Cooks Mill Road (Route 623). The winery will be on the right after another mile.

The Williamsburg Winery
5800 Wessex Hundred
Williamsburg VA 23185

Hours: M–Sa 10:00–6:00, Su 11:00–6:00 (Apr–Oct)
M–Sa 10:00–5:00, Su 11:00–5:00 (Nov–Mar)
Closed New Year's, Thanksgiving, Christmas

757-258-0899
www.williamsburgwinery.com
E-mail: wine@wmbgwine.com

Located just minutes from Colonial Williamsburg, Williamsburg Winery is one of Virginia's largest wine producers. The winery was founded in 1985 by the Duffeler family of Belgium, with Patrick Duffeler Sr. and Patrick Jr. overseeing its production of over sixty-thousand cases per year. The winery offers guided tours and an onsite wine museum. Guests may dine at the winery's Gabriel Archer Tavern or the Café Provençal. The winery's facilities are available for private parties, dinners, and weddings.

Williamsburg Winery also offers guests the option of overnight stays at the twenty-eight-room Wedmore Place hotel on the winery grounds.

White Wines: Acte 12 Chardonnay, Chardonnay, Governor's White, James River White, John Adlum Chardonnay, Sauvignon Blanc, Sir Christopher Wren White, Traminette, Viognier.

Rosé Wines: Plantation Blush.

Red Wines: Adagio, Arundell Cabernet Sauvignon, Burgesses' Measure Merlot, Gabriel Archer Reserve, Hening's Statute Claret, J. Andrewes Merlot, Lord Botetourt Red, Merlot, Susan Constant Red, Syrah, Two Shilling Red, Trianon *(Cabernet Franc)*.

Sweet/Dessert Wines: Licoreux de Framboise *(raspberry)*, Licoreux de Mûres *(blackberry)*, Late Harvest Vidal.

Seasonal Wines: Settlers' Spiced Wine.

Price Range: $9–$65

Tastings: $10 per person, $36 for reserve tasting.

Wheelchair accessible.

Purchasing: Online purchasing for residents of AK, CA, CO, FL, GA, IL, LA, ME, MO, MI, MN, MO, NY, NC, OH, VA, DC, and WI; some wines available only to VA residents.

Wine Club members receive regular shipments, discounts at varying levels.

Directions: From I-64 Eastbound, take Exit 234 onto Route 199 East and drive 8 miles. Turn right onto Brookwood Drive and make the first left onto Lake Powell Road (Route 617). Drive about 1 mile and turn left onto Wessex Hundred and the winery.

From I-64 Westbound, take Exit 242 onto Route 199 West. Drive 5 miles and turn left onto Brookwood. Turn left onto Brookwood Drive and make the first left onto Lake Powell Road (Route 617). Drive about 1 mile and turn left onto Wessex Hundred and the winery.

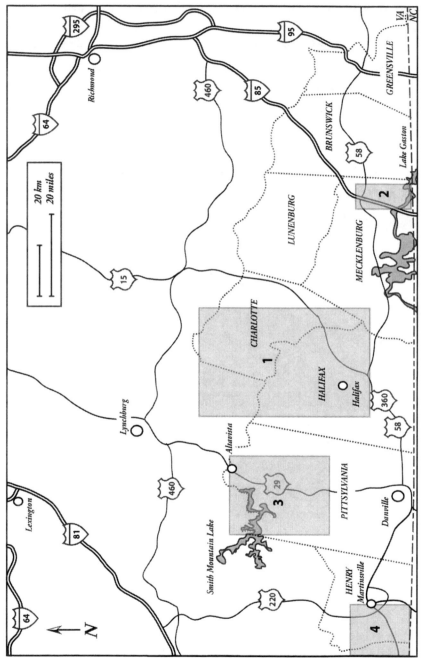

Map 10.1. South Virginia Region: (1) Halifax; (2) Rosemont;
(3) Danville-Alta Vista; (4) Danville-Martinsville.

10. SOUTH VIRGINIA REGION

Centered along the Virginia-North Carolina border, the South Virginia region is farm country, dotted with lakes, state parks, and small towns. Sometimes called the Southside of Virginia or the Southern Piedmont, the area is characterized by a rolling landscape, a long growing season, mild winters, and an average of 43 inches of precipitation annually, the second highest average in the state. The wineries in this region are all family-run farm wineries that are well worth a visit for those looking for a slower pace and a chance to explore sites that are a little off the beaten path.

<u>Things to see and do</u>: Many of the region's towns offer driving and walking tours that highlight historic homes and sites. Nature lovers will appreciate the Staunton River, a popular canoeing and tubing venue, and Lake Gaston's ample boating and sport fishing possibilities. History buffs may be interested in Red Hill, the home of Patrick Henry of "Give me liberty or give me death!" fame. Historic Noland Village near Nathalie is a restored mid-19th century village that recaptures life in rural Virginia.

The area is also home to a growing number of Old Order Amish families that began settling in the Nathalie area around 2005. Several have established several small businesses offering fresh-baked goods, furniture, and plants. Visitors may also encounter Amish horse-drawn buggies on roadways, so slow down and keep an eye open!

<u>Winery Trails</u>: The SoVA Wine Trail includes most of the region's wineries.

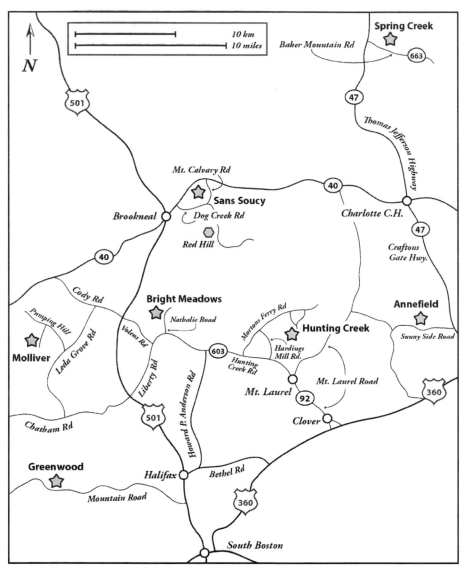

Map 10.2. Halifax

HALIFAX

Annefield Vineyards
3200 Sunny Side Road
Saxe VA 23967

Hours: Sa 11:00–5:00 (until 6:00 in summer)   434-454-6017
Closed Nov–Mar   www.annefieldvineyards.com
Stay Tuned: Facebook, Twitter   E-mail: info@annefieldvineyards.com

Annefield Vineyards was founded in 2006 by Stephen Ballard and Michael Leary on the site of the nineteenth-century Annefield Plantation. Their initial three-acre Arrowhead Vineyard, named for a white quartz Sappony Indian arrowhead found on the site, was planted to Cabernet Franc, Cabernet Sauvignon, and Viognier in 2006, with plans to expand the range of varietals grown. Winemaking is currently being done by Michael Shaps of Virginia Wineworks.

White Wines: Annefield White, Chardonnay, Viognier.

Rosé Wines: Rosé.

Red Wines: Annefield Red *(Bordeaux-style blend)*, Cabernet Franc, Cabernet Sauvignon.

Price Range: $15–$24

Purchasing: Online ordering is available for VA residents only.

Wine club members receive regular shipments, discounts on purchases.

Directions: From U.S. Route 360, take Craftons Gate Highway (VA 47 North) and drive 2.6 miles. Turn left at County Road 612 (Sunny Side Road). The winery entrance will be 3.5 miles on the right.

Bright Meadows Farm Vineyard & Winery
1181 Nathalie Road
Nathalie VA 24577

Hours: W–Sa 11:00–6:00, Su 1:00–6:00 (Apr–Dec)   434-349-5349
Closed Jan–Mar, Thanksgiving, Christmas   www.brightmeadows.com
Stay Tuned: Facebook   E-mail: BrightMeadowsFarm@yahoo.com

Boyd and Shirley Archer opened their family-owned and operated winery to the public in 2005. Located on the grounds of a nineteenth-century tobacco plantation, Bright Meadows' winery production facility and tasting room are in a restored 117-year-old barn. Visitors are welcome to enjoy the walking paths and picnic areas on the property after their tastings. The facilities are available for private parties and weddings. Children and pets are welcome.

Fruit Wines: Apple, BAG *(blackberry, apple, grape)*, Blackberry, Sangria *(apple, blackberry, Bright Meadows Red)*.

White Wines: Bright Leaf White *(Vidal Blanc)*, Bright Meadows White *(Niagara)*.

Red Wines: Bright Meadows Red *(Concord)*, Burley Red *(Chambourcin)*, Dan River Noir *(Chambourcin)*, Halifax Red *(Concord)*, Rebellion Red *(Norton)*.

Price Range: $12–$17

Purchasing: Online ordering is available via VinoShipper to AK, FL, ID, LA, MN, MO, NE, NV, NH, NM, ND, OH, OR, DC, WV , and WY.

Directions: From Halifax, take U.S. Route 360 East and turn left onto Howard P. Anderson Road. Drive 8.7 miles and turn left onto Lennig Road (Route 603). Continue 3.7 miles and turn right onto Nathalie Road. The winery will be on the left in 3/4 mile.

Greenwood Vineyards
9050 Mountain Road
Vernon Hill VA 24597

Hours: W–Sa 12:00–5:00, Su 1:00–6:00   434-454-9219
Closed New Year's, Thanksgiving, Christmas   www.greenwood-vineyards.com
         E-mail: info@greenwood-vineyards.com

Greenwood Vineyards was launched when Paul Greenwood returned to his native Halifax County in 1984 and planted a vineyard on his sixth-generation family farm. He first began selling grapes to other area wineries and ultimately decided to open to the public in 2010. Greenwood's tasting room is in a 145-year-old restored tobacco barn that also includes the barrel room and production facilities. The winery is available for private parties. Children and leashed pets are welcome.

White Wines: Chardonnay.

Rosé Wines: Molly's Mountain Rosé, Sweet Samantha Rosé.

Red Wines: Cabernet Franc, Merlot, Mountain Road Red, Sangiovese.

Price Range: $15

Directions: From U.S. Route 501 at the town of Halifax, drive west on VA Route 360 (Mountain Road) for 8.9 miles. Turn right into the winery entrance on the right.

Hunting Creek Vineyards
2000 Addie Williams Trail
Clover VA 24534

Hours: W–Su 11:00–5:00 (mid-Apr–mid-Dec) 434-454-9219
Closed Thanksgiving, mid-Dec–mid-Apr www.hcwines.com
Stay Tuned: Facebook E-mail: info@huntingcreekvineyards.com

Hunting Creek Vineyards is owned and operated by Milton and Sandy McPherson, who originally planted their three-acre vineyard in 2002 with the intent to sell grapes to other vintners while also reserving enough grapes to make wine for themselves. Seven years later, they decided to open their own winery to the public. Their newly built tasting room offers seating both indoors and out, with works by local artists adorning its walls. Hunting Creek has an annual "harvest party" to welcome volunteers who help harvest grapes. The McPhersons recommend calling first as they may be in the vineyard working. Children and leashed pets are welcome.

White Wines: Pure Luck *(Viognier)*.

Red Wines: Decadence *(Petit Verdot, Viognier)*, Indulgence *(Merlot, Petit Verdot)*, Repentance *(Cabernet Franc, cranberry)*, Temptation *(Merlot)*.

Other: Dare *(jalapeño)*.

Price Range: $15

Purchasing: Online ordering is available for Virginia residents and via VinoShipper to AK, FL, ID, LA, MN, MO, NE, NV, NH, NM, ND, OH, OR, DC, WV, and WY.

Directions: From U.S. Route 360, drive north on either Moseley Ferry or Clover Road into the town of Clover; the two merge to become Main Street and then Mt Laurel Road (Route 92). Follow Mt. Laurel Road about 4 miles to the village of Mt. Laurel. Turn left onto Hunting Creek Road (Route

603). Drive two miles and turn right onto Hardings Mill Road. Continue another 2 miles and turn right again onto Mortons Ferry Road. Drive 3 miles and turn right onto Addie Williams Trail (portions unpaved). The winery will be on the right after 1 mile.

Molliver Vineyards & Winery
2046 Waller Road
Nathalie VA 24577

Hours: Daily 1:00–6:00
Closed New Year's, Thanksgiving, Christmas
Stay Tuned: Facebook, Twitter, newsletter

434-349-1000
www.molliver-vineyards.com
E-mail: finewines@molliver.org

Marshall Molliver established his namesake winery on his 134-acre property on the Banister River. The winery hosts a number of events, including a Labor Day barbecue weekend, harvest festivals, and wine appreciation movie nights. The Mollivers dedicate a portion of their proceeds for animal rescue groups and sponsor various fundraisers for the local chapter of the humane society. Nature-lovers are welcome to fish in the winery pond, raft on the nearby Banister and Staunton Rivers, or hike in the adjoining woods. With advance reservations, RVs may park overnight. Children and leashed pets are welcome. Advance phone calls before tastings are appreciated.

Fruit Wines: Blackberry.

White Wines: Chardonnay, Pinot Grigio, Riesling, Sauvignon Blanc, Vidal Blanc, Viognier.

Red Wines: Cabernet Franc, Cabernet Sauvignon, Chambourcin, Merlot, Norton.

Sweet/Dessert Wines: Vin Chocolat.

Price Range: $14–$18

Tastings: $5 per person.

Groups: Reservations requested for groups of 8 or more.

Purchasing: Online ordering available via VinoShipper by AK, FL, ID, LA, MO, NE, NV, NH, NM, ND, OH, OR, DC, WV, and WY.

Directions: From U.S. Route 501, turn west onto Cody Road and drive about 2 miles. Turn left onto Leda Grove Road. After 1.5 miles, turn right on Pumping Hill Road (Route 667). After 1.5 miles, turn left onto Waller Road. The winery will be 1.9 miles on the right. (Note: Some GPS units misidentify Waller Road as Walker Road.)

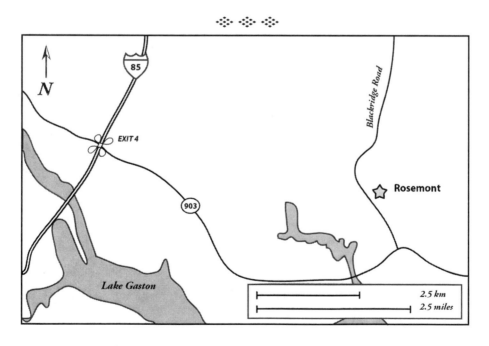

Map 10.3. Rosemont

Rosemont Vineyards & Winery
1050 Blackridge Road
LaCrosse VA 23950

Hours: M–Sa 11:00–6:00, Su 1:00–6:00   434-636-9463 (WINE)

Closed New Year's, Thanksgiving, Christmas   www.rosemontofvirginia.com

Stay Tuned: Facebook, e-newsletters   E-mail: sales@rosemontofvirginia.com

Rosemont Vineyards & Winery is located on the 450-acre Rosemont Estate, a working farm that has been in the Rose family since 1858. The family first began planting the vineyard in 2003 and produced their first vintage five years later. All Rosemont's wines are from estate-grown fruit, with the exception of its Chardonnay, which is produced from grapes from other Virginia vineyards. The winery features special tasting menus on the weekends and also hosts an annual Harvest Festival, the Wine and Art Festival, and occasional live music and barbecues. Tours of the production area and barrel room are available. The winery may be rented for special events and weddings. Children and leashed pets are welcome.

White Wines: Chardonnay, Pinot Grigio, Traminette, Vidal Blanc.

Rosé Wines: Rosé of Chambourcin.

Red Wines: Cabernet Franc, Kilravock, Lake Country Red, Meritage, Merlot, Syrah.

Sweet/Dessert Wines: Blackridge Red, Lake Country Blush *(Chambourcin)*, Lake Country Sunset.

Price Range: $9–$25

Groups: Reservations required for groups of 6 or more.

Purchasing: Online ordering available via VinoShipper for AK, FL, ID, LA, MD, MO, NC, NE, ND, NH, NM, NV, OH, OR, VA, DC, WV, and WY.

Wine club members receive regular shipments, discounts on purchases.

Directions: From I-85, take Exit 4 (Bracey/Lake Gaston) onto Route 903 East. Drive about 7.5 miles and turn left onto Blackridge Road. The winery will be on the right after 1 mile.

Sans Soucy Vineyards & Winery
1571 Mount Calvary Road
Brookneal VA 24528

Hours: M–Sa 11:00–5:00 (Mar–Dec) 434-376-9463
Closed Jan–Feb, Thanksgiving, Christmas www.sanssoucyvineyards.com
Stay Tuned: Facebook E-mail: tastingroom@sanssoucyvineyards.com

Owner-winemaker Paul Anctil and his wife, Jackie, started their winery in 2004 on a farm near Patrick Henry's Red Hill estate and Appomattox Court House. Paul oversees the 5.5-acre vineyard and wine production with their son Paul. Sans Soucy's winery and tasting room are in a hundred-year-old barn with seating indoors in the tasting room loft as well as outdoors on the porch and lawn. Cheeses and sausages are available for purchase in the tasting room. Sans Soucy sponsors the monthly Summer in the Vineyard concert series, as well as Bark & Wine benefits for the All-American Mutt Rescue. The winery is available for private parties and weddings, and offers free Wi-Fi for visitors. Children and leashed dogs are welcome.

Fruit Wines: Blackberry.

White Wines: Chato-O White, Traminette, Viognier.

Red Wines: Cabernet Franc, Legacy, Paint the Town Red, Petit Verdot, Tempranillo, Chateau Weuf du Pup.

Sweet/Dessert Wines: Ginger.

Price Range: $13–$26

Tastings: $5 per person.

Groups: Reservations requested for groups of 8 or more for tastings and pairings.

Wheelchair accessible.

Purchasing: Online purchasing is available via VinoShipper for AK, FL, ID, LA, MO, NE, NV, NH, NM, ND, OH, OR, DC, WV, and WY.

Legacy Wine Club members receive quarterly shipments, special discounts.

Directions: From U.S. Route 501, turn east at the town of Brookneal onto Lynchburg Avenue (Route 40) which bends to the left and becomes Wickliffe Road. After about 1 mile, turn right onto Dog Creek Road and continue 2.3 miles. Make a left onto Mount Calvary Road. The winery will be 1/3 mile on the left.

Spring Creek Wine Cellar
3628 Baker Mountain Road
Pamplin City VA 23958

Hours: Sa–Su 1:00–6:00 (early Apr–mid-Dec)   434-248-6981
Closed Thanksgiving, mid-Dec–early Apr   www.springcreekwinecellar.com
E-mail: info@springcreekwinecellar.com

Spring Creek Wine Cellar is a small boutique winery that features all estate-grown, vegan-friendly, pure varietals aged in stainless steel. The winery is owned and operated by Texas natives Gene and Evelyn McCluney on their Canongate Angus Farm located not far from Appomattox Courthouse. The lower level of the McCluneys' house serves as the winery's tasting room, which also offers snacks for purchase. The facilities may be rented for private events. Children are welcome.

White Wines: Cayuga White, Chardonel, Chardonnay, Johannisberg Riesling, Pinot Gris, Seyval Blanc, Traminette, Vidal Blanc.

Red Wines: Cabernet Franc, Cabernet Sauvignon, Chambourcin, Chancellor, Maréchal Foch, Merlot.

Price Range: $12–$17

Tastings: Complimentary basic tasting; $3 for reserve tasting.

Groups: Reservations required for groups of 8 or more.

Directions: From U.S. Route 360, turn north onto Craftons Gate Highway (Route 47), which will change names several times before becoming Thomas Jefferson Highway after passing through Charlotte Court House. Drive another 15.5 miles and turn right onto Baker Mountain Road (Route 663). The winery will be 1/2 mile on the left; the tasting room is at the back.

TASTING TIPS

Getting the most from what a wine has to offer is a truly sensory experience that fully engages your senses of sight, smell, and taste to appreciate the full range of characteristics of the wine in your glass. Wine tasting can be broken down into five simple steps:

1. Look at the color of the wine by tilting the glass slightly away from you and holding it above a white background. Notice the depth of color and, for reds, whether you can see your fingers through the wine or not. This may give a hint as to the richness or fullness of the wine.

2. Swirl the wine in the glass to help release the aromas.

3. Smell the wine, first about chin level and then by sticking your nose into the glass. Notice whether it is delicately scented or highly aromatic. Does it have a fruity or jammy aroma? Does it smell grassy or spicy? Does it have vanilla or oaky overtones? Is the aroma simple and straightforward, or is it complex, with several different smells?

4. Taste the wine by getting at least a couple of tablespoons of wine in your mouth. Hold it there for at least several seconds. Notice whether the wine is light or full-bodied. Is it sweet, tannic, crisp, or fruity? As with smell, is the taste simple and straightforward, or is it more complex, with different aspects to the flavor?

5. Reflect on the overall taste and balance of the wine, once you have swallowed it (or spit it out into a tasting bucket, if you're tasting many different wines). How long do the flavors last in your mouth? Does one flavor stand out or is the wine balanced? Does the taste seem to evolve and change?

While wineries include their own descriptions on tasting sheets, try not to be influenced by them. Rather, think about what the wine smells and tastes like to you, and jot down your own comments on the page.

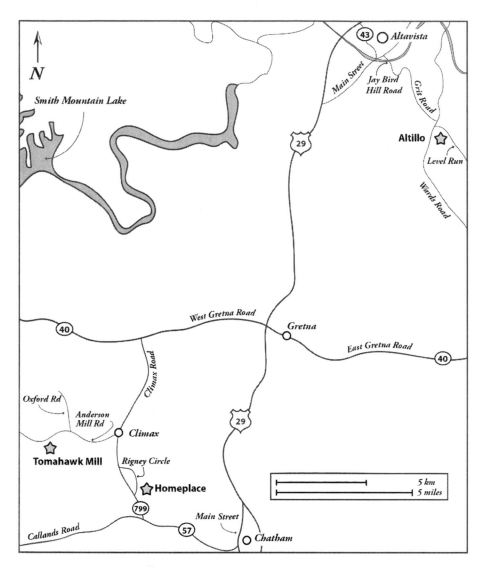

Map 10.4. Danville (Altavista section)

DANVILLE

Altillo Vineyards
620 Level Run Road
Hurt VA 24533

Hours: Th–F 12:00–6:00, Sa 12:00–6:00 (to 8:00 in summer)   434-324-4160

Closed New Year's, Thanksgiving, Christmas   www.altillovineyards.com

Stay Tuned: Facebook   E-mail: altavistavineyards@yahoo.com

Altillo Winery is a small family-owned and operated vineyard that opened its doors to the public in 2010. Originally named Altavista, Altillo was launched by Bob and Eric Schenkel, who bought the property in 2000 and produced their first vintage in 2009. Altavista produces all Virginia-grown wine using both fruit from their own vineyards and from other nearby growers. The winery sponsors occasional live music and special events, both at their Hurt winery and at The Overlook on Mountain Lake Road (VA Route 700), two miles south of the Mountain Lake Hotel (May through October). Dogs are welcome.

White Wines: Chardonnay, Viognier, Vista Blanca.

Rosé Wines: Vista Rosa.

Red Wines: Cabernet Franc, Meritage, Shiraz.

Price Range: $15–$20

Tastings: $5 per person.

Directions: From U.S. Route 29, take the Route 43 exit onto Bedford Avenue and drive into the town of Altavista. Turn left onto Main Street (U.S. Route 29 Business) and take the third right onto Pittsylvania Avenue (Route 668) which becomes Ricky van Shelton Drive after crossing the Roanoke River, then Jay Bird Hill Road and finally Grit Road, driving 4 miles in all. Turn left onto Level Run Road. Continue about 1/2 mile to the winery entrance on the right.

Homeplace Vineyard
568 Rigney Circle
Chatham VA 24531

Hours: M–Sa 11:00–6:00 (Mar–Nov),   434-432-9463 (WINE)
Closed Jan–Feb, Thanksgiving, Christmas   www.thehomeplacevineyard.com
Stay Tuned: Facebook   E-mail: thehomeplacevineyard@yahoo.com

Joe and Brenda Williams established Homeplace Vineyard in 2005 on a farm that has been in the Williams family for four generations. After converting the tobacco fields into a vineyard, the couple began selling grapes to other wineries in the area before establishing their own winery and opening their doors to the public in 2010. They built their tasting room on the site of the original family homestead (or, "homeplace" in Southern parlance), using timbers from the old tobacco barns that had been used in the farm's previous incarnation. Homeplace sponsors Flip Flop Fridays in the summer that feature live music and sangria and wine tastings. The facility may be rented for weddings and private parties.

Fruit Wines: Cabin Sunset *(strawberry).*

White Wines: Traminette, Viognier.

Blush Wines: Rockin' Rosé.

Red Wines: Cabernet Sauvignon, Chambourcin, Old Red Tractor *(Cabernet Sauvignon, Chambourcin)*, ShamRaz.

Price Range: $10–$15

Tastings: $5 per person.

Directions: From Chatham, take Route 57 west for 4.5 miles. Turn right onto Climax Road (Route 799) and drive 1.4 miles. Turn right onto Rigney-Circle and drive 1/2 mile. The winery entrance will be on the right.

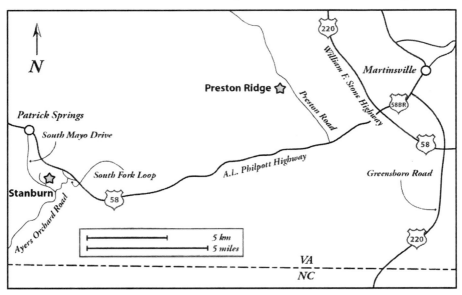

Map 10.5. Danville (Martinsville sections)

Preston Ridge Winery
4105 Preston Road
Martinsville VA 24112

Hours: W–Su 10:00–6:00, (summer); F–Sa 12:00–5:00 (winter)   276-957-2100
Closed New Year's, Thanksgiving, Christmas   www.prestonridgewinery.com
Stay Tuned: Facebook   E-mail: PrestonRidge@comcast.net

Preston Ridge was established by Lawrence and Lois Penn, who opened their small winery to the public in March 2010. After spending several years honing his skills as a home winemaker, Lawrence decided to branch out with a tasting room. Preston Ridge currently uses grapes from vineyards in the region to produce its eight wines while its own vineyard matures. Visitors are welcome to bring their own picnic lunches to enjoy on the grounds. The winery gift shop includes a range of winemaking supplies for purchase.

Fruit Wines: Apple, Blueberry.

White Wines: Chardonnay, Riesling, Vidal Blanc.

Blush Wines: Blushing Katie (Chambourcin).

Red Wines: Cabernet Franc, Chambourcin, Rosie Ryan *(Chambourcin, Cabernet Franc)*.

Price Range: $14

Tastings: $5 per person.

Purchasing: Phone orders available for VA residents only.

Directions: From Martinsville, take the A.L. Philpott Highway (U.S. Route 58 Business) south for about 5 miles. Turn right onto Preston Road and drive 4 miles. The winery driveway will be on the left.

Stanburn Winery
158 Conner Drive
Stuart VA 24171

Hours: Sa 12:00–6:00, Su 1:00–6:00, Apr–Dec   276-694-7074
Closed Dec–Mar   www.stanburnwinery.com
Stay Tuned: Facebook, Twitter   E-mail: david@stanburnwinery.com

Nelson and Elsie Stanley began operations in 1999 when they planted a ten-acre vineyard on their hundred-acre property. After selling their grapes to other wineries for over a decade, they opted to open their own winery, whose name combines Stanley with Elsie's maiden name of Burnette. The family is converting an old farmhouse on their Patrick County property to serve as a larger tasting facility. Son David and daughter Dawn Stanley Osborne oversee the vineyard and are currently working with Michael Shaps at Virginia Wineworks to produce Stanburn's wines.

White Wines: Chardonnay, Meadow Breeze, Traminette.

Blush Wines: Bull's Blush.

Red Wines: Big A Red, Cabernet Franc, Chambourcin, Poorhouse.

Price Range: $12–$16

Tastings: $6 per person, with souvenir glass.

Purchasing: E-mail ordering for Virginia residents only.

Directions: From U.S. Route 58, turn south onto the South Fork loop **and** then south again onto Ayers Orchard Road. Drive 2.2 miles and turn right onto South Mayo Drive. After 3/4 mile, turn right onto Conner Drive. The winery entrance will be on the right.

Tomahawk Mill Winery
9221 Anderson Mill Road
Chatham VA 24531

Hours: Tu–Sa 11:00–5:00, Su 1:00–5:00 (15 Mar–15 Dec)   434-432-1063
Closed Thanksgiving, 15 Dec–15 Mar   www.tomahawkmill.com
Stay Tuned: Facebook   E-mail: info@tomahawkmill.com

Tomahawk Mill is housed in a grist mill founded in 1888 by Sergeant James Anderson, a Confederate Civil War veteran. The mill was in continuous operation by the family until 1988, when Anderson's cousin closed the mill and planted a vineyard. Now owned by Corky and Nancy Medaglia, Tomahawk Mill offers tastings in the restored mill; guests may also picnic on the grounds. The winery sponsors several special events, including a summer festival; Halloween in the Gristmill, with wine and gourmet food and readings from Edgar Allen Poe; and a Holiday Open House in December.

Fruit Wines: Apple.

White Wines: Chardonnay, Riesling, Vidal Blanc.

Blush Wines: Country Blush.

Red Wines: Sergeant Anderson's Red *(Concord)*, Tobacco Road Blues *(Cabernet Sauvignon, Cabernet Franc, Chambourcin)*.

Sweet/Dessert Wines: Earl of Chatham Mead, Sweet Concord.

Price Range: $11–$20

Purchasing: Online ordering is available via VinoShipper for AK, FL, ID, LA, MO, NE, NV, NH, NM, ND, OH, OR, DC, WV, and WY.

Directions: From the town of Chatham, turn west on Depot Street (Route 57) and drive 4.5 miles. Turn right onto Climax Road (Route 799) and drive 3.5 miles. Make a sharp left onto Anderson Mill Road (Route 649) and continue 3 miles to the winery on the left.

SERVING TEMPERATURES

A commonly held rule of thumb is that sparkling, white, and rosé wines should be served chilled, while red wines are served at room temperature. But what do "chilled" and "room temperature" really mean? And how much does temperature really matter?

To test the effect of temperature on wine flavor for yourself, pour equal amounts of a white wine and a red wine into glasses, cover them with plastic wrap, and refrigerate the glasses for at least one hour. Have a friend blindfold you so that you cannot see the wine. Can you tell which is the red and which is the white?

According to many wine experts, the ideal serving temperatures for white and rosé wines range from about 45 to 55 degrees Fahrenheit, and reds from 50 to 65 degrees Fahrenheit. In general, that means whites and rosés are often served much too cold, while reds could be slightly cooler than they often are.

Colder serving temperatures tend to reduce the aroma of a wine, while warmer temperatures let it blossom. Cooler temperatures also tend to bring out the acidity and tannins in a wine, while warmer serving temperatures reduce them.

To test this, pour a glass of a tannic red, such as Cabernet Sauvignon, cover with plastic wrap, and let it chill in the refrigerator for an hour. You'll probably find that the chilled Cabernet is so astringent as to be barely drinkable. Let it warm to room temperature, however, and the tannins will soften.

Similarly, chilling a very fruity white wine will add crispness to balance out the fruit and give it better structure. Pour two glasses, cover both with plastic wrap, and put one in the refrigerator while leaving the other on the counter. After an hour, compare them. The colder wine will have a bit more acidic crispness to it.

For sparkling wines, serving temperature is also important. Colder temperatures help reduce the release of the carbon dioxide bubbles in sparkling wines, helping them keep their bubbliness longer.

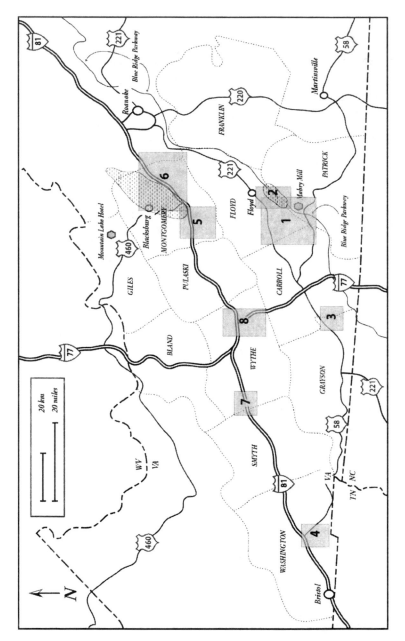

Map 11.1. **Blue Ridge Region and Rocky Knob AVA:** (1) Blue Ridge
Parkway (western section); (2) Blue Ridge Parkway (eastern section);
(3) Blue Ridge Parkway (Mt. Vale); (4) Blue Ridge/I-81 (Abingdon);
(5) Blue Ridge/I-81 (Attimo); (6) Blue Ridge/I-81 (Beliveau);
(7) Blue Ridge/I-81 (Rural Retreat); (8) Blue Ridge/I-81 (West Wind).

11. BLUE RIDGE & ROCKY KNOB AVA

The Blue Ridge Mountains stretch from Virginia's border with Maryland down into North Carolina. The Blue Ridge is the easternmost ridge of the Appalachian Mountain chain, and its southern stretches have some of the highest elevations in the United States east of the Rocky Mountains, with some peaks in North Carolina and Tennessee reaching over six thousand feet above sea level. As one would expect given the elevations, summer temperatures in the Blue Ridge wine region are cooler than elsewhere in the state. Along with the Heart of Appalachia region, this area has the highest precipitation in all Virginia, with just over forty-seven inches per year.

The Blue Ridge's wineries capture the full range of winery sizes and experiences in Virginia. From Chateau Morrisette's expansive grounds and on-site restaurant to the more intimate experiences at Blacksnake Meadery and Foggy Ridge Cider, the Blue Ridge offers something for every visitor's tastes and preferences. Two of its wineries—Chateau Morrisette and Villa Appalaccia—are in the Rocky Knob AVA, which is the smallest AVA in Virginia.

<u>Things to see and do</u>: Rich in natural beauty, the Blue Ridge area is perfect for nature lovers, offering multiple trails, camping sites, and fishing spots. The 469-mile Blue Ridge Parkway stretches from Waynesboro down into North Carolina; its northern extension, the Skyline Drive, meanders north-

ward to Front Royal. It is a lovely driving tour that is popular in summer for its access to outdoor activities and in the fall for its colorful foliage displays. The Parkway's website (www.blueridgeparkway.org) lists special events and programs, fishing and hiking information, and weather closures.

Mabry Mill in Floyd County at Blue Ridge Milepost (MP) 176 is one of the most picturesque and photographed structures in the area. In addition, there are several living history sites along the Parkway in the summer, including the mid-19th century Johnson Farm and Aunt Polly's Ordinary at MP 85 in the Peaks of Otter. The Blue Ridge region is also home to one of Virginia's only two natural lakes, Mountain Lake, whose size can vary considerably due to leakage from a natural crevice in the lake bottom. The Mountain Lake Conservancy Hotel was featured in the 1987 film *Dirty Dancing* and offers special *Dirty Dancing* weekends in the summer for guests.

The Blue Ridge Region is also home to the eastern and southern portions of the Crooked Road Heritage Trail, a scenic trail that winds from Rocky Mount to Floyd, then to Stuart, where it follows U.S. Route 58 westward through Abingdon and Bristol. The trail features numerous events and places highlighting the region's deep bluegrass music history and culture. Downloadable maps and other information can be accessed at www. thecrookedroad.org.

<u>Wine Trails</u>: There are two wine trails that include wineries in the Blue Ridge region. The Blue Ridge Wine Trail features wineries in both Virginia and North Carolina, while the Mountain Road Wine Experience focuses on seven wineries in the Blue Ridge and South Virginia regions. More details are included in Appendix 1.

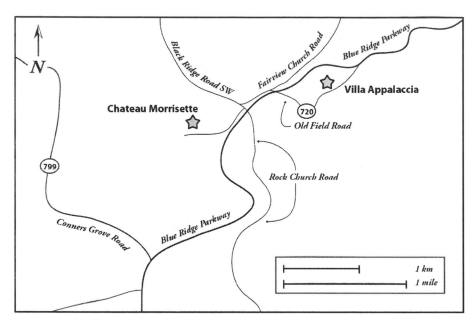

Map 11.2. Blue Ridge Parkway (eastern section)

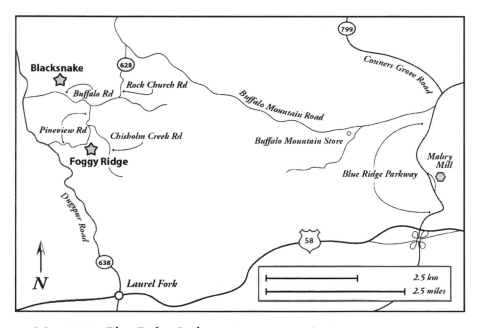

Map 11.3. Blue Ridge Parkway (western section)

BLUE RIDGE PARKWAY

Blacksnake Meadery
605 Buffalo Road
Dugspur VA 24325

Hours: 11:00–5:00 Sa–Su (always call first to confirm)   540-834-6172
Closed Nov–Apr   www.blacksnakemead.com
Stay Tuned: Facebook, Twitter   E-mail: blacksnake@blacksnakemead.com

Teachers Steve and Joanne Villers started their meadery after spending several years making their own home brews. Honeybees on their Blue Ridge property now supply about half of the honey used in their production. Their meads include traditional mead as well as cyser (pressed apple cider and honey), melomel (mead with fruit), and hydromel (light mead). Blacksnake offers honey tastings and Thanksgiving and Holiday (December) open houses. Children are welcome.

Blacksnake meads may also be sampled in nearby Floyd at The Tasting Room (www.thetastingroomva.com), which is open on Fridays (4:00–9:00), Saturdays (11:00–6:00), and Sundays (1:00–4:00).

Meads: Meloluna, Sweet Traditional, Sweet Virginia, Tupelo Honey Wine, Wildflower Honey Wine.

Cyser: Crabapple, Cyser.

Melomel: Squashed *(pumpkin)*.

Hydromel: Hoppy Bee Brew, Lime Bee Brew.

Price Range: $12–$18

Purchasing: Online ordering available to CA and VA only.

Directions: From the Blue Ridge Parkway, turn between Milepost 174 and 175 onto Buffalo Mountain Road (Route 628) and drive 7 miles, staying straight at the Buffalo Mountain Store. Turn left onto Rock Church Road. At the Buffalo Presbyterian Church, the road becomes Buffalo Road (portions unpaved). Continue 1/2 mile and bear right to stay on Buffalo Road. Turn in 0.8 miles into the driveway on the right.

Chateau Morrisette Winery
287 Winery Road SW
Floyd VA 24091

Hours: M–Th 10:00–5:00, F–Sa 10:00–6:00, Su 11:00–5:00 540-593-2865
Closed Thanksgiving Eve & Day, Christmas Eve & Day www.thedogs.com
Stay Tuned: Facebook, Twitter, newsletter E-mail: info@thedogs.com

Chateau Morrisette was established in 1978 when the Morrisette family planted their first vines. Now selling well over sixty thousand cases of wine annually, the winery produces fifteen different wines from 150 acres of vineyards across Virginia. Chateau Morrisette sponsors live music, food and wine pairing dinners, and festivals, and has become a popular stop for Virginia wine tourists. The winery also sends a portion of its proceeds from several special wine label series to various charities, including the Blue Ridge Parkway Foundation (MP series), a Virginia Tech scholarship fund (Hokie series), medical research into canine EPI disease (For The Love of Dogs), and Service Dogs of Virginia and St. Francis Service Dogs (Service Dogs series). Lunch and dinner are available at the in-house winery restaurant. The facilities may also be rented for private parties and weddings. Children and leashed pets are welcome.

Fruit Wines: Apple, Blackberry, Peach.

Sparkling Wines: Star Dog *(Chardonnay)*.

White Wines: Angel Chardonnay, BRP Milepost 000 Chardonnay, Chardonnay, Hokie Bird White, Hollins Rocking Chair White *(Chardonnay)*, Independence, Our Dog Blue *(Riesling, Traminette, Vidal Blanc)*, Parkway Chardonnay, Vidal Blanc, Viognier.

Rosé Wines: Blushing Dog *(Vidal Blanc, Riesling, Chambourcin)*, Dry Rosé *(Chambourcin)*.

Red Wines: Black Dog, BRP Milepost 469 Dry Red, Cabernet Franc, Cabernet Sauvignon, Chambourcin, Hokie Bird Red, Hollins Rocking Chair Red, Merlot, Petit Verdot, Pinot Noir, Reserve Tannat, Parkway Dry Red.

Sweet/Dessert Wines: Frosty Dog *(Traminette, Vidal Blanc)*, Red Mountain Laurel, Sweet Mountain Laurel.

Price Range: $10–$48

Tastings: $5 per person with souvenir glass.

Groups: Reservations required for groups of 12 or more.

Wheelchair accessible.

Purchasing: Online purchasing for residents of all states and Washington DC, *except* AK, AZ, HI, KY, MA, MO, ND, and UT.

Kennel Club members receive discounts on wines and members-only events.

Directions: From the Blue Ridge Parkway, turn west onto Black Ridge Road between Milepost 171 and 172. Take an immediate left onto Winery Road; the winery will be about 1/2 mile on right.

Foggy Ridge Cider
1328 Pineview Road
Dugspur VA 24325

Hours: Sa 11:00–5:00, F, Su 12:00–5:00 (Apr–Dec) 276-398-2337
Closed Jan–Mar www.foggyridgecider.com
Stay Tuned: Facebook, Twitter, newsletter E-mail: cidermaker@foggyridgecider.com

Chuck and Diane Flynt first began planting their orchard in 1996 and now grow over thirty varieties of apples on two hundred acres on elevations reaching three thousand feet. Their apples include Harrison, Graniwinkle, Roxbury Russet, Virginia Hewe's Crab, Dabinett, Tremlett's Bitter, Muscadet de Berney, and Cox's Orange Pippin. Diane is the cidermaker and currently produces four ciders made only from apple juice and yeast. Foggy Ridge's outstanding website offers much interesting information and history about apples and cider.

Foggy Ridge ciders may also be sampled at The Tasting Room in Floyd, Virginia; see entry under Blacksnake Meadery for more information.

Foggy Ridge's First Fruit *(American heirloom apples)*

Foggy Ridge Handmade *(Newtown Pippin)*

Pippin Black *(Newtown Pippin, Arkansas Black)*

Pippin Gold *(Newtown Pippin, Apple Brandy)*

Serious Cider *(Tremlett's Bitter, Dabinett, Ashmead's Kernel, Roxbury Russet)*

Sweet Stayman Cider *(Stayman, Grimes Golden, Cox's Orange Pippin)*

Price Range: $15–$25

Purchasing: Shipping to Virginia residents only.

Directions: From Blue Ridge Parkway, turn west between Milepost 174 and 175 onto Buffalo Mountain Road (Route 628). Drive for 7 miles, staying straight at the Buffalo Mountain Store. Turn left onto Rock Church Road (Route 628). Pass the Buffalo Presbyterian Church and then turn left onto Pineview Road (Route 656) to the cidery 1/2 mile on left.

❖ ❖ ❖

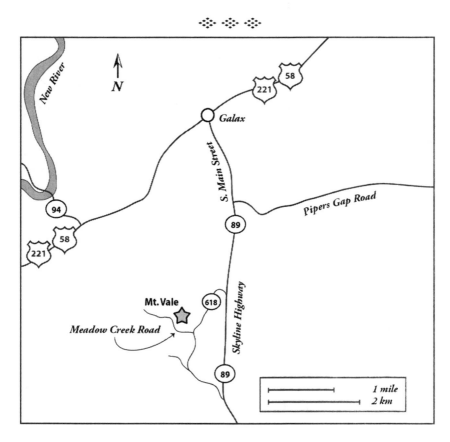

Map 11.4. Blue Ridge Parkway (Mt. Vale)

Mt. Vale Vineyards
3222 Meadow Creek Road
Galax VA 24333

Hours: Th–Sa 10:00–6:00   276-238-9946
Closed New Year's, Thanksgiving, Christmas   www.mtvalewine@gmail.com
Stay Tuned: Facebook   E-mail: mtvalewine@gmail.com

Mt. Vale Vineyard was opened to the public in late 2011 by Noel and Peggy Belcher, who decided to establish Mt. Vale to fulfill a long-held dream after both retired from their construction and nursing professions in Raleigh, North Carolina. The couple found their ideal property on a scenic setting just off the Blue Ridge Parkway. North Carolina vintner Mary Simmons is serving as Mt. Vale's winemaker. Visitors are welcome to linger in the tasting room or outdoor patios and gazebos. The winery sponsors wine dinners and live music, and may be rented for weddings or special events. Light fare is available for purchase.

Mt. Vale also has a guest house for overnight stays on the property.

Fruit Wines: Cranberry Delight *(Chardonnay, cranberry)*.

White Wines: Cellar Door *(Chardonel)*, Chardonnay, Misty Morning.

Red Wines: Cabernet Sauvignon, Table for Two.

Price Range: $15–$24

Tastings: $5 per person.

Purchasing: Online ordering available to VA residents or via VinoShipper to AK, FL, ID, LA, MN, MO, NE, NV, NH, NM, ND, OH, OR, DC, WV, and WY.

Directions: From U.S. Route 221, turn south onto Main Street (VA 89) at the town of Galax. Drive 3.3 miles and turn right onto Mt. Vale Road. After 1/2 mile, turn left onto Meadow Creek Road. The winery entrance will be 1/2 mile on the right.

Villa Appalaccia Winery
752 Rock Castle Gorge
Floyd VA 24091

Hours: F 11:00–5:00, Sa 11:00–6:00, Su 12:00–4:30 (May–Nov) 540-593-3100
Sa 11:00–5:00, Su 12:00–4:30 (Mar–Apr) www.villaappalaccia.com
Closed Dec–Mar E-mail: chianti@swva.net
Stay Tuned: Facebook, newsletter

Located just one mile from Chateau Morrisette, Villa Appalaccia opened to the public in 1995, six years after Stephen Haskill and Susanne Becker planted their first two-acre vineyard. The winery focuses on Italian varietals, including Primitivo, Malvasia, Aglianico, Corvina Veronese, and, most recently, Vermentino. Visitors are welcome to relax in the music garden or play on the bocce court. Cheeses, meats, and breads are available for purchase. Villa Appalaccia hosts several events for which reservations are required or have a fee, including All Things Olive, progressive tastings (with other area wineries), Flatbreads of the World, Cheeses of the World, Brick Oven Weekends, and Antipasta Weekends.

Villa Appalaccia wines may be sampled at The Tasting Room in Floyd, Virginia; see the entry under Blacksnake Meadery for more details.

Stephen and Susanne also own a villa in Tuscany that is available for rent by the week. See the website for more details.

Sparkling Wines: Allegra.

White Wines: Lirico, Pinot Grigio, Simpatico *(Malvasia Bianca, Pinot Grigio, Trebbiano)*.

Red Wines: Aglianico, Francesco Cabernet Franc, Primitivo, Sangiovese, Toscanello *(Cabernet Franc, Sangiovese, Primitivo)*.

Sweet/Dessert Wines: Alba Late Harvest Vidal, Raspberry Beret.

Price Range: $16–$20

Tastings: $5 per person.

Groups: Reservations required for groups of 6 or more.

Purchasing: Online ordering to VA only.

Directions: From the Blue Ridge Parkway, turn east onto Old Field Road (Route 720) between Milepost 170 and 172; there are two entrances to Old Field Road, one between MP 170 and 171, and another between MP 171 and 172. Follow Old Field Road (unpaved) to the winery driveway.

⥤⥢

WINE AROMAS

One of the most important elements of appreciating wine comes from the fragrance of the wine. Indeed, our sense of smell is so critical that we can perceive very little flavor from food or beverages without it.

Most wineries use tasting sheets to describe the aromas and tastes of the wines they present. These descriptions can be a helpful way to build our wine vocabulary, but it is important to also think about what the wine smells and tastes like to you. Each of us has distinct preferences in terms of smells and tastes; some people love green peas, for instance, while others loathe them. Wine is no different.

Wine aromas can be sorted into five broad clusters: fruit, floral, vegetal and spice, animal, and roasted.

Fruit aromas include citrus (orange or grapefruit, for instance), tropical (banana or pineapple), red berry (strawberry, raspberry), black berry (blackberry, blueberry, black currant), and stone fruit (apricot, peach). Floral tones include flowers (rose, violet), trees (hawthorn or linden), and even honey.

Vegetal and spice aromas encompass green pepper, earthy smells (mushroom or truffle), spicy tones (cedar or licorice), herbs (thyme, clove), and even vanilla. A wine may have a leathery or buttery smell; these, along with musk, are in the animal group. The roasted category includes toast, roasted nuts (hazelnut or almond), coffee, chocolate, and even smoke.

One way to build an aroma vocabulary is to start by identifying which broader category best categorizes the wine, then a subcategory, and finally a specific aroma. For example, if a wine smells fruity, think about whether that fruity aroma is a citrus or berry or stone fruit smell. Then decide which specific flavor you detect, such as peach or raspberry or pineapple. Over time, you'll develop a broader set of terms to describe the wines that you are tasting.

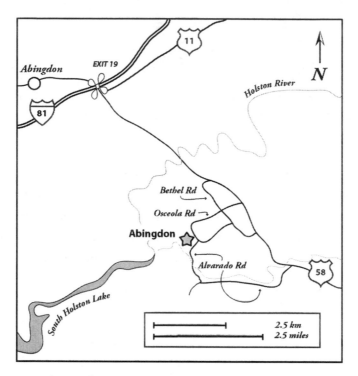

Map 11.5. Blue Ridge/I-81 (Abingdon)

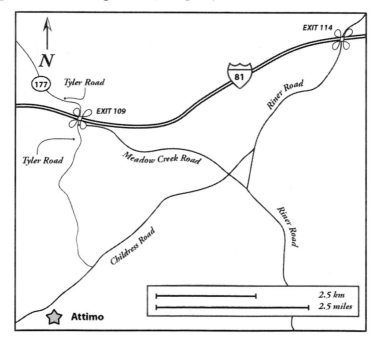

Map 11.6. Blue Ridge/I-81 (Attimo)

BLUE RIDGE/I-81

Abingdon Vineyard & Winery
20530 Alvarado Road
Abingdon VA 24211

Hours: Tu–Sa 10:00–6:00,   276-623-1255

Su 12:00–6:00 (mid-Mar to mid-Dec)   www.abingdonwinery.com

Closed Thanksgiving, mid-Dec to mid-Mar E-mail: info@abingdonwinery.com

Abingdon Winery is a small farm winery along the scenic South Holston River. The winery is owned and operated by Ron Carlson and his wife Janet Lee Nordin, who began planting their first vines in 1998 on the fifty-three-acre property. Abingdon is near a number of boating, hiking, and camping sites, with the Virginia Creeper Trail a mere half-mile away and the Appalachian Trail just five miles down the road in Damascus, Virginia. Snacks are available for purchase in the tasting room.

White Wines: Bare Chardonnay, Chardonnay, Chardonel, Misty River, Riesling, Traminette, Viognier.

Blush Wines: White Pinot Noir.

Red Wines: Bare Chambourcin, Cabernet Franc, Cabernet Sauvignon, Chambourcin, Norton, Red Hawk *(Chambourcin, Chardonel)*, Royal Blend, Special Red *(Cabernet Franc, Chambourcin, Norton)*.

Sweet/Dessert Wines: Alvarado Rouge, Appalachian Autumn, Appalachian Sunset *(Niagara, Cayuga)*, Creekside Blush, Dazzle, Misty River II, Razzle, Triple Duck.

Price Range: $11–$16

Tastings: First six tastes are complimentary; $1 per taste afterwards.

Groups: Reservations required for groups of 15 or more.

Purchasing: Online ordering available via VinoShipper to AK, FL, ID, LA, MO, NE, NV, NH, NM, ND, OH, OR, DC, WV, and WY; phone ordering available to NC and VA.

Directions: From I-81, take Exit 19 onto U.S. Route 58 East. Turn right after 5 miles onto Osceola Road (Route 722). Drive 2.4 miles and turn right onto Alvarado Road, immediately after a sharp turn; the winery driveway will be on the right.

Attimo Winery
4025 Childress Road
Christiansburg VA 24073

Hours: M, Th–Sa 11:00–6:00, Su 12:00–5:00
Closed New Year's, Thanksgiving, Christmas
Stay Tuned: Facebook, Twitter

540-382-7619
www.attimowinery.com
E-mail: wine@attimowinery.com

New Jersey natives Rik and Melissa Obiso established Attimo Winery in 2007 after returning to southwestern Virginia where they had attended Virginia Tech some years earlier. They first began planting their sixteen-acre vineyard that same year, harvesting their first grapes in 2010. Their interest in winemaking began as a hobby that grew into a desire to expand to the commercial side. Light snacks are available for purchase at the tasting room, which offers both indoor and outdoor seating for visitors.

Fruit Wines: Just Kissed *(Vidal Blanc, raspberry)*, Sudden Downpour *(apple, white wine)*, Sweet Berry Sunset *(raspberry, red wine)*.

White Wines: Bull Frog Symphony, I Do *(Traminette, Petit Manseng)*, Masquerade *(Chardonnay)*, Off The Cuff, Sonnet *(Vidal Blanc)*, Yesterday's Song *(Chardonnay)*.

Orange Wines: Blaze *(Vidal Blanc)*.

Rosé Wines: Firefly Dance *(Cabernet Franc)*.

Red Wines: A.D. 325 *(Chambourcin)*, After Midnight, Aviator, Deep Silence *(Cabernet Franc)*, Vertex *(Cabernet Sauvignon)*.

Fortified Wines: Seduction.

Price Range: $15–$26

Tastings: $5 per person; $1 per taste for reserve tasting.

Groups: Reservations requested for groups of 10 or more.

Directions: From I-81, take Exit 109 (Radford) south onto Tyler Road (Route 177). Drive 3 miles and turn right onto Childress Road. The winery entrance will be 1 mile on the left.

Beliveau Estate
5415 Gallion Ridge Road
Blacksburg VA 24060

Hours: F–Su, holiday M 12:00–6:00	540-961-0505
Closed New Year's, Christmas	www.beliveauestate.com
Stay Tuned: Facebook, Twitter	E-mail: info@beliveauestate.com

Joyce and Yvan Beliveau opened their winery in 2012, three years after planting their first vineyard and five years after establishing their bed & breakfast inn on a 165-acre property located between Roanoke and Blacksburg. Visitors can enjoy scenic views of the hills and ponds from the tasting room's verandas. Beliveau sponsors a Lavendar Festival the last Sunday in June, as well as Tapas Nights and other special events. The facilities are available for weddings and private events.

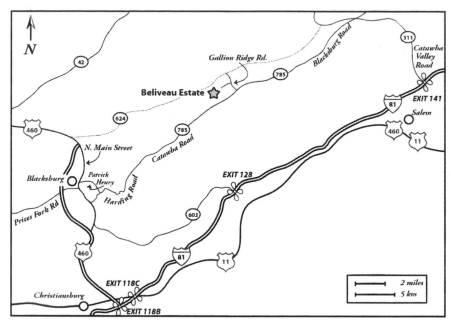

Map 11.7. Blue Ridge/I-81 (Beliveau)

The Inn at Beliveau Estate offers five guest rooms for overnight stays; special packages are available.

White Wines: Afternoon Delight *(Vidal Blanc)*, Destiny *(Vidal Blanc)*, Lovers' Quest *(Vidal Blanc)*, Reflection *(Traminette)*.

Red Wines: A Cappella *(Landot Noir)*, Rainbow *(Zinfandel)*, Serenity *(Chambourcin)*, Silhouette *(Cabernet Sauvignon)*, Summer Rose, Sunset Slipper *(Zinfandel)*.

Price Range: $15–$26

Tastings: $5 per person.

Wine club members receive discounts and invitations to special events.

Purchasing: Online ordering is available via VinoShipper to AK, FL, ID, LA, MN, MO, NE, NV, NH, NM, ND, OH, OR, VA, DC, WV, and WY.

Directions: From I-81 Northbound, take Exit 118B toward Christiansburg/ Blacksburg and merge onto U.S. Route 460 West. Drive 9.4 miles and exit onto Prices Fork Road (VA 412 East) into Blacksburg. Drive 1.5 miles and turn left onto North Main Street (U.S. Route 460 Business). After about one mile, turn right onto Patrick Henry Drive and continue 0.8 miles. Turn left onto Harding Avenue which will become Harding Road and then Catawba Road. Drive 10.9 miles in all and turn left onto Gallion Ridge Road (portions unpaved). Drive 1.2 miles and turn left into the long winery drive; the winery will be 3/4 mile ahead.

From I-81 Southbound, take Exit 141 (New Castle) and merge onto Catawba Valley Road (Route 311 North). Drive 7 miles and turn left onto Blacksburg Road (Route 785). Drive 10 miles and turn right onto Gallion Ridge Road (portions unpaved). Continue 1.2 miles and turn left into the long winery drive; the winery will be 3/4 mile ahead.

Davis Valley Winery & Vineyard

1167 Davis Valley Road

Rural Retreat VA 24368

Hours: M–Sa, 10:00–5:00, Su 12:00–5:00   276-686-8855
Closed New Year's, Thanksgiving, Christmas   www.davisvalleywinery.com
                                                E-mail: info@davisvalleywinery.com

After Rusty and Ruth Rhea Cox purchased this scenic hilltop property, they converted the former dairy farm to a vineyard, with plantings that include Maréchal Foch, Norton, Corot Noir, and Steuben. Visitors can sample a flight of wines on a hundred-year-old bar in their tasting room. The winery may be rented for special events, dinners, and weddings.

White Wines: Chardonnay, Davis Valley White, Virginia Breeze White.

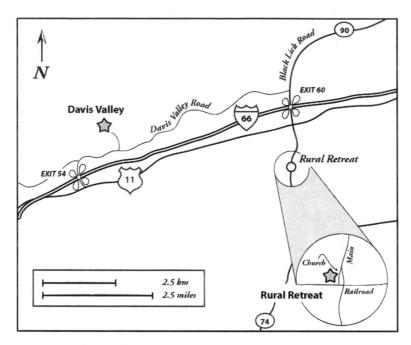

Map 11.8. Blue Ridge/I-81 (Rural Retreat)

Rosé Wines: Davis Valley Blush.

Red Wines: Autumn Red, Cabernet Franc, Chambourcin, Corot Noir, Davis Valley Red *(Maréchal Foch)*, Virginia Breeze Red *(Steuben)*.

Sweet/Dessert Wines: Appalachian Breeze.

Price Range: $11–$19

Tastings: $4 per person.

Directions: From I-81, take Exit 54 (Grose Close). Turn north onto Winsor Road, which will bend right and become Davis Valley Road (portions unpaved). Continue 1.4 miles to the winery on the left.

Rural Retreat Winery & Dye's Vineyards
201 Church Street
Rural Retreat VA 24368

Hours: M–Th 11:00–5:30, Fr–Sa 11:00–6:30, Su 12:00–5:30   276-686-8300

Closed New Year's, Thanksgiving, Christmas   www.ruralretreatwinery.com

Stay Tuned: Facebook, Twitter   E-mail: info@ruralretreatwinery.com

Rural Retreat is owned and operated by Scott and Linda Mecimore, who purchased Dye's Vineyards and Winery in 2007. The tasting room is located in a combination gift shop and eat-in deli, with the tasting bar toward the back. Children are welcome. The winery also offers a two-bedroom suite for overnight stays.

White Wines: Chardonnay, Golden Muscat, Riesling, Traminette, Vidal Blanc.

Rosé Wines: Chambourcin Rosé, Russell Rosé, Sainte Marie Rosé.

Red Wines: Cabernet Franc, Cabernet Sauvignon, Cardinal Red, Chambourcin, Depot Red *(Steuben, Concord)*, Cripple Creek, Sweet Gracie Red.

Price Range: $10–$24

Tastings: $4.50 per person.

Purchasing: Online shipping available via VinoShipper to AK, FL, ID, LA, MO, MN, NE, NV , NH, NM, ND, OH, OR, DC, WV, and WY; direct shipping to VA residents.

Directions: From I-81 take Exit 60 onto Route 90 South toward Rural Retreat and drive 1.6 miles. Turn right onto Railroad Avenue and make an immediate right onto Church Street and the winery on the left.

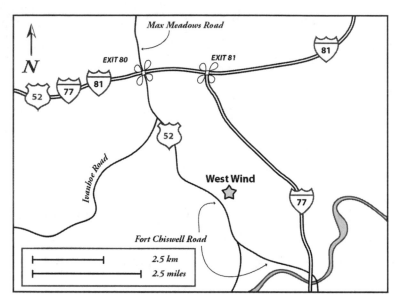

Map 11.9. Blue Ridge/I-81 (West Wind Farm)

West Wind Farm Winery
180 West Wind Drive
(Alternate GPS address: 2228 Fort Chiswell Road)
Max Meadows VA 24360

Hours: M–Sa 11:00–6:00, Su 1:00–6:00

276-699-2020

Closed New Year's, Easter, Thanksgiving, Christmas

www.westwindwine.com

Stay Tuned: Facebook, Twitter, newsletter

E-mail: info@westwindwine.com

West Wind is owned and operated by Paul and Brenda Hric on a family farm that has been in Brenda's family for four generations. The Hrics began planting their five-acre vineyard in 2003 and made their first wine in 2005. West Wind's tasting room offers both indoor and outdoor seating for visitors, as well as a gift shop with candles, glassware, and pottery. The winery hosts live music at Summer Saturdays concerts, as well as various festivals, including a fall Wine and Swine barbecue. The facilities may be rented for private events and dinners. The winery is certified Virginia Green. Children and leashed dogs are welcome

Fruit Wines: Galena Creek Blackberry *(with Merlot, Chambourcin)*, Galena Creek Peach *(with Vidal Blanc)*, New River Red *(Concord)*.

White Wines: Galena Creek White *(Vidal Blanc)*, Pinot Gris, Riesling.

Red Wines: Cabernet Sauvignon, Chambourcin, Galena Creek Red *(Cabernet Sauvignon, Cabernet Franc, Chambourcin)*, Heritage Reserve.

Price Range: $13–$19

Tastings: Complimentary tasting of 3 wines, $3 for additional tastes.

Groups: Reservations requested for groups of 8 or more, $5 per person.

Restrictions: Reservations required for buses.

Directions: From I-80/I-77, take Exit 80 at Fort Chiswell. Follow Fort Chiswell Road (U.S. Route 52) south for 4 miles to the winery entrance on the left, just past Archer Drive.

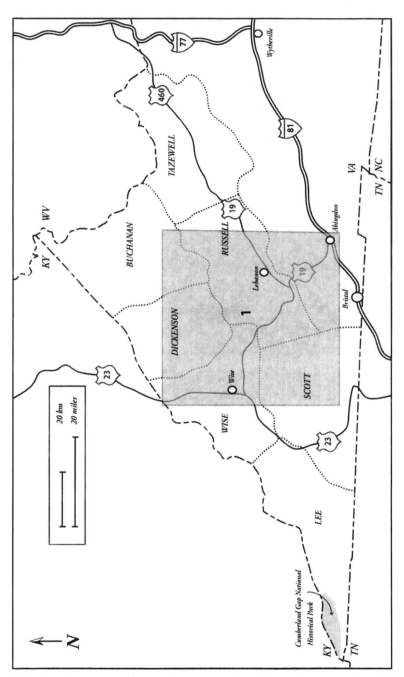

Map 12.1. Heart of Appalachia Region: (1) Heart of Appalachia

12. HEART OF APPALACHIA

The mountainous southwest corner of Virginia is an area of scenic and rugged natural beauty where river gorges cut through spectacular sandstone cliffs and rich coal seams streak through the rock formations. With its high elevations, the region has the coolest summer temperatures and highest precipitation in the state. The region's two wineries offer an intimate experience unique to the region. MountainRose honors the region's long coal-mining history in its wine names, while Vincent's Vineyard is a haven for fly-fishermen (and women).

Things to see and do: Multiple scenic drives allow nature lovers to enjoy the region's fall foliage. The area offers many opportunities for hiking, camping, and fishing. The region's coal mining history was depicted in John Fox's *Trail of the Lonesome Pine*, a 1913 novel adapted for film in 1936. The Heart of Appalachia Driving Tour leads visitors through various sites and towns through the region's counties; tour stages can be printed from Virginia's tourism website (www.virginia.org/heartofappalachiadrivingtour/).

The independent-minded people who settled this region brought with them a rich culture that endures in the rhythms and cadences of bluegrass and country music. This is the birthplace of country music legends June Carter Cash and the Carter Family, and Ralph Stanley. Visitors can experience the history and music of the region on the Crooked Road Heritage Trail which winds through ten counties and even more towns with local music festivals and jams; more information, including a map, is available at www.crookedroad.org.

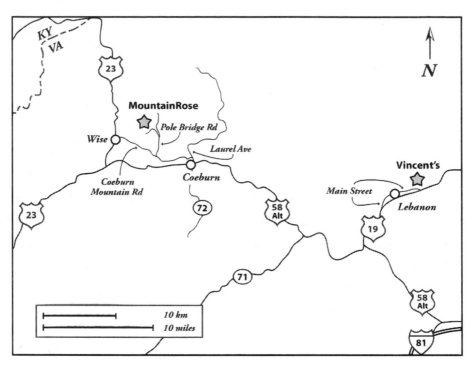

Map 12.2. Heart of Appalachia

HEART OF APPALACHIA

MountainRose Vineyards
10439 North Reservoir Road
Wise VA 24293

Hours: M–Sa 10:00–6:00
Closed New Year's, Thanksgiving, Christmas
Stay Tuned: Facebook, Twitter

276-328-2013
www.mountainrosevineyard.com
E-mail: swlawson@comcast.net

MountainRose got its start in 1997 when David Lawson first rooted one hundred grape vines from an eighty-year-old Concord vine on land his family has owned since the 1850s. The winery vineyard has now expanded to include plantings in Niagara, Traminette, and Vidal Blanc; the tasting room and production facility were completed in 2004. In honor of the area's long coal history, the Lawsons have named their wines after old coal seams in nearby mines and are active advocates of reclaiming old stripmined lands through grape and apple cultivation. MountainRose hosts a variety of events at the winery, including festivals, grape stomps, live music, and quilt shows. The winery facilities are available for rental for private parties or weddings. Children are welcome.

White Wines: Blair White, Gladeville White, Riesling, Traminette, Sweet Mountain Rose White *(Niagara)*.

Blush Wines: Darby Blush *(Chambourcin)*.

Red Wines: Cabernet Franc, Dorchester Red *(Chambourcin, Tannat)*, Gladeville Red, Jawbone Red, Pardee Red *(Chambourcin, Chancellor)*, Pocahontas Red.

Sweet/Dessert Wines: Autumn Gold.

Price Range: $9–$18

Wheelchair accessible.

Purchasing: Online ordering available for VA residents or via VinoShipper to AK, FL, ID, LA, MN, MO, NE, ND, NH, NM, NV, OH, OR, WV, WY, and DC.

Directions: From U.S. Route 23, take Business 23 into the town of Wise. Once in Wise, turn right at the first traffic light onto Main Street. Take a right at the third light onto Darden Drive. Just past the University of Virginia campus, Darden Drive becomes Coeburn Mountain Road (Route 646). Continue for four miles and turn left onto Pole Bridge Road at Hard Rock Contractors. Follow Pole Bridge Road 1.8 miles and turn left onto North Reservoir Road. The winery driveway will be 1/2 mile on right.

Vincent's Vineyard
2313 East Main Street
Lebanon VA 24266

Hours: M–Sa 11:00–6:00
Closed New Year's, Thanksgiving, Christmas
Stay Tuned: E-newsletter

276-889-2505
www.vincentsvineyard.com
E-mail: vincentsvineyard@yahoo.com

Vincent and Betsy Gilmer established this small family winery on their sixth-generation family farm in Russell County. The winery's three-acre vineyard and tasting room are located adjacent to Big Cedar Creek, a favorite spot for fly fishing in the foothills of Clinch Mountain. Visitors can sit and enjoy the view of the mountains and the farm's Katahdin sheep from the tasting room, which offers snacks and artisanal crafts for sale. Leashed pets are welcome.

White Wines: Angler's Choice, Shepherd's White *(Chardonel)*, Traminette.

Blush Wines: Make Me Blush *(Chambourcin).*

Red Wines: Cabernet Franc, Ambrosia *(Steuben),* Shepherd's Red.

Price Range: $10–$12

Groups: Please call ahead for group tastings.

Purchasing: Online ordering available via VinoShipper to AK, FL, ID, LA, MO, NE, NV, NH, NM, ND, OH, OR, DC, WV, and WY; direct shipping to VA residents.

Directions: From I-81, take Exit 17 (Abingdon/South Holston Dam) onto U.S. Route 19 North/U.S. Route 58 Alt. Stay on U.S. Route 19 North for 21.6 miles into Lebanon. Turn left onto East Main Street (U.S. Route 19 Business) at the first light after Walmart. Drive 1/2 mile to the winery entrance on right, just past Big Cedar Creek Bridge.

APPENDIX 1
VIRGINIA WINE TRAILS

Virginia has a number of wine trails that offer visitors a nicely packaged way of visiting the many wineries in the state. The wine trails all have different features and attractions, including several with passport programs that offer reduced tasting fees for visits to multiple wineries.

Appellation Trail (http://theappellationtrail.com)
Wineries: Glass House, Grace Estate (opening 2013), Moss Vineyards, Mountfair, Stinson, White Hall

Small family-run boutique wineries bordering on the Blue Ridge Mountains and Appalachian Trail. Website includes links to wineries, a printable map, and an events calendar.

Artisanal Wineries of Rappahannock (www.artwinerc.com)
Wineries: Chester Gap, Gadino Cellars, Narmada, Rappahannock Cellars, Sharp Rock

Family-run wineries that focus on small-lot production. Website includes a printable map and trail guide, events calendar, and links to wineries.

Bedford County Wine Trail (www.bedfordwinetrail.com)
Wineries: Hickory Hill, LeoGrande, Peaks of Otter, Savoy-Lee, White Rock

Family-run wineries in Bedford County. The trail's passport program offers a free wine glass for visiting all five wineries. Website includes a map and links to local festivals, attractions, lodgings, and restaurants.

Blue Ridge Whiskey Wine Loop (www.discovershenandoah.com/whiskey-wine-loop)

Wineries & Distilleries: Chester Gap, Copper Fox Distillery, DuCard, Gadino, Glen Manor, Rappahannock, Sharp Rock, Wisteria Farm

Wineries and one distillery near Shenandoah National Park, from Front Royal to Luray. Website includes a printable driving map and a list of attractions. On Facebook.

Blue Ridge Wine Trail (www.blueridgewinetrail.com)

Wineries: AmRhein, Blacksnake, Chateau Morrisette, Fincastle, Foggy Ridge, Peaks of Otter, Valhalla, Villa Appalaccia (in Virginia); Brushy Mountain, Laurel Gray, Old North State, Raffaldini, Round Peak, Shelton (in North Carolina)

Fourteen wineries along the Blue Ridge Mountains in both Virginia and North Carolina. Website includes links to bluegrass music events, local attractions, lodgings, and restaurants.

Blue Ridge Wine Way (www.blueridgewineway.com)

Wineries: Gray Ghost, LaGrange, Mediterranean, Molon Lave, Narmada, Oasis (by appointment only), Pearmund, Rappahannock, Unicorn

Website has a printable trail map, an e-newsletter sign-up, and an events calendar, as well as links to restaurants, lodgings, and local attractions. On Facebook.

Chesapeake Bay Wine Trail (www.chesapeakebaywinetrail.com)

Wineries: Athena, Belle Mount, Dog & Oyster, General's Ridge, Good Luck, Hague, Ingleside, Jacey, New Kent, Oak Crest, Saudé Creek, Vault Field

Trail centers on Northern Neck wineries with one nearby winery in the Hampton Roads region. Passport program offers discounts and entry for prizes for those who visit six of the trail's wineries. Website includes links to a printable map, dining, lodging, and local attractions.

Eastern Shore Wine Trail (www.easternshorewinetrail.com)
Wineries: Bloxom, Chatham, Holly Grove

Website has links to a printable map, local attractions, limo services, lodgings, and dining.

Fauquier County Wine Trail (http://fauquierwines.com)
Wineries: Aspen Dale, Barrel Oak, Chateau O'Brien, Delaplane, Desert Rose, Hume, Mediterranean, Miracle Valley, Molon Lave, Naked Mountain, Pearmund, Philip Carter, Piedmont, Rogers Ford, Three Fox, Vint Hill Craft, Winery at La Grange

Website offers an events calendar, a printable map, printable tasting sheets for each winery, and an option for entering online tasting notes for members. Links to restaurants, dining. On Facebook, Twitter.

Foothills Scenic Wine Trail (www.foothillsscenicwinetrail.com)
Wineries: DuCard, Sharp Rock

Website has an events calendar and downloadable maps. Newsletter.

Heart of Virginia Wine Trail (http://hovawinetrail.com)
Wineries: Cooper, Grayhaven, James River, Lake Anna

Passport program ($10) includes tastings at all four wineries, souvenir glass, entry for prize drawing. Website includes a downloadable trail map, an events calendar, and links to wineries.

Loudoun Wine Country (www.visitloudoun.org/Experience-Loudoun/wine-country)
Wineries: 8 Chains North, 868 Estate, Above Ground, Barns at Hamilton Station, Barrel Oak, Bluemont, Bogati, Boxwood, Breaux, Cana, Casanel, Catoctin Creek (by appointment only), Chrysalis, Corcoran, Crushed Cellars, Doukénie, Dry Mill, Fabbioli, Hidden Brook, Hiddencroft, Hillsborough, Lost Creek, Loudoun Valley, North Gate, Notaviva, Otium

Cellars, Quattro Goomba's, Sunset Hills, Swedenburg, Tarara, Village, Willowcroft, Zephaniah Farm

Website has links to downloadable and printable touring guide, wineries, wine tour services, local attractions, and driving tour maps. Passport program includes a chance for prize drawings after visits to five wineries.

Monticello Wine Trail (www.monticellowinetrail.org)

Wineries: Afton Mountain, Barboursville, Blenheim, Burnley, Cardinal Point, DelFosse, Early Mountain, First Colony, Flying Fox, Gabriele Rausse (not open to public), Glass House, Horton, Jefferson, Keswick, Kilaurwen, King Family, Lovingston, Mountfair, Pippin Hill, Pollak, Prince Michel, Reynard Florence, Stinson, Stone Mountain, Trump, Veritas, Virginia Wineworks, White Hall, Wisdom Oak

Website has printable Google maps for its five different sub-trails, an events calendar, links to restaurants, and lodgings. E-mail newsletter.

Mountain Road Wine Experience (www.mountainroadwineexperience.com)

Wineries: AmRhein, Attimo, Blacksnake, Chateau Morrisette, Foggy Ridge, Stanburn, Villa Appalaccia

Two-day ticket program ($25 if purchased in advance, $35 if purchased on site) includes tastings at all wineries. Website includes links to wineries and some local lodgings and restaurants.

Nelson 151 (http://nelson151.com)

Wineries and breweries: Afton, Cardinal Point, Flying Fox, Hill Top, Pollak, Veritas, Wintergreen; Blue Mountain Brewery, Devil's Backbone Brewing Company, Wild Wolf Brewing Company

Website includes a calendar of events, links to wineries and breweries, restaurants, and lodgings along Route 151, as well as a printable map and directions. Facebook, Twitter.

Shenandoah County Wine Trail (www.shenandoahtravel.org—select "Wine Trail" under Things to Do>Agri-tourism)
Wineries: Cave Ridge, North Mountain, Shenandoah, Wolf Gap

   Website has printable Google maps of winery locations, links to local attractions, and an online Shenandoah County travel guide.

Shenandoah Valley Wine Country Trail (http://shenandoahvalley winetrail.com)
Wineries: Barren Ridge, Blue Ridge, Bluestone, Cave Ridge, Cedar Creek (by appointment only), Cross Keys, Lexington Valley, North Mountain, Ox-Eye, Rockbridge, Shenandoah, Valerie Hill, Wisteria Farm, Wolf Gap

   Website includes an events calendar, links to wineries, local attractions, and a printable Google trail map. On Facebook.

Southern Virginia Wine Trail (www.sovawinetrail.com)
Wineries: Annefield, Bright Meadows, DeVault, Greenwood, Hickory Hill, Homeplace, Hunting Creek, Molliver, Rosemont, Sans Soucy, Tomahawk Mill, White Oak Mountain Meadery

   Website includes a printable passport, a list of bed & breakfast inns, a trail map, and an events calendar.

Tuskie's Wine Trail (www.tuskies.com/WineTrail2011/)
Wineries: 8 Chains North, Barrel Oak, Bluemont, Bogati, Boxwood, Breaux, Casanel, Catoctin Creek (by appointment only), Chrysalis, Corcoran, Crushed Cellars, Delaplane, Doukénie, Dry Mill, Fabbioli, Hidden Brook, Hiddencroft, Hillsborough, Lost Creek, Loudoun Valley, North Gate, Notaviva, Pearmund, Quattro Goomba's, Sunset Hills, Swedenburg, Tarara, Veramar, Village, Willowcroft, Winery at La Grange, Zephaniah Farm

   Website includes an interactive trail map with wineries, restaurants, and bed & breakfast inns; a coupon book for discounts is also available.

Vintage Piedmont (http://vintagepiedmont.com)
Wineries: Barrel Oak, Desert Rose, Naked Mountain, Philip Carter, Rappahannock
   Website has a map and links to wineries.

Virginia Sesquicentennial Winery Project (www.virginiawine.org/sesquicentennial)
Wineries: Bright Meadows, Byrd, Casanel, Democracy, DuCard, Fox Meadow, General's Ridge, Gray Ghost, Ingleside, James River, Keswick, Lake Anna, MountainRose, Oak Crest, Prince Michel, Spring Creek, Tarara, Three Fox, Tomahawk Mill, Veramar, West Wind Farm, Winery at La Grange, Woodland Farm
   Website includes a map of the wineries and Civil War battlefields.

Wine Trail of Botetourt County (www.botetourtwinetrail.com)
Wineries: Blue Ridge, Fincastle, Virginia Mountain
   Website includes a downloadable trail map, links to wineries, places to stay, and local attractions. On Facebook, Twitter, YouTube.

APPENDIX 2
VIRGINIA WINE BLOGS

Since the number of wine blogs seems to grow by the month, the following list represents a quick selection of the most frequently visited sites that focus either exclusively or predominately on Virginia wines and wineries. These bloggers have a wide range of styles and opinions; try several on for size to see which seem to mesh well with your own experiences and preferences.

Beltway Bacchus (http://beltwaybacchus.blogspot.com)
Authored by a Washington D.C.-based blogger who wishes to remain anonymous. Blog entries cover Virginia wines and wineries, as well as wine tastings and wineries in other states. Includes photos, search engine. Twitter.

Charlottesville Uncorked (http://cvilleuncorked.com)
Authored by Tricia Traugott, a realtor and Texas native who focuses on Virginia wine and winery events in the greater Charlottesville area. Includes photos and links. Facebook, Twitter, RSS feed.

Drink What You Like (http://drinkwhatyoulike.wordpress.com)
Frank Morgan blogs about wine and wineries (and breweries) in Virginia, as well as others he may visit during his business travels to other states and countries. Twitter, e-mail updates.

Hagarty on Wine (www.hagarty-on-wine.com)
Produced by John Hagarty, the events manager at Rappahannock Cellars.

Blog entries range from interviews with winemakers and other wine industry figures to tasting notes on various wines. RSS feed.

My Vine Spot (http://vinespot.blogspot.com)
Written by Dezel Quillen, My Vine Spot includes entries and reviews of Virginia wineries, with a focus on those in the northern and central parts of the state, as well as some wineries in Georgia and New York. Includes photos, video spots, background information on wineries, "quick sips" tasting notes, search engine. Facebook, Twitter, RSS feed, YouTube, e-mail updates.

Richard Leahy's Wine Report (http://www.richardleahy.com)
Author Richard Leahy posts blogs on a wide range of topics, from Virginia wines and wineries to tasting notes to developments in the Virginia wine industry as a whole. RSS feed, e-mail updates.

Swirl, Sip, Snark (http://swirlsipsnark.com)
Published by a couple that wishes to remain anonymous, this blog covers Virginia wineries exclusively, with entries and comments that range from entertaining to, well, sometimes a little snarky. Well-organized site includes photos, links to previous postings, links to wineries, search engine. Facebook, Twitter, RSS feed, YouTube.

Virginia Pour House (http://virginiapourhouse.com)
Tony Marocco blogs about Virginia wineries, including rating the wines he has tasted. Includes photos, interviews, tasting notes. Twitter, e-mail updates.

Virginia Wine Dogs (http://vawinedogs.blogspot.com)
Virginia wineries seen through the eyes of Munchkin (Yorkshire Terrier) and Pomeroy (Pomeranian) and their blogger Terri Hauser. (Munchkin,

sadly, passed away in 2012.) Includes winery reviews, photos, search engine. Facebook, Twitter.

VA Wine in My Pocket (http://vawineinmypocket.com)
Written by travel writers Nancy Bauer and Rick Collier, this excellent blog site includes information about wineries they have visited, as well as a link to purchase their iPhone application of the same name. Includes information about local places of interest, photos, lodging, and restaurants. RSS feed, e-mail updates on blog entries.

Virginia Wine Time (www.virginiawinetime.com)
Warren Richard and Paul Armstrong are the duo behind Virginia Wine Time, which focuses exclusively on Virginia wines and wineries. Nicely designed site includes search engine, photos of wineries visited. Facebook, Twitter, RSS feed, YouTube.

Wine About Virginia (http://wineaboutvirginia.blogspot.com)
Written by an anonymous couple from Fairfax County, this blog focuses mainly on Virginia wines and wineries, with tasting room and wine reviews. E-mail updates.

Wine Compass (www.wine-compass.com)
Wine Compass covers wineries across the country, including reviews and photos of Virginia wineries and wines. Offers specialized content for registered users.

Wine Trail Traveler (www.winetrailtraveler.com)
This blog site by Terry and Kathy Sullivan includes reviews of wineries in multiple states with a particularly nice section on Virginia. Includes photos, wine routes, wine information, search engine. Facebook, Twitter, YouTube.

BIBLIOGRAPHY

Frye, Keith. *Roadside Geology of Virginia*. Missoula: Mountain Press Publishing Company, 2001.
Good introduction to the geologic structure and history of Virginia; includes numerous driving trails and maps.

Halliday, James and Hugh Johnson. *The Art and Science of Wine*. New York: Firefly Books, 2007.
An in-depth exploration of winemaking techniques for a range of noble grape varieties.

Heinemann, Ronald L., et al. *Old Dominion, New Commonwealth: A History of Virginia, 1607-2007*. Charlottesville: University of Virginia Press, 2008.
A good basic overview of the history of Virginia.

Kliman, Todd. *The Wild Vine: A Forgotten Grape and the Untold Story of American Wine*. New York: Clarkson Potter, 2010.
The dual-track story of Virginia's Norton grape and of Jennifer McCloud of Chrysalis Vineyards, who is perhaps the Norton's strongest champion.

Kramer, Matt. *Making Sense of Wine*. Philadelphia: Running Press, 2003.
Elegantly written essay on wine appreciation; includes a number of good recipes and wine pairings.

Kupperman, Karen Ordahl. *The Jamestown Project*. Cambridge: Belknap Press, 2007.
Very readable study of the origins, challenges, and economic development of the Jamestown Colony.

Lukacs, Paul. *American Vintage: The Rise of American Wine*. Boston: Houghton Mifflin, 2000.
Excellent short history of the American wine industry.

Mapp, Alf J., Jr. *The Virginia Experiment: The Old Dominion's Role in the Making of America, 1607-1781*. Lanham: Madison Books, 1990.
Detailed history of colonial Virginia, from its founding to the American Revolution.

McCusker, John. *The Economy of British America, 1607-1789*. Chapel Hill: University of North Carolina Press, 1991.
Scholarly examination and comparison of the economic development of the original thirteen American colonies and the Caribbean.

Pinney, Thomas, *A History of Wine in America, Volume One: From the Beginnings to Prohibition*. Berkeley: University of California Press, 1999. And *A History of Wine in America, Volume Two: From Prohibition to the Present*. Berkeley: University of California Press, 2005.
An outstanding and highly detailed two-volume history of winemaking in the United States.

Robinson, Jancis. *How To Taste: A Guide to Enjoying Wine*. New York: Simon & Schuster, 2000.
Very good introduction to wine tasting aimed at helping readers develop good palette pictures of the noble grape varieties.

Robinson Jancis. *Jancis Robinson's Wine Course*. New York: Abbeville Press, 1996.
Excellent broad introduction to wine, grapes, and wine tasting.

Robinson, Jancis, ed., *The Oxford Companion to Wine*. Oxford: Oxford University Press, 2006.
A comprehensive wine encyclopedia for the true wine geek.

Rowe, Walker Elliott *A History of Virginia Wines: From Grapes to Glass*. Charleston: History Press, 2009.
A short general overview of Virginia's wine industry, including some winemaker interviews (no index).

Simonetti-Bryan, Jennifer. *The Everyday Guide to Wine* (DVD). Chantilly: The Great Courses, 2010.
An entertaining and informative video introduction to wine and wine tasting (Great Courses has frequent sales).

GLOSSARY

Aglianico *(ah-lee-AH-nee-koh)*: A dark-skinned grape variety of Greek origin generally cultivated in the south of Italy, known for its dark ruby color and assertive flavor; the name is a corruption of *Ellenico*, Italian for "Greek."

Albariño *(ahl-bah-REE-nyoh)*: An aromatic white grape variety commonly grown in Spain's Galicia region as well as Portugal's Vinho Verde area.

Alcohol strength: The amount of alcohol in wine as measured in parts per one hundred; the alcohol strength of most wines falls between 9 and 15 percent.

Alicante Bouschet *(ah-lee-cahnt boo-shay)*: A black grape from southern France, generally known simply as Alicante and originally bred in the mid-1800s by Henri Bouschet, who crossed the Petit Bouschet and Grenache grape varieties.

American Viticultural Area (AVA): Since 1983, a geographic designation generally defined by geographic and climatic boundaries; approval for an AVA designation must be granted by the Bureau of Alcohol, Tobacco, and Firearms. At least 85 percent of wine with an AVA designation must originate from grapes grown in that AVA.

Barbera *(bar-BEAR-ah)*: A late-ripening dark-skinned grape, originally from Italy's Lombardy region; one of the most commonly planted varieties in Italy.

Blaufränkisch *(blaw [rhymes with "how"] fren-kish)*: One of the most widely planted black grape varieties in Austria, particularly in Burgenland; known in Germany as Limberger and in Washington state as Lemberger.

Blend: Any wine made from two or more different grape varieties.

Blush wine: A very pale pink and often sweet wine, noticeably lighter than rosé, often made from black-skinned grapes.

Bordeaux-style blend: Generally used to designate a dry red wine made from a blend of two or more of five grape varieties: Cabernet Sauvignon, Cabernet Franc, Merlot, Petit Verdot, and Malbec.

Brut: Designation for a sparkling wine made with little or no residual sugars.

Buffalo: A blue-black native American hybrid, often used for making grape juice.

Cabernet Franc *(ca-behr-nay frahn)*: A French black grape with long historic roots in France, lighter in color and tannins than Cabernet Sauvignon; it is one of the five varieties commonly used in Bordeaux blends.

Cabernet Sauvignon *(ca-behr-nay soh-vee-nyon)*: One of the most widely known red wine grapes, determined in 1997 by DNA analysis to be a cross of Cabernet Franc and Sauvignon Blanc; the primary variety used in Bordeaux, it produces wines that are often deep in color with good potential for aging.

Carmine: A cross between Carignan and Cabernet Sauvignon, first produced in California.

Catawba: A pink-skinned hybrid from an unknown native American *la brusca* and European *vinifera* grape, first identified in North Carolina in 1802.

Cayuga: A white hybrid bred from a Seyve-Villard grape and the North American Schuyler grape, first produced in the Finger Lakes region of New York in 1945.

Chambourcin *(shahm-boor-sehn)*: A French-American hybrid grape that produces deep red wine with an aromatic nose; commercially available since 1963.

Chancellor: A red hybrid grape first bred in France where it is known as Seibel 7053; now more commonly grown now in the central and eastern United States.

Chardonel *(shar-doh-nel)*: A cross between Seyval Blanc and Chardonnay, first bred in New York in 1953 and commercially released in 1990.

Chardonnay *(shar-doh-nay)*: A white grape variety originating from the Burgundy region of France; one of the most widely planted white wine grapes in North America.

Cider: Fermented apple juice, ranging from 2 to 8.5 percent alcohol content.

Claret: An English term for red wines from the Bordeaux region in France.

Concord: A highly aromatic native American *labrusca* grape widely grown in the eastern United States and named after the town of Concord, Massachusetts; commonly used in producing grape juice and grape jelly.

Corot Noir *(koh-roh nwahr)*: A red wine hybrid between a European Seyve-Villard and American Steuben grape; first produced in New York in 1970.

Corvina Veronese *(kohr-VEE-nah veh-roh-NAY-zay)*: A red wine grape that is the predominate component of several Italian wines, including Valpolicella, Bardolino, and Amarone; also known simply as Corvina.

Cross: The result of crossing two grapes of the same species; for example, two *Vitis vinifera* grapes.

Cyser: Fermented honey and apple juice.

Dessert wine: In the United States, dessert wines are defined as wines between 14% and 24% alcohol strength; dessert wines may or may not be fortified. In Europe, often defined as sweet wines.

Dornfelder: A red grape that is a cross between the Helfensteiner and Heroldrebe varieties, first propagated in Germany in 1956 by August Herold; known for its deep color and aromatic fruit.

Dry: A wine tasting term meaning a lack of sweetness.

Eau-de-vie *(oh-duh-vee)*: A grape-based distilled spirit, such as brandy.

Fer Servadou *(fair sehr-vah-doo)*: A black grape variety from southwest France; also known simply as Fer. The Fer variety cultivated in Argentina is not related to the French variety.

Filtration: A winemaking process in which sediments and particles are filtered out of the wine; wines that do not undergo filtration are said to be unfiltered.

Fining: A winemaking process intended to clarify and stabilize the wine by use of a fining agent, such as bentonite or egg whites.

Finish: A wine-tasting term signifying how long the wine lingers on the palate after swallowing. Finishes are often said to be short (no lingering taste) or long (taste lingers).

Fortified wine: Wine whose alcohol strength has been increased by the addition of grape spirit; port and sherry are examples of fortified wines.

Fruit forward: A wine tasting term indicating a noticeable fruitiness with the first taste of a given wine; also called "up-front fruit"; a characteristic of many New World wines.

Fumé Blanc *(foo-may blahn)*: Another name for Sauvignon Blanc, first coined by Robert Mondavi in the 1970s; Fumé Blanc wines often have undergone some oak aging.

Gewurztraminer *(geh-VOOHRTS-trah-mee-ner)*: A pink-skinned aromatic mutation of the Traminer grape, first reported in the Italian Tyrol region around 1000 and widely planted in Alsace and Germany; also spelled Gewürztraminer.

Golden Muscat *(moos-kah)*: A green-golden grape that is a hybrid between Muscat Hamburg and the North American Diamond grape; first bred in New York.

Graciano *(grah-see-AH-noh)*: A black grape variety from the Rioja region in northern Spain; also known as Graciana.

Grauburgunder *(graw [rhymes with "how"]-boor-goon-der)*: The Austrian name for Pinot Gris.

Grenache *(gruh-nahsh)*: A black grape variety most commonly planted in France's southern Rhone Valley and Languedoc-Roussillon region, as well as in Spain where it is known as Garnacha.

Hybrid: The result of crossing two grapes of different species; for example, a *Vitis vinifera* grape with a *Vitis labrusca* grape.

Hydromel: Pure mead, often light or low-alcohol.

Ice wine: Sweet wine made from ripe grapes that are picked when frozen on the vine; also includes wines made by artificially freezing the grapes.

Isabella: An American hybrid of unknown origin, thought to have been first developed in 1816 in South Carolina; also known as Isabelle.

Jeropiga *(zheh-roh-pee-gah)*: Traditional Portuguese-style wine made by adding grape spirits to unfermented grape must.

Kvevri: Large earthenware vessels lined with beeswax and traditionally used in the Republic of Georgia for making wine; also spelled *qvevri*.

Landot Noir *(lan-doh nwahr)*: A red grape variety that is a hybrid of Landal Noir and Seyve Villard; most commonly grown in New York and Ontario, Canada.

Late harvest: Wine made from grapes left on the vine beyond the regular harvest time in order to concentrate the fruit and natural sugars.

Lemberger *(lame-bear-ger)*: The name given in Washington state to the Limberger grape variety, also called Blaufränkisch in Austria.

Library Wines: Wines that have been put aside by a winery to age, generally of higher quality than ordinary vintages; may also refer to a home collection of wine.

Madeira *(mah-DARE-uh)*: A fortified wine originally from the Portuguese island of the same name.

Malbec *(mall-beck)*: A black grape variety grown in the Bordeaux and Loire regions of France, and one of the five varieties used in Bordeaux blends; now commonly associated with wine from Argentina and Chile.

Malolactic fermentation: A secondary fermentation during which malic acid is converted to the smoother tasting lactic acid in both red and white wines; produces greater flavor and smoothness in the final product.

Malvasia *(mall-vah-ZEE-ah)*: An ancient grape varietal family of Greek origin that includes mostly whites and some light-colored reds; wines are often characterized by higher residual sugars and alcohol strength.

Maréchal Foch *(mar-eh-shall fosh)*: A red grape hybrid of uncertain parentage first propagated in France.

Mataro: A synonym for Mourvedre, often used in the United States.

Mead: A fermented drink made from honey and commonly believed to predate either beer or wine.

Melomel: Honey and fruit-based mead.

Metheglen: Mead blended with herbs or spices.

Méthode champenoise *(meh-tode sham-puh-nwahz)*: Sparkling wine made in the style of the Champagne region of France.

Meritage: A term coined in 1981 for American wines made from a Bordeaux-style blend of Cabernet Sauvignon, Cabernet Franc, Merlot, Malbec, and/or Petit Verdot; sometimes also used for white blends of Sauvignon Blanc, Semillon, and/or Muscadelle; rhymes with "heritage."

Merlot *(mehr-loh)*: A black grape variety that is the predominate red wine grape in France's Bordeaux region and widely planted in northern Italy, among other regions.

Montepulciano *(mon-tay-pool-CHA-no)*: A red grape variety widely planted in central Italy.

Moscato: Another name for Muscat.

Mourvedre *(moor-veh-dra)*: The second most planted black grape variety in Spain, where it probably originated near the town of Murviedro near Barcelona; also known as Mataro, particularly in the United States.

Muscat *(moos-kah)*: An ancient grape variety from the Mediterranean region with multiple varieties in different colors; known in Italian as Moscato.

Muscat Blanc *(moos-kah blahn)*: One of the earliest grapes grown in France, dating from ancient Roman times; also known as Muscat Canelli and White Muscat, among other names.

Muscat Canelli: Another name for Muscat Blanc.

Muscat of Alexandria: An ancient Muscat variety unrelated to Muscat Blanc and believed to have been first cultivated in Egypt.

Muscat Orange *(moos-kah oh-rahnzh)*: A white grape variety often used to produce dessert wines; unrelated to Muscat Blanc.

Muscat Ottonel: A white grape variety first bred in 1852 in France from Chasselas and Muscat de Saumur.

Must: The unfermented mixture of grape juice, pulp, skins, stem fragments, and seeds produced after grapes have been crushed at the start of the winemaking process.

Nebbiolo *(neh-bee-OH-loh)*: A black grape from the Piedmont region in northwest Italy and the variety used in Italy's great Barolo and Barbaresco wines.

Niagara: A green grape that is a cross between the native American Concord grape and the white Cassady hybrid.

Norton: A native American, dark-skinned grape variety bred in the 1820s by Dr. Daniel Norton on his farm near Richmond; the variety was first recognized for its winemaking potential by George Husmann of Hermann, Missouri, in the 1850s.

Orange Muscat: See Muscat Orange.

Orange Wine: Wine made from white grape varieties; it is kept in contact with the grape skins for an extended period, giving the finished product a deeper golden hue.

Petit Manseng *(puh-tee mahn-sang)*: A white grape variety from southwest France and the Pyrenees region, noted for its flavor.

Petit Verdot *(puh-tee vehr-doh)*: A black grape variety used in Bordeaux and Bordeaux-style blends, noted for its rich color.

Pinotage: A hardy red grape variety first bred in South Africa by A.I. Perold, who crossed Pinot Noir and Cinsaut, the latter also known as Hermitage.

Pinot Grigio *(PEE-noh GREE-joe)*: The Italian name for Pinot Gris.

Pinot Gris *(pee-noh gree)*: A mutation of Pinot Noir with greyish blue to brownish pink berries; known in Germany as either Ruländer when sweet or Grauburgunder when dry.

Pinot Meunier *(pee-noh muh-nee-aye)*: A black grape variety often used to produce classic French champagne.

Pinot Noir *(pee-noh nwahr)*: The classic black grape variety of the Burgundy region of France, noted for lower tannins and a somewhat fruity taste.

Port: A fortified wine originally from the Douro region or Portugal, made by adding brandy to wine; may be either red or white.

Primitivo: A red grape variety grown extensively in southern Italy, principally in Apulia, and confirmed by DNA analysis to very closely related to Zinfandel.

Reserve wines: Generally intended to designate wines of superior quality, although they are few controls on how and when the term may be used.

Residual sugar: The amount of natural grape sugar remaining in wine after fermentation, measured in percent per liter.

Retsina: A resinated wine common in Greece and Cyprus; protected by the EU as a traditional appellation.

Riesling *(reece-ling)*: The classic white wine grape of Germany, known for its aroma and flavor; also called White, Rhine, or Johannisberg Riesling.

Rkatsiteli *(ahr-kat-sah-teh-lee)*: A white grape variety first documented in the country of Georgia and widely planted in Russia and many of the former Soviet republics.

Rosé: Pink-colored wine made either by leaving dark grape skins in contact with the juice just long enough to color it, or by pressing the juice from red wine grapes in a process called "saignée."

Roussanne *(roo-sahn)*: A reddish-skinned aromatic white grape from the Rhone region in France.

Saignée *(sen-yeah)*: French term meaning "bled" and designating a process for making rosé wines in which a certain amount of juice is pressed or "bled" from dark-skinned grapes.

Sangiovese *(sahn-joh-VEH-seh)*: A red grape that is the most commonly planted variety in Italy, where it is used in producing Chianti's wines.

Sauvignon Blanc *(sew-vee-nyohn blahn)*: An aromatic white grape variety, often crisp and sometimes even grassy in taste.

Semillon *(seh-mee-yohn)*: A golden grape variety from southwest France, frequently used in blending with other varieties; spelled Sémillon in Francophone countries.

Seyval Blanc *(say-vahl blahn)*: A white grape Seyve-Villard hybrid often producing crisp wines and popular in Canada and the United States.

Sherry: A dry fortified wine from Spain, ranging in style from the pale *fino* to darker *oloroso*.

Shiraz *(shih-RAZZ)*: Name given in Australia and South Africa to the Syrah grape; Shiraz-style designates a wine that is somewhat sweeter and riper than French Syrah.

Sparkling wine: Effervescent wine made according to the méthode champenoise; only wines made in France's Champagne region may bear the name "Champagne."

Steuben: A blue-black native American grape that is a cross between the Wayne and Sheridan grapes; first propagated by Cornell University's Geneva experiment station.

Super-Tuscan: Term used to describe wines made by blending Cabernet Sauvignon with Sangiovese, the traditional grape variety used in Chianti.

Symphony: An aromatic white grape that is a cross of Muscat of Alexandria and Grenache Gris, first propagated in California.

Syrah *(see-rah)*: One of the premier black grape varieties, thought to have originated in either Sicily or ancient Persia; widely grown in the Rhone region of France.

Tannat *(tah-nah)*: A black grape variety of Basque origin; noted for its deep color and high tannins.

Tannins: Chemical compounds from grape skins and pips that give wine an astringent taste.

Tempranillo *(tem-pra-NEE-yoh)*: A red grape variety from Spain that produces wines rich in color and often high in alcohol.

Terroir *(tehr-wahr)*: A French term that describes the totality of a vineyard's environment, particularly its climate and soil.

Tinta Cão *(TEEN-tah KAWM)*: A black grape once widely planted in Portugal's Douro region and one of the five varieties traditionally used to produce port; Portuguese for "red dog."

Touriga Nacional *(too-REE-gah nah-see-oh-NAL)*: A black grape that is generally considered the finest variety for port; also used to produce dry red wines.

Traminer Aromatico *(trah-mee-ner ah-roh-mah-tee-koh)*: A synonym for Gewurztraminer.

Traminette: An aromatic white grape that is a hybrid of Gewürztraminer and a Seyve hybrid, first cultivated in 1968 at the University of Illinois.

Trebbiano *(treh-bee-AH-noh)*: A white grape variety, also called Ugni Blanc, that is the most widely planted white variety in Italy.

Varietal: A wine named for the dominant grape variety from which it is made; varietals may be pure (100%) or a blend consisting of at least 75% of the grape for which the wine is named.

Verdejo *(vehr-DAY-hoe)*: An aromatic white grape that is the primary variety in Spain's Rueda region.

Vermentino *(ver-men-TEE-noh)*: An aromatic white grape grown in Sardinia, Corsica, and the Languedoc-Roussillon region of France.

Vidal Blanc *(vee-dahl blahn)*: An aromatic white grape hybrid between Ugni Blanc and one of the parent grapes of Seyval Blanc that lends itself to sweet and late harvest wines; widely grown in Canada because of its hardiness.

Vignoles *(veen-yole)*: A French-American hybrid between the French-American Seibel 8665 grape and Pinot de Corton, a Pinot Noir clone; originally propagated in France in 1922 and named after the French town of Vignoles, the grape is now more commonly planted in the United States.

Villard Blanc: A white grape Seyve-Villard hybrid.

Vin de Paille *(van duh pie)*: French term designating a sweet white wine, traditionally made by drying grapes on mats of straw (*paille* in French).

Vin Gris *(van gree)*: A pale pink wine made from dark-skinned grapes, characterized by little skin contact with the juice.

Vinho Verde *(vee-nyo ver-day)*: A Portuguese wine that is light, acidic, and traditionally sold soon after fermenting; the term means "green wine" in English.

Viognier *(vee-oh-nyee-eh)*: An aromatic white grape variety from the Rhone region in France and increasingly planted in California and Virginia.

Virginia Green: A state-wide program whose aim is to preserve and protect the environment by promoting eco-friendly practices in Virginia's tourism industry.

Viticulture: The science and practice of growing grapes.

Yeast: A single-celled agent whose key role in fermenting grape juice into wine was first described by Louis Pasteur; yeast strains may be cultivated or naturally occurring.

White Moore's Diamond: A white native American cross between the Concord and the Iona; grown primarily in New York and Pennsylvania for juice and dry white wine.

Wine: Any fermented fruit juice, most often associated with grapes; in the United States, table wines are between 7% and 14% alcohol strength.

Zinfandel: A black grape variety widely planted in California; determined by DNA analysis to be closely related to the Italian Primitivo variety.

ALPHABETICAL INDEX OF WINERIES

GENERAL INDEX

ABOUT THE AUTHOR

Donna R. Gough has enjoyed learning about and appreciating wines since she spent a year living in France. She has visited vineyards in the United States, Canada, Germany, and Chile. A geographer and linguist, she lives in Northern Virginia with her family. She blogs about wine and Virginia wineries at www.facebook.com/goughpubs and about writing in general at goughpubs.wordpress.com.

Back cover photos: Sunset Hills Vineyard (top), Chateau O'Brien at North-point (bottom)

CPSIA information can be obtained at www.ICGtesting.com
Printed in the USA
LVOW06s1551120314

377119LV00008BA/165/P